Praise for *Almost Somewhere: Twenty-Eight Days on the John Muir Trail* by Suzanne Roberts

"Roberts dares to combine a hiking adventure with a healthy dose of humor and female bonding in all its complicated and turbulent best. . . . An utterly refreshing outdoors memoir free of the seemingly manufactured drama so many similar titles contain. A delightful and quite literary diversion."

—COLLEEN MONDOR, *Booklist*

"At all turns, a gratifying read. It is intimate and funny, sharp and pensive, and its readers—if not inspired to undertake their own adventures—will certainly be sad to leave Roberts at the trail's end."

—MICHELLE SCHINGLER, *ForeWord*

"Suzanne Roberts sets off on a remarkable Sierra journey that will test the limits of physical endurance, of friendship, and of faith in self. . . . This is not the usual wilderness story of independence, competition, and violence. Here, thankfully, is the more urgent story of intimacy, community, and compassion. A loving, and lovely, ode to life."

—JOHN T. PRICE, author of *Not Just Any Land*

"A 260-page journey that is bound to take you beyond the John Muir Trail."

—KATHRYN REED, *Lake Tahoe News*

"In *Almost Somewhere* we get to travel both the physical John Muir Trail—its history, its flowers and trees and shadowy peaks—and the gritty emotional landscape of the three women who make the journey. Where are we in the world, anyway? Suzanne Roberts helps us know that the only place we can be is here, giving it all we have, day by day."

—FLEDA BROWN, author of *Driving with Dvořák*

"A contribution to the growing body of women's nature writing, and a worthwhile, entertaining and occasionally funny story of the California wilderness."

—JULIA JENKINS, *Shelf Awareness*

"This is not a backpacking primer, but rather one on young females in search of themselves as they prepare for life after college. We read about insecurities, jealously, lust, self-esteem, tears, bingeing, self-realization, learning to appreciate oneself for oneself, and interpersonal relationships. And come away with the author's realization that mountains in general, and the [John Muir Trail] specifically, provide a spectacular backdrop to work through these issues and absorb the associated lessons."

—KURT REPANSHEK, *National Parks Traveler*

"Readers who have walked sections of the John Muir Trail will appreciate Roberts's accurate descriptions of lakes and passes, of trail-worn feet, and of the fleeting moments when you seem to float down the trail."

—BRADLEY JOHN MONSMA, *ISLE: Interdisciplinary Studies in Literature and Environment*

"Will appeal to readers of travel and nature books, as well as those who enjoy reading about social interactions and group dynamics."

—*KIRKUS*

"*Almost Somewhere* will not disappoint. It is a wonderful read for outdoor lovers and inspirational for anyone experiencing self-doubt. The message that resonates is as Roberts says, 'It's not just in the having done but in the doing . . . being 'Almost Somewhere.'"

—GLORIA SINIBALDI, *North Lake Tahoe Bonanza*

"[Roberts's] writing is filled with wonderful descriptions and is often sprinkled with lovely self-deprecating humor. Her voice . . . is realistic and rings true: A woman who is vulnerable and understands her limitations but is also determined to overcome challenges."

—TIM HAUSERMAN, *California's Adventure Sports Journal*

"This book is one I didn't want to end. I felt as if I were hiking with Roberts. When she finished, I would be finished, and like her, I would be sad to be done."

—EVE QUESNEL, *Moonshine Ink*

BAD TOURIST

Bad Tourist

Misadventures in Love and Travel

~~~~~~

SUZANNE ROBERTS

University of Nebraska Press

Lincoln

Publication of this volume was assisted by a grant from the
Friends of the University of Nebraska Press.

Library of Congress Cataloging-in-Publication Data
Names: Roberts, Suzanne, 1970– author.
Title: Bad tourist: misadventures in love and travel /
Suzanne Roberts.
Description: Lincoln: University of Nebraska Press, 2020.
Identifiers: LCCN 2020004131
ISBN 9781496222848 (paperback)
ISBN 9781496223968 (epub)
ISBN 9781496223975 (mobi)
ISBN 9781496223982 (pdf)
Subjects: LCSH: Roberts, Suzanne, 1970– —Travel. |
Roberts, Suzanne, 1970– —Relations with men. | Travel—
Psychological aspects. | Tourism—Psychological aspects. |
Self-actualization (Psychology)
Classification: LCC G155.A1 R56 2020 | DDC 910.4092—dc23
LC record available at https://lccn.loc.gov/2020004131

Set in Filosofia by Laura Buis.

Although this book is true to the author's fallible memory,
some names and distinguishing characteristics have been
changed to protect the identities of both the innocent and
the guilty.

For Thomas,
with love and a lifetime
of adventure

Contents

BAD TOURIST

Sights

~~~~~~~~~~~~~~~~~~~~~~~~~~~~~~~~~~~~~~

The real voyage of discovery consists
not in seeking new landscapes, but in
having new eyes.

MARCEL PROUST

Life is either a daring adventure or
nothing at all.

HELEN KELLER

The Love Test

Everglades National Park, United States,
February 2007

I had a suspicion then, which has since been confirmed, that this was my relationship test. Don't pretend you have never been subjected to one or devised one yourself. We were camped at the deserted Highland Beach, 100 miles into a 150-mile kayaking trip in the Gulf of Mexico, paddling from Florida's Everglade City to the Flamingo Visitor's Center and back. My practical-to-the-extreme and water-savvy new boyfriend had been a kayaking instructor with Outward Bound, and he wanted to make sure his new girlfriend could make such a trip.

By the third twenty-mile kayaking day, my forearms squeaked like rusty door hinges when I tried to move my wrists or my hands. Later I learned the medical term for this, "crepitus," making it sound like the death of an arm, which in some ways it was. On the fourth day, we ran over a shark in the shallow waters between mangroves, and I had a tantrum, which is quite a feat considering I was squeezed into my kayak compartment like a wrapped mummy.

"It's just a nurse shark," Practical Boyfriend said.

"So?" I screamed. "Shark. Shaaaarrrk."

"Calm down. I don't even think they have teeth."

I grew up at the height of the *Jaws* paranoia, so the sight of a dorsal fin brought me back to my six-year-old self and the trochaic meter of that Jaws music, the thrashing, and blood blooming like red begonias under the sea. One has to wonder why parents ever let their small children see such a film.

And for the record, nurse sharks do have teeth.

I was surely passing the test. I had paddled through my crepitus and didn't sink the boat during our shark encounter. I even agreed to hitting a fellow boater over the head with my paddle, if needed. A school group was out at a rough point, not ironically called Shark Point. Their canoes had tipped in the wind, and the waves lashed at their boats and their now-submerged bodies. They were screaming. A lot.

"Listen," Practical Boyfriend said, "I have a tow line. We've got to go out and get them."

"We do?" I asked. My question was not rhetorical.

Apparently, this particular corner of ocean was popular with the hammerheads, who even Practical Boyfriend admitted had teeth. But he had been a Boy Scout and an Outdoor Trip Leader, and there was no way we were going to paddle past the group in their time of need. They were all bobbing about the angry gray sea like eggs boiling in a pot. One of their canoes was upside down, the other beyond their reach.

"But if they try to grab at you," Practical Boyfriend warned, "hit them with your paddle, so they don't capsize the boat."

I was poised but still full of doubt. How could I crack the head of someone in need with my hard-plastic paddle? I certainly would have failed that test. Thankfully, Practical Boyfriend saved the day with his tow line and his quick wits, and no head-smashing was called for.

That night we arrived at Highland Beach on our way back up to Everglade City and set up Practical Boyfriend's small blue tent between two palm trees. We watched bald eagles steal fish from osprey. The salty sky turned blue to pink, and a mackerel jumped from the sea, glinting silver. Crab shells littered the edge of the shore, shining white like bones. The sun streaked across the sea, a tunnel of light reaching the sand. The wind whistled the palm fronds above and kept the blackflies away. A hawk caught in a draft of wind, flashed a brown triangle of wing, a red tail.

We drank red wine from a box, and I watched as Practical Boyfriend cooked dinner. Three pelicans glided by, and the line between sea and sky shined like glass. I dug my toes into the sand, the million tiny broken stones and shells. An osprey called overhead. A flock of orange-beaked oystercatchers darted above the water. We looked out over the horizon; pelicans were silhouettes in the darkening sky. As the constellations appeared, Practical Boyfriend pointed to them, deciphering the syntax of stars—Cassiopeia, Andromeda, Orion's Belt. The tide unrolled a curtain onto the sand, surging and retreating, leaving behind beautiful corpses of conch shells, pink and temporal. Raccoons scurried to the tide pools, pulling the flesh from shells.

Then the wind carried clouds, obscuring the stars, as if they were covered by the gauzy net of a veil. And then flashing light bloomed in the distance. "Are those explosions?" I asked.

"I'm not sure what that is," Practical Boyfriend said. "Maybe lightning."

"How could *that* be lightning? It looks like a fireworks show."

The light erupted like a volcano, a commotion of orange and yellow along the line between the black sky and gray sea.

We listened to the marine radio with its mechanical warnings to small craft about electrical storms, high seas, and winds.

"I guess you were right," I said, "but I've never seen lightning like that before."

We sat on the sand, looking out at the flashing horizon; the storm still seemed so very far away.

We woke at dawn, and the radio issued new, more urgent warnings to the small craft that had not heeded the initial announcement. The rain fell in pleats against the nylon roof and walls of the tent. The ground beneath us shook with the rumble of thunder. But still an ocean away. Or so it seemed. Practical Boyfriend wasn't worried, and so we reached for each other.

Then the rain turned to hail stones, and the small tent lit up with each new bolt of lightning. The distant thunder became detonations on our sandy beach, between our two lovely palms, around our little love tent. "Listen," Practical Boyfriend said. "If anything happens, here's how you call out on the radio." He showed me.

"What do you mean anything? Why would I call? Who would I call?"

"If anything happens to me," he said. This was not a man who overreacted, so I tried to concentrate on what button to push and when.

"And we better get in lightning position," he said between cracks of thunder and flashes of lightning. The air smelled like burning things, and my hair stood on end. Until that moment, I had always thought of this as a cliché. But sometimes, there's truth in cliché.

"Okay," I said. "Lightning position. What's that?"

Practical Boyfriend demonstrated. He rolled up his sleeping pad, kneeling on it. I copied him. "You have to have your knees and feet together," he warned. "So if we're hit by ground current, there's one entry and exit place. It's safer that way."

"Ground current?" I asked.

"Yes," he said. "Kneel like this."

So I did.

I didn't find out what this meant until later—that if the lightning struck close enough, it could reach us by traveling down one of our palm trees and through the sand. Practical Boyfriend knew a fellow Outdoor Leader who had died exactly this way. One point of entry and exit means less burning of the body.

There we kneeled, naked and knees together on our camping pads. Now closer, the thunder sounded like bombs exploding nearby.

When it got to be too much, I started to cry.

"It'll be okay," Practical Boyfriend said. The blue tent lit up with each strike, followed by another crashing *ka-boom*. And the smell of something like sulfur. I was scared, but it wasn't that—well, at least not exactly that.

"I have to go poo," I finally admitted. The fear plus this crouching, knee-together kneeling position meant I might not be able to hold it. It's one thing to be scared of sharks in front of a new boyfriend or even fail to smash a fellow boater's head with your paddle should you need to.

This was another thing entirely.

But Practical Boyfriend reached for his knit beanie, and he said those six words every woman longs to hear: "You can poop in my hat."

Practical Boyfriend had not yet told me he loved me, nor even said that he liked me.

But because of my practiced yoga postures, a strong will, sheer embarrassment, and an offering of the hat that I interpreted as true love, I was able to hold off until the storm finally moved on, and I could sprint from the tent and squat in privacy behind a palm. In the end, it was Practical Boyfriend who passed the test.

Practical Boyfriend would eventually become Practical Husband, and for the record, I have never pooped in his hat.

Scared Shitless

Aguas Calientes, Peru, April 2007

I thought Sandra waited for me because she wasn't as scared as I was, but I later learned that she thought we would die right then and there. The bartender was already hammering boards across the windows when I locked myself in the bathroom, cursing myself for such bad timing. My hiking group had run out of the bar and left me there, except for my friend Sandra, who is one of those unflappable travel partners who meets you on your travels when she says she will and who can handle just about anything. She knocked on the door, saying, "Girl! You'd better hurry up in there."

As it turns out, "scared shitless" isn't just another cliché.

Our final day hiking the Inca Trail had concluded at dawn at Machu Picchu, where Sandra and I admired the ruins and green mountainscape until the busloads of tourists arrived; then we boarded a local bus for nearby Aguas Calientes, a town in a box canyon so narrow that passing trains seemed like they might scrape the pastel-colored buildings on their way through. Jungle-clad mountains crouched above, notching the sky.

The Inca Trail was more beautiful than we had expected but also more difficult. When we weren't climbing granite stairs, we hiked steep hills that our guides ironically called Andean flat. Even though I was used to hiking, the rugged trail was harder than I thought it would be. After a few days, my calves burned and my toes blistered. But we loved it all—the jungle-draped mountains with their countless species of wild orchids along the trail and even the rain. It was early April, the changeable season, the time between the wet and dry seasons, but our hike proved to be more wet than dry. Our last night, it rained so hard (the Spanish word for this is *aquacero*) that our guides and porters were up in the middle of the night digging trenches around our tents, which made me feel like a *princesa* and not in a good way—I felt spoiled.

After hiking over thirteen-thousand-foot passes, most notably Warmiwañusca (or Dead Woman's Pass), we looked forward to relaxing in the natural hot springs that gave Aguas Calientes its name. We dropped off our muddy hiking clothes at a laundry, found a hostel, and changed into bathing suits and shorts. We met our hiking group and guides at the bar El Gringo Feliz for a couple of celebratory Pisco Sours before heading to the springs.

As we finished our drinks and exchanged email addresses, a train shrilled to a halt. People jumped from the train and scattered across the canyon, running along the pebbled tracks. Vendors abandoned their wares—blankets, walking sticks, ponchos, and postcards—on the narrow sidewalk. Shopkeepers began hammering boards over their windows. One man fell onto the wet train tracks, smashed his head on the rail, then stumbled to his feet and continued. Blood stained the rocks where he had fallen. We asked people running past, "¿Que pasó?" What happened?

A woman shouted, "¡Avalancha de lodo!" A man in khakis and a floppy hat translated as he ran past: LANDSLIDE.

That's when I hurried back into the bar with the immediate urge to go. The lights had gone out, and the bartender nailed boards across the windows. Sandra pounded on the bathroom door, shouting: "Get out of there. *Now.*" I finished up and followed Sandra through the dark bar and out the front door. The air outside thickened with humidity, drenched with the smell of wet earth. Everyone darted across the tracks. Sandra and I crossed over, joining the others who had gone in search of higher ground, but we didn't know the exact location of the mudslide. Was it on the other side of the canyon or was it on our side, oozing toward us from *somewhere up there?*

Anna, a British woman from our hiking group, seemed unreasonably calm. She reminded me of the *Titanic* passengers who were sipping their after-dinner drinks and insisting on dessert, even though they knew the ship had collided with an iceberg. She told me the guides had said not to worry, that if there was danger, the town sirens would sound. "So not to worry," Anna said. "No sirens."

We breathed the heavy air, chewy and primal with the smell of mud. *No sirens, no sirens, no sirens*—I repeated this mantra until the ring of the high-pitched alarms bounced off the canyon walls. The police hurried toward us, shouting something in Spanish. Our hiking guides, Romulo and Chaya, translated: "Run!"

Ten minutes earlier, my legs had been sore and my toes so bruised I could hardly walk. Now I ran, my sandals flip-flopping through muddy puddles. The adrenaline, a cold snake down my spine. The rain picked up again, and shards of gray sky seemed to break off and fall in a downpour. The crowd bustled along, and Anna stopped to take a photograph. I squinted through the rain and finally saw the mudslide, the watery earth slithering a brown trail through the green mountainside above us.

We ran with the crowd across the bridge over the Rio Urubamba, bubbling in a cold, muddy boil, slopping over the rusted metal in murky waves, the sounds of the turbulent brown water like the static of a radio turned on maximum volume. I ran with my arms flapping about like wings, as if that would somehow lift me into flight and save me. Sandra's sprint was more dignified, void of arm flurry; she didn't knock into fellow evacuees the way I did. We followed the *ruta de evacuación*, past the evacuation gates about a mile upstream and to a train stopped up canyon, waiting.

We stood in a rustling line, not sure if the surrounding hillsides would rupture and slide onto us, sweeping us away in a brown waterfall, enveloping us in mud. I brought only my prescription sunglasses; I had left my regular glasses and my backpack at the hostel, along with my passport and credit cards. My swimsuit, shorts, and the towel draped over my shoulders were soaked. I worried because I didn't have a ticket for the train. Did I need a ticket to evacuate? People pushed into each other, trying to board.

A young Dutch-Australian couple in front of us in line argued. The husband spoke in English and said, "Get a hold of yourself. It's going to be fine." The wife answered in Dutch, but with all her crying, even a native Dutch speaker wouldn't have understood her. She crossed herself and began praying. Then more crying, this time the hyperventilating kind. Her hysteria gave me a strange sense of calm. She demonstrated exactly what I felt, so I didn't have to. But I wasn't nearly as composed as Sandra, who later asked me this: "Why panic? Being smothered with mud would be the ultimate horror, but it's not like we could do anything to stop it."

The husband tried to soothe his frantic wife. He said, "We *will* have children. We *aren't* going to die on our honeymoon." The opposite effect was achieved by this mention of their future; the wife's frenzy now included convulsive moaning and choking sobs.

That was when he slapped her, and she resumed a silent weeping.

Remembering back, I can feel the sting of that slap with a glassy sharpness, though unflappable Sandra would say, "If I were him, I would have slapped her sooner." At the time, I felt nothing more than surprise and a mild dismay; it all seemed part of the surreal drama unfolding around us.

Now I see that there's nothing like fear to reveal all the parts of ourselves—sometimes beauty but also the horror.

When we made it to the train's door, I tried to explain in my broken Spanish that we didn't have tickets, but the conductor waved us tourists on board. The guides and porters, however, were turned away. Evacuating the tourists was the priority. This upset me but not so much that I gave up my seat. As we filed down the aisle, I looked out the rain-spotted window with shame. The river was still rising and rumbling in chaotic brown waves.

It would be easy to say there was nothing I could do and that our guides and porters would probably be all right (and thankfully they were). While that was true on some level, it was also not true; it was the lie I relied on. It's harder to say you would do the right thing after you've already been tested and failed. Sandra later asked, "What else could we have done?"

I'm still not sure. I only know that getting to board that train while the porters and guides stood there in the rain next to the rising river felt wrong. It still does. But looking back at my younger self, that terrified tourist, I can tell you there was nothing that could have made me get off that train. I can't even say I would do better now, because we can only know these things in the moment we are tested.

Sandra and I sat across from the Dutch-Australian couple. The woman ordered a bottle of wine and asked us if we wanted to share it. Sandra said no because she sold wine for a living, and she wasn't about to drink cheap swill. Although I had also worked in the wine business, I wasn't quite so discerning. The Dutch woman and I took turns passing the red wine across the table between us, swigging it straight from the bottle.

We waited there on the still unmoving train, wondering if the land would buckle above us, sending the train into the river. I asked the waiter if everything would be okay, and he shrugged and said, "No sé." But that certain squint of his eyes, the voice cracked in a whisper, gave away his fear.

I took another gulp from the bottle of cheap Malbec. The British group showed each other digital images of the mudslide. As they shared photographs, they didn't seem at all bothered that the train wasn't yet moving, that we remained in a box canyon in the pouring rain. They were like my own British mother, who worried incessantly about a thing until it happened, and then when there was actual danger, she pretended like nothing was wrong.

The train eventually started to lumber through the canyon toward Cusco, and everyone clapped, which took me by surprise. But then I clapped along—because we were moving out of the box canyon, because it seemed like we might be okay after all. The husband apologized to the wife, who accepted with a wine-happy smile. Sandra fell asleep, as she has been known to do during exceptionally turbulent flights and on small boats in rough seas. I sat there in my sunglasses and swimsuit, wet towel draped around my shoulders; I swayed with the din of the rocking train, watching the black hollow of night slide past my reflection in the window.

My Mother Is My Wingman

Santorini, Greece, July 2005

"Oh no you don't. You're not going to jump off from there," Mother called out to me. I stood teetering on the edge of the schooner, the Aegean Sea below. In the distance, the white-washed buildings clinging to the caldera's edge looked like a dusting of snow.

"It's deep enough," I said.

"I forbid it." She put one hand on her hip and pointed at me with the other.

"Mom, I'm thirty-four."

"Then act like it." My mother shook her head. I leapt into the sea.

As I climbed the ladder and into the boat, a sandy-haired stranger smiled at me and winked. I had noticed him as soon as my mother and I boarded the sunset cruise. He had smiled at me then, and being my mother's daughter, I smiled back. He didn't look like the usual Santorini tourist—sunburned, tennis-shoe clad, a face tinged with an expression of awe and indigestion.

"What do you think you are, a bloody mermaid?" Mother asked.

"Maybe," I said and looked at the sandy-haired stranger.

My mother caught me and said, "What are you looking at?" even though she already knew.

After a hiking trip up Nea Kameni volcano and a swim in the cloudy warm springs, the tourists were settled back in the boat, drinks in hand, and the sandy-haired man played the saxophone, serenading the setting sun. My mother and I sipped Greek wine and listened to the breathy music, a sound both sassy and serious.

Mother was scared of most things, which was why she didn't hike the volcano or swim in the sea, but she was also bold and brave in other ways, so it was my mother who introduced herself to the saxophone player. It was my mother who asked Benny— that was his name—to ride the rickety cable car back up to Fira with us and then invited him to dinner. My mother got away with this behavior because she was a former beauty queen, and even as an older woman, she was still beautiful. Her British accent made her sound charming and funny even when she was being pushy.

It was as if my mother wanted to make sure somebody was going to have a *Shirley Valentine* experience in Greece. But communication with Benny proved to be an ordeal, since he had a repertoire of about ten English words. He was Albanian but also spoke Greek and Italian. We managed on Benny's Italian and my broken Spanish, understanding about 7 percent of what the other said. We made it through dinner this way, eating take-out gyros on a park bench. My mother shared her cigarettes with him. She pretended she didn't smoke until she had someone to smoke with. "I don't smoke much," she would say, though anytime she deemed it appropriate, she would light up. And then she would blame me, saying, "I only smoke because you make me nervous."

And according to her, her high blood pressure had nothing to do with the cigarettes; that, too, was because of me.

"That Benny sure is nice, isn't he?" my mother said when he invited us to have drinks later at Enigma, the nightclub where he worked.

"I guess so. It's hard to talk to him," I said. Flirting with him on the boat seemed fun, but I didn't need it to go any further.

"He's handsome."

"Did you see he's missing teeth? In the back?" I asked.

"Don't be so judgmental," Mother said, which was what she often said to me when I disagreed with her about something.

We wandered the cobbled streets, past the tourist shops and bougainvillea, and then went for a couple of drinks at Murphy's Irish Pub. When we thought it was late enough, we headed for Enigma, but still, the bouncer told us we were too early. It was 10 p.m., but things wouldn't get started until midnight. Or later.

"Can we just come in for a drink?" my mother asked. "We *know* Benny."

We entered through a neon-lit cave that looked like the tunnel where you wait in line for Disneyland's Space Mountain—low, curved ceilings, the purple neon glowing on the white walls.

Mother and I were the only patrons in the club.

We walked to the bar and ordered retsina, which tasted like acetone. I asked the bartender how long the bottle had been open, and he gave me a blank look. My mother told him, "We're *friends* with Benny, you know." Then she turned to me and said, "Why are you always such a wine snob? It's fine." She smiled at the bartender, and he smiled back.

"I used to work in the wine industry," I said, "that's why."

"You have an answer for everything," she told me, still smiling at the bartender.

I knew I couldn't have been the first woman to come in looking for Benny after the boat ride, but I may have been the first woman who had come to the bar accompanied by her mother as wingman.

We sat at one of the white vinyl sofas with our acidic wine, and my mother said, "You're boy crazy, you know that?"

"Me? *You* invited Benny to dinner. What are you talking about?"

"You know what I'm talking about. In high school, you said you wanted to live with that boyfriend of yours."

"I was probably just trying to shock you. Besides, I was a child."

"Of course you were. You're still a child to me. And didn't I find condoms in your purse the night of your prom?"

"You know the answer," I said.

"Do I?" she asked, all innocence. "You know," she added, "I'm only passive aggressive because if I'm not, you accuse me of being critical of you."

"Being direct doesn't mean you have to be insulting," I said.

"Kill 'em with kindness, that's what I always say."

For my mother, different truths existed in different rooms of the brain. At any given time, she decided which room to live in and whether or not secrets and lies decorated the walls. I'd learned to go along with whatever she wanted. So it didn't seem as strange as it might have when my mother and I danced with Benny on the empty dance floor, the bartender looking on with an amused smile. Or when Benny started calling my mother "Mama," which she tried—unsuccessfully—to discourage because she thought it made her sound old enough to be his mother, which of course she was.

When we returned to the couches, Benny squeezed in next to me. He went in for the kiss, and I gave him my cheek. "Want to see the rooftop terrace?" he asked in Italian. The word "terrace" is the same in Spanish, so I translated for my mother.

"You two go ahead," she said, waving toward the door. "I'll stay here." She took a sip of wine.

"Thanks, Mama," Benny said with a grateful smile.

I followed Benny up to the rooftop terrace. The lights of Santorini glimmered on the purple Aegean Sea. I breathed in the sea air, and Benny tried to kiss me again. I squirmed away, not because of modesty. I liked Benny more from afar; the saxophonist's allure wasn't in the fulfillment of a love affair but in its promise.

"I want to kiss you," he said. These were among his ten English words, and he didn't need them because the way he tried to press his mouth to mine made his intent obvious enough.

"We haven't even had a date," I tried, as if that had ever stopped me before. And admittedly, it would have been easier to kiss him than to converse with him.

"But I love you," he said, trying to kiss me.

"You don't love me. You want to fuck me."

He nodded as if I finally understood. "Yes!" he said. "I want to make fuck, but also I love you."

"Uh-huh."

"You are beautiful, and I want to make fuck," he repeated, now that this option was on the table.

"I'm sure you do," I said. For every backward step I took, Benny took one forward. He nodded and twisted his face into what could pass for sincere. Our bodies projected shadows in the yellow blaze of a nearby streetlamp; we stood at the edge of the terrace against a stone wall, the sea shimmering far below.

"That's fine," I said, "but I don't want to leave my mother for too long. We should go back."

When he looked at me, confused, I said, "Mama," and pointed toward the club.

He nodded and said in Italian, "We will have a date tomorrow. I will pick you up on my moto. We will go to the beach."

"Where?" I asked, catching all of it but the last part because the Spanish and Italian words for "beach" are nothing alike.

"To the sea," he said in English.

"What time?" I asked in Spanish.

"Dieci," he said.

"Diez?" I held up all of my fingers, and Benny nodded. I told him the name of our hotel. It was one of those third-drink decisions. And I reasoned that most of us just want to make fuck; at least Benny had been up-front about it. Sometimes the fewer words we are able to exchange with each other, the more honest we become.

Benny smiled and said, "Back to work now."

When I got back to the club, the dance floor was still empty. I didn't really want to go on a date with Benny, but I wasn't sure how to say no. I also knew my mother wanted to be witness to my Greek love affair, and I didn't know how to say no to her either—it had always been that way with us. She had such a profound influence on me, and in some ways, I wanted to be just like her. But in other ways, I wanted to learn who I was separate from her.

I found my mother at the bar and said, "Let's go."

"But I just ordered another drink." The club's neon lights strobed across my mother's face.

"It's like vinegar."

"It cost me good money," Mother said.

"Bring it with you."

"How can I?"

I took the glass off the bar and held it inside my jean jacket. "This is how. Let's go."

"Suzanne!"

"This way it won't be wasted. We can give the glass to Benny tomorrow," I told her as we left the club.

"Tomorrow?"

"I sort of made a date with him."

"That's good," Mother said.

We ended up getting lost on the way back to the hotel, and Mother asked, "Why are you leading me through the back alleys of Greece?"

"I'm not trying to."

"You're not lost, are you?"

"No," I lied. We walked past a group of stray cats, eating what looked like noodles off sheets of newspaper. Ahead of us, an old woman distributed the food, and cats competed for it, snarling and hissing at one another.

"It smells like urine," my mother whispered. "Oh, why did you bring me into the back alleys?"

"Mom, this is Santorini. There are no back alleys. Stop saying that. Here, have some wine." I handed her the glass. My mother nodded and drank. A man walked toward us on the path, and my mother spun around and ran the other way, up the cobbled stairs, spilling wine as she went. I followed her, shouting, "Mom, Mom!"

The next morning, my mother asked if I was going to have a date with Benny. I told her I wasn't. "That's good," she said. "But do give him back the wineglass."

"Last night you were trying to set me up with him."

"I was not. I wouldn't do that. Don't be daft." She rifled through her suitcase and pulled out her bathing suit.

"You did."

"Well, you got us lost in the back alleys with the stray cats," she said. "Luckily, I found the right way to go."

"By running away," I said.

"It got us going in the right direction, didn't it? And away from the hobos."

"Hobos? What hobos?"

"You know what hobos. Why do you ask me things you already know the answer to?"

"Why are you so afraid of everything?" I asked.

"Why are you so mean?"

We stood there looking at each other, neither of us willing to answer the other's questions. I knew the answers would have been too difficult, so I ended the standoff by apologizing. She nodded and went to the bathroom to change.

I waited in front of the hotel and heard the motor of Benny's moped straining up the hill before I saw him. He wore faded jean cutoffs, a white t-shirt, and sandals made from woven straw. He motioned for me to get on the back of the bike. I tried to explain first in English and then in Spanish that I wasn't coming, but Benny just half-smiled, patting the vinyl seat behind him.

"I changed my mind," I said.

And when Benny still didn't seem to understand, I said in Spanish, "I change my mind," mixing up verb tenses so it came out in the present tense, making it seem more right than before.

"You don't like the beach? We'll have coffee instead," Benny said, patting the seat again.

"No, it's not that. It's just that I don't want to leave my mother. She's sick," I lied. "Mama sick. Mama enferma." I hoped the Italian word for "sick" resembled the Spanish.

It doesn't, so Benny stared at me, pressing his lips together. Then he exhaled and asked, "So we are finished?"

Because I didn't have the words to explain, I said, "Yes."

Benny shook his head, not trying to conceal his disappointment. "But I like you too much." He crossed his arms over his chest.

I nodded. He started his moped and sped back down the hill. I stood there holding the empty wineglass. I couldn't figure out how to explain and give it to him, so I left it at the hotel bar on my way back up to the room.

I know it would have made a better story had I gone with Benny to the sea. Sometimes my students wonder what a character in a novel might have done in another circumstance. Or what might have happened if a character had acted differently, chosen another path. What if Edna Pontellier could have divorced her husband? Would she still have walked into the sea? The point, I tell them, is not what didn't happen but what did; anything else is off the page.

That evening, my mother and I went for appetizers at a balcony restaurant under the windmill in Oia. The sun dropped like a stone into the water; the sunset cruise sailed by below the white-washed buildings, the blue-domed roofs, and the rocky caldera. An older gentleman at the next table smiled at my mother. She smiled back at him and then whispered to me, "See! I can still get an old codger."

"Or a young one," I said, and we laughed.

Saxophone music rode the wind. "Do you hear that?" Mother asked. "I wonder if that's Benny?"

"How many saxophone players are in Santorini?" I asked, and we both laughed again.

My body felt full of *what ifs* and *why nots*. I'd liked Benny from afar—the smile, the wink, the boundary of desire. I wondered what would have happened if I had gone with him on the back of his bike, winding paths to the sea.

But that's off the page.

The ending of my Greek story was right there, sitting in the salty, pink sunlight, laughing with my beautiful mother, listening to the far-off notes of a saxophone.

Three Hours to Burn a Body

Varanasi, India, January 2007

The calloused hands of the oarsman worked a rhythmic sluice in the Ganges River. The rising sun cast an orange hue through the fog. The small boat docked, and we walked a short distance to Manikarnika Ghat, one of the cremation sites, to meet our guide. He said, "No photos, here." Though I saw many other tourists taking pictures, I vowed to capture this holy ritual only on the screen of my memory. A tourist pointed his giant telephoto lens at a man in prayer, but I would refrain from distancing myself by watching through a camera. Just being there as outsiders—voyeurs of the sacred—seemed wrong. Although I knew we'd be coming to Varanasi, I didn't imagine the guide would bring us so close to the cremations, to walk among the dead.

The guide shooed away beggars and children selling small shells that cradled candles and marigolds—an offering for Mother Ganga. The murky river held a thousand such lights, stars drifting in the dawn waters. The real stars were hidden by a tent of clouds. The air smelled of incense, spices, and cow dung.

Three barefoot girls approached us with baskets of candles. A skinny street dog followed them. "A wish for you," the girls said.

Our guide told them to leave, but my friend Sholeh said, "No, it's okay. I want to buy them."

We each bought two shells, filled with marigolds and candles. Sholeh wanted to take a picture of the three girls, but they would not stand together. The taller girl, the one with some English, told us she could not stand with the other girls—they were Dalits, Untouchables, the lowest Hindu caste. The taller girl belonged to a higher caste. We took pictures of the two smaller girls together and then one of the taller girl alone. When Sholeh showed the girls their digital images, they huddled around her, standing on their tippy-toes to see, squealing with laughter, momentarily forgetting to keep their distance from one another. I handed out chocolates to the children. I made sure to give more to the smaller girls. I now understand that we shouldn't have been giving out the chocolates at all; it's not like we would give out candy to children at home. These are the peccadillos—the seemingly harmless things we do in another culture that we would never do in our own—that make us bad tourists.

Sholeh placed her shells on the water's surface and watched them sail away. I bent down to the Ganges to float my candle, making a wish for the children I had seen begging the day before in the train station.

In the train station, a little boy—no older than seven or eight—had approached us; he held a plastic shopping bag in one hand and a sick baby in the other. The baby had matted hair, a dirty bare bottom, and her eyes were glued shut with dried pus. The boy held out his bag. "Shampoo," he begged, "soap." I had taken the travel-sized shampoos from our hotels, so I dug through my purse to give them to him. Sholeh took a photograph of the two children in the slant of morning light, the juxtaposition of the beautiful with the horrific making the scene all the more tragic. I handed over the shampoo, and the boy dropped it into his bag. A group of children saw this exchange and surrounded us. They begged us for school pens, soap, shampoo, one rupee. A little boy showed us miniature carved animals and said, "Elephants. Very good luck." A beautiful young girl with brown, feckless eyes and unevenly shorn hair held out postcards and said, "For your family." Sholeh bought a few sepia postcards, and I bought a tiny wooden elephant. The children didn't seem to notice each other, their eyes set on us.

A beggar sat on the concrete, looking up at us. His nose seemed melted into his face, his fingers fused together. I didn't know leprosy still existed but would later learn that India had the highest number of new leprosy cases in the world. I reached into my purse and fished out a PowerBar I had brought from home and handed it to him. He held it with his wrists, looking at the shiny wrapper. I realized there was no way he could open it. I took the bar back, telling him in English (which was perhaps more ridiculous than the PowerBar itself) that I would do it for him.

I unwrapped the bar and placed it back between his wrists. He looked at the congealed energy bar with what seemed like curiosity. It didn't resemble any of the food I had seen in India. "Let's go," Sholeh said, tired of watching the absurdity and the horror of this scene. Since I didn't know what else to do, I waved a goofy half-wave as we walked on. He nodded.

I wanted to believe I had done something good, but I knew I hadn't.

Sholeh and I waited for the train, and a teenaged boy, holding a small wooden box, caught my eye from the other side of the station. He strode over to me, passing stray cows and a turbaned man reading from the Koran. The boy weaved around a small girl who had lifted her skirt and was peeing on the concrete platform. The boy reached me and pointed to his boxful of blackened rags and shoe polish and then to my sandals. "No thank you," I told him.

"You need a shoe shine," he said, motioning to my sandals. "Very dirty."

Although he was right about my shoes—they were dirty—I said, "I'm fine."

"I have very good polish."

"It's not that," I said, knowing there was no way to explain. A cow with an injured leg limped by.

Sholeh could tell I was wavering, so she said, "I wouldn't let him do it. Just tell him no." She wasn't being unkind; she was originally from Iran and went to school in the Caribbean and Europe, so she was much more educated about the ways of the world than I was.

She also let me make my own mistakes.

"Please?" he begged.

"What could be the harm in it?" I asked.

"Don't say I didn't warn you," Sholeh told me. While the boy set to work on my leather sandals, I looked at Sholeh's pictures of the Taj Mahal, built by the Mughal emperor Shah Jahan for his favorite wife after she died in childbirth. Artisans spent twenty-two years building the domed mausoleum and decorating its walls with intricate patterns of semiprecious jewels; the Taj glitters in the moonlight, sparkles in the reflecting pools. Our guide had told us the artisans' hands were cut off at the completion of the project, so they couldn't betray the emperor by recreating the elaborate designs.

I felt a tug at my foot and glanced away from the camera's digital screen and down at the boy. He pointed to a large rip in my sandal, telling me in his limited English that it would cost extra for the repair. I spotted the pointed instrument he had used to tear the leather; it was already tucked back into his wooden box.

Later I would wish I had listened to Sholeh, but more than that, I would be ashamed that I didn't just pay the extra money and have the boy sew up the tear. But in the moment, I was travel-raw and tired, so I thought instead of my own loss in the transaction—my new travel sandals, ruined. And I thought about how I didn't want him to trick anyone else, and about what was right and what was wrong, which of course is much easier when you have the means to buy yourself a pair of $100 shoes. What was really wrong was the inequality in this, but at the time I said, "I know you did that on purpose. You tore my shoe with that tool. You sew it up right now, or I'll scream."

The boy quickly stitched up the sandal, and I didn't pay extra for the "repair." Only later would I realize his family could have lived for three months off what I paid for those sandals. He didn't rip my shoe out of meanness but from desperation. Sholeh didn't say, "I told you so," even though I deserved it. And I didn't tell her I should have listened to her because that was obvious, too. The train arrived, and a middle-aged couple stepped off with their guide. The husband told the guide, "I hope we're staying somewhere nice. My wife likes opulence, you know."

"Deserves," the wife corrected him.

"Well then," the guide said, "she shall have the sky."

I leaned down to the Ganges River to make a second wish for the boy who ripped my sandal, but I dropped my shells into the water, and they turned upside down, extinguishing the flames. I watched the dark ripple where the shells disappeared.

The sadhus, or holy men, congregated at the river's edge. They were unmistakable—either naked or in loincloths with long, tangled locks and beards, they covered their bodies with the ash from the cremations, making their mouths and eyes look like black holes. "You are lucky," our guide told us. "You have come during holy ceremony. Many holy men giving advice."

A sadhu is a man who has given up all worldly possessions, living a life of renunciation. He is considered dead both to himself and to the country of India. "They go to live in caves in the mountains, saying good-bye to all life," our guide said. One big-bellied sadhu drew a crowd. He stood on a block above the audience, rolling his ashy penis around a stick. A few videotaped his stunt. "They show that their bodies are unimportant in this way," the guide explained. "They are attached to nothing."

A Western woman—a traveler in the requisite zip-off pants and floppy hat, the tourist uniform I had so often seen and tried to avoid wearing—sat with a group of ash-covered sadhus. They were all smoking something, and she was laughing. I asked Sholeh, "Should we save her?"

"From what?"

I couldn't answer her.

My life at home, the one I called my real life, seemed far away. It was as if the pathways in my brain had started to navigate different channels, and the world itself shifted—ever so slightly, but enough to feel the tilt. Enough to show me that everything I believed was now up for question.

We walked past a dying cow. Someone had draped a blanket over the moaning animal, its large brown eyes already filled with flies, and three children tended a nearby fire. This cow might have ingested too many plastic bags, painfully blocking its intestines— the sad fate of many cows in India.

Our guide explained that once the cow died, it would be pushed into the river. "Cows, in this country, are very sacred," he said.

Anything considered sacred is not cremated but rolled into the river whole—not just holy cows but also children, pregnant women, and sadhus. Everyone else is cremated, promising liberation from the endless cycle of life and death, or *moksha*—an express ticket to paradise. Exceptions are those who are bitten by venomous snakes; they are sent down the river on bamboo stretchers for purification. If the body is caught as it floats by, it is then cremated when it has been determined that the individual is in fact dead and not just under the spell of the snake. Judging by the number of snake charmers I saw in India, I imagined there were many such stretchers bobbing along the Ganges.

Our guide led us down a narrow path to the burning bodies. He explained that the vips were burned in a separate area, opting for the more expensive sandalwood for their pyres. But once charred by flame, all the bodies looked alike. All smelled of rosewater, fire, and ash.

Every few minutes, men traveled barefoot down the steps of the ghat with another silk-shrouded body on their shoulders. They chanted, and the family followed. The oldest son, shaved from heel to head and robed in white, bathed in the river. It was his job to bring the eternal fire to the body and then throw the bone fragments in the river, telling his father, "You go your way now, and I'll go mine," preventing his father from becoming a ghost.

We weaved around small fires at the river's edge, the basket of the hips in one smoldering pile, the curved lower backbone in another. Our guide said, "This one's almost finished." He pointed to a burning pyre. A flame twisted from the ghostly socket of an eye. Fire ate the saffron cloth, the skin, the flesh. I looked at the other pyres; one held a pelvis, another a skull. "Three hours," our guide said, "to burn a body." The flames burned hot on my legs, and ash rained into my hair. "Very good luck. Good luck indeed." He pointed to the ash, the dead caught in my curls.

The Dalits tended to the eternal fire, a 3,500-year-old flame that must never die. Our guide told us a Dalit inherited the flame and now was a millionaire since cremations do not come cheap. Because the wood must be transported by boat along the Ganges to Varanasi, cremations on the banks of the river cost upwards of 40,000 rupees—nearly 900 U.S. dollars at the time, the average per capita income in India the year we visited. Families save their money, hoping for a cremation at the Varanasi ghats. The less expensive, though perhaps more environmentally friendly, cremations are done in large concrete crematoriums, the smoke billowing from their distant chimneys.

Varanasi is sometimes called "the city of death," and bodies were indeed everywhere. The dead were carried on bamboo stretchers along the streets, tied to the luggage racks of suvs. We traveled behind a body-topped car in traffic, and a foot peeked out from underneath the death shroud. I couldn't help but stare. The hummock of an ankle, the white ball of the heel, the curled toes—the bare foot of the dead felt like a stranger's secret overheard in passing, something that should have been kept private but wasn't.

"Come," our guide said, leading us past large stacks of wood. Cows and goats snuffled around in the embers. We entered a cold concrete building where the elderly sat on wooden pallets, waiting to die. As we walked past, their murky eyes followed our legs.

We met a woman with a toothless mouth and a creased face. She held out her hand, and a wrinkled breast sagged from her sari. She tucked it back in without apology. Our guide explained, "She needs money for her pyre. Good karma for you." We gave her 1,000 rupees, about 20 U.S. dollars at the time, a large sum by Indian standards but perhaps not enough to make her deadline. The guide said, "Not enough. You must give more for your karma." We shook our heads, saying we had given her enough. He wobbled his head, and I wondered about my karma.

Nothing will force you to face the reality of your life, and what to do with your aliveness, like the fact of a burning body. My eyes burned, and I felt a thickening in my throat, a breathlessness, and a more complicated mix of emotions than I knew was possible, including all the hard things I saw traveling through India, witnessing the world as it was, as well as my recognition of my privileged place in it—and all the difficult feelings that go along with this: guilt, relief, and a heavy sense of responsibility.

We left for the shore where the boatman waited. The azan rang in a chorus from nearby mosques, the call to prayer. The sun was a pink orb in the smoky sky. As we floated down the Ganges, I looked back toward the burning bodies, the black splotches on sand. We drifted through the smells of water and smoke, the living and the dying and the dead.

Children ran along the rooftop of the concrete building where an old woman waited to die. The fires below created hot wind that lifted their colorful kites and their laughter into flight.

Sleeping

~~~~~~

Our deeds still travel with us from afar, and
what we have been makes us who we are.

GEORGE ELIOT

Sometimes when I wake,
I'm shaping the world with my hands.

Sometimes when I sleep,
the world shapes me.

ILYSE KUSNETZ

Hotel Cádiz

Cuernavaca, Mexico, July 2002

We were in the Cuernavaca station, waiting for another bus, going on another date that we called an "excursion," as if renaming it could turn it into something else, something permissible.

As if I didn't have a husband at home.

David and I both attended the Spanish language school in Cuernavaca, though we weren't in the same class. He was fluent, a Spanish teacher taking classes toward his credential. I was trying to learn enough Spanish to fulfill the language requirement for my doctoral work. We had met our first weekend in Mexico on one of the program's cultural outings, a trip to Teotihuacán, an ancient Mayan city. Strolling along the Avenue of the Dead, David made me laugh harder than I had in months.

We made excuses to see each other most days after class. We talked about our lives—our families, our teaching jobs, even our day-to-day routines at home—without mentioning Craig, the husband we both knew I had; we were like magicians who made the stage's centerpiece disappear while the audience paid attention to the details of something else.

The weekend before, David went to Mexico City, and I went to Acapulco with my new friend Mina, and though I didn't want to admit it, I thought about David most of the time. Now we were headed to Las Grutas de Cacahuamilpa, a large network of underground caves. I watched the curve of David's face. He wiped his forehead and said, "I sweat a lot. Sorry."

"Sweating is good for you," I said, and David smiled.

We sat on a wooden bench among other travelers and sipped bottled water. Women with baskets full of fruit and bread weaved through the crowds. Taxi drivers leaned against old cars, waiting for fares. Dogs sniffed the streets for food, noses buried in garbage. A neon sign flashed red and blue.

I moved my hand from my lap and onto the bench, hoping gravity would pull David's hand to mine. Instead, he held a ripe grapefruit between his fingers and peeled it, exposing the naked flesh. He handed me a triangle of fruit, red and wet, with skin as soft as tissue paper. As we ate, the peels curled on the bench like question marks. I wiped my sticky hands on my shorts.

Eventually, the bus rattled down the dusty road.

"Vámonos," David said. "To the caves." I followed him to the bus.

David and I shared a too-small bus seat even though there were plenty of options. The Mexican landscape moved past the windows, and I watched ladies selling sundries on the side of the road and construction crews repairing asphalt. It seemed as if every American love song from the 1980s played on the radio: REO Speedwagon's "Can't Fight This Feeling" and Foreigner's "I Want to Know What Love Is." When Journey's "Open Arms" came on, I felt like I was back at a junior high roller-skating party, where my talent for skating backward had gone unrecognized because nobody had ever asked me to couples skate. I remember standing there in my *Flashdance* sweatshirt, hoping I looked approachable but not desperate.

Now somebody was clearly asking me to skate. What a feeling! I was a teenager again, in that dorky-but-alive way. Did I have to go backward to go forward?

Would I have to cheat on my husband to feel alive again?

I had carefully crafted the life I'd always imagined—the tenured teaching job, the husband who liked to ski, the cabin in the woods, our large network of friends, even the furry mountain dog.

I'd told myself this two-week solo trip to Mexico was a break from my life and that once I returned, I would be happy again. I'd told myself that all the arguments where we both started sentences with, "You're the one who . . ." would magically end.

David held my hand and read to me from his guidebook. According to it, Las Grutas was one of the largest cave systems in the world.

When we arrived, David led the way past other tourists, mostly Mexicans, to the entrance. We went through the turnstiles where the Chontalcoatlán and San Jeronimo Rivers merged and learned we could not enter the caves without a guide. A Spanish-language tour was leaving momentarily. My Spanish wasn't very good, but David could translate what I missed.

We crowded with the other tourists into the living Cacahuamilpa caves, where water still cut into rock. Inside, the air felt sparse, quiet, humid, still. David reached for me through the darkness. When our hands met, both were damp with sweat.

The guide told us, "Automatic lighting will be triggered by movement sensors." As we descended, the rocky aisle lit up, and our bodies cast charry shadows on the walls. Underground rivers splashed below. Our guide pointed out rock formations, fanciful resemblances of cave pearls, asparagus, broomsticks, tortillas.

We walked down the narrow pathway, single file. David's breath wafted against the back of my neck, and the hot air sent tremors down my spine. I became my desire; nothing else mattered but my own body in relation to this other body. My heart seemed to pump closer to the surface of my skin. Every last bit of reason was now crowded out by longing.

I have heard people say that they "couldn't help" cheating, but I could have helped it. I could have said no to that final date. I had renegotiated what was acceptable: "excursions," hand-holding. But I kept pushing at the invisible boundary. Once I entered those caves, the choice had been made. I would not go back to the little house my husband and I shared in Lake Tahoe, nor to our life together. It scared me, but in that moment desire took over, and I didn't have to think. David and I were like magnets hovering in a state of attraction and resistance before they collide. The air between us felt like that—a force field of torque and spark.

One of my favorite novels is Milan Kundera's *The Unbearable Lightness of Being*. In it, Tomas, a fantastic womanizer, cheats on his wife, Tereza. He carries no guilt. The burden, which manifests itself as bizarre dreams, is entirely on Tereza.

I saw myself in both characters. I was acting like Tomas, but like Tereza, I couldn't help but carry the burden of my own guilt.

The guide told us the decay of isotopes occurs at a predictable rate, something formed and destroyed at the same time—the ways of the earth. We continued to walk, and David pressed his palm into the small of my back. We passed through the Goat, Throne, and Cathedral salons, named for their formations. The guide pointed out other features: gypsum flower, Medusa's head, tangled vines. David muttered these translations into my ear and then pulled me to the side and whispered, "Vámonos."

We veered down another passageway, away from the group. The guide was busy clarifying how stalactites and stalagmites are formed, so he didn't notice us stray.

David and I stumbled upon a giant underground amphitheater, one with theater-style chairs used for concerts and other events. Eventually, the motion-sensing lights went out, and we sat down in the dark stillness. I realized we could easily get lost in the labyrinthine caves, and the thought excited me. Alone with David, underground, not just in another country but in another world, my other life—the one where my husband and I grocery shopped together, sat down to meals with friends, backcountry skied or hiked on the weekends—seemed so very far away, burrowed into a small corner of my brain.

I had spent so many years building the life I was about to destroy.

The smells closed around us: mineral earthiness, underground rivers, our own salty sweat. Desire is dependent on the wanting but not yet having, the body's tingle and ticking and tumble. The maybe-ness of possibility.

After a first, hesitant kiss—the space between us finally broken—we nearly devoured each other. Hands moved over bodies, hard and wet and trembling. I felt like a school of small silver fish swam in my veins. I don't know how long we were there; time disappeared, and what was left was one body frantic for the other.

Our group eventually approached the amphitheater, and we had to pull ourselves apart. We slipped back in with the others unnoticed, our bodies still full of yearning. The guide said we could return on the lighted path at our own pace, so we wandered back slowly.

At the mouth of the cave, the two subterranean rivers reemerged above ground, forming the Amacuazac River. Pale green leaves of amate trees fluttered in the wind. Our pupils wide, we blinked at the bright sunlight and walked into it.

The following evening would be David's last night in Mexico, so we made plans to meet up with our friends from the language school for happy hour. It was *dos por una*—two-for-one beers. I chose a seat across from David, and we stole glances at each other and smiled. I hoped no one would notice, but I'm sure they did. When Mina smiled at me across the table, I felt like I'd been caught.

A group of mariachis in powder-blue tuxedos played for us, and we reached into our pockets for pesos to tip them.

"Let's go dancing at MamboCafé," Mina said.

Even as the rest of our friends got up to go, David and I stayed at the table. "We'll meet you there," David told them.

Once everyone else had left, I said, "It's hard to believe you're leaving tomorrow."

"I know." He got up and sat next to me, taking my hand under the table.

"Happy hour's almost over," I said. "It's your last chance to get dos por una."

"I'm okay. I don't want anything else."

"Do you want to go to the dance club?" I asked. The mariachis started up a song for a couple on the other side of the restaurant.

David shook his head. "I think I'd rather walk around Cuernavaca with you."

"In the rain?"

"I have an umbrella."

We strolled the streets, past the Capilla del Carmen and the Templo de la Tercera Orden de San Francisco, through the water-soaked Jardín Borda with its red-blooming trees that my teacher had called *llama del bosque*—the flame of the forest. The misty rain glowed in the yellow light of the streetlamps. Taxis passed us, sounding their horns, flashing their lights, wondering if we wanted a ride. We kept walking, entering unfamiliar neighborhoods.

A street dog skittered out of the way of a car, its claws *click-clacking* on pavement. I couldn't help but think of my own dog, Riva, at home with my husband. I clutched David's hand and noticed that his fingers, his hands, were smaller than my husband's.

The rain picked up, falling in gray sheets. Despite the umbrella, we were drenched. Somewhere near midnight, we stumbled upon a small group of pink stucco cabañas with red tile roofs—the Hotel Cádiz—and paused at the front gate. Palms rustled in the courtyard. The sign read "Libre." Vacancy. "Bienvenido a Casa." Welcome Home.

I followed David down the red concrete, jig-sawed by weeds. I told myself, *Just to get in from the rain*. We walked into the hotel office. Fluorescent bulbs flickered from the ceiling. A man with deep wrinkles and tired-looking eyes asked us if we wanted a room. David told him yes.

"And your luggage?" he asked.

David shook his head, saying, "No, no tenemos." We have none.

The man pointed to a shelf behind him, asking us what we needed: bottled water, toothbrushes, toothpaste, shaving cream, razors, soap? David told him we'd take two bottles of water, a toothbrush, and toothpaste. When David pointed at the condoms, I looked at the tile floor.

We followed the man through the courtyard, past a sputtering fountain, to the room. He unlocked the door and asked us if the room was okay. David told him it was, and the man left us. The room was sparse but clean. The walls were an earthy red; the lamps on the bed tables were ceramic, cut with shapes so the light scattered circles and triangles on the red wall. The rain bounced off the metal roof in tin echoes. I sat on the edge of the bed—full-size, with a carved wooden headboard, the *cama matrimonial* David had asked for. Even with my limited Spanish, I knew the direct translation: wedding bed.

David came to me. "Is everything all right?"

I nodded, got up, and walked to the bathroom to dry off and brush my teeth with our shared toothbrush. I took off my wedding ring and placed it on the counter. I glanced into the mirror at my rain-soaked hair, then looked back at the silver ring. I decided this gesture was useless; I wasn't fooling anyone, not even myself. I slipped it back on my finger.

I took off my wet clothes and slid between the sheets. There was no reason to play coy. The truth was there in the room—a body wanting a body. David's bare feet padded across the red tile floor as he walked to the bed.

Outside the window, crickets called through the light rain. I turned off the lamp, and the shapes on the walls disappeared, replaced by shadows and flashes of lightning.

"What's 'lightning' in Spanish?" I asked.

"Relámpago."

"And 'thunder'?"

"Truenos." He took off his t-shirt and shorts and pulled back the sheet. "Guapa," he said, looking at me in the darkness.

"Thanks."

I remember the rain on the metal roof, the lightning and claps of thunder, the break in the storm and the crickets' song rising into the mist. I remember the shadows the palm trees cast across the floor. But I don't remember the sex. I do know it was over so quickly the first time that we waited and tried again. After that, I assured myself that the sex would improve once we got to know each other better. But longing leaves once you have gotten what you wanted. Without a body full of desire, I felt only shame.

I didn't sleep, and near dawn I told David I had to go, that I couldn't stay the night. The cloudy sky had already shifted from black to blue, and I wanted to be alone. I told David my homestay parents would worry about me. David agreed. He needed to go pack, anyway. In a few hours, he would be on a bus to Mexico City and then a flight home to Illinois.

I took my journal from my purse and ripped a page from it. "Write your information here," I said. David took the piece of paper. When he finished, I shoved the sheet into the pocket of my jeans without looking at it.

We took a taxi, and I was dropped off first. I told him we'd see each other again. He nodded. I kissed him good-bye and tried my key to the house, but I couldn't get the door to open. After some jiggling, the lock unfastened and my host father stood there in his robe at the door. "Lo siento," I said, apologizing. He nodded and walked upstairs. I felt terrible for waking him but also for everything else.

When I got to my room, I unfolded the journal page with David's address and telephone number. Across the top, he had written "Te quiero," which I thought meant "I want you." This didn't make sense; he'd already had me. Then I remembered *te quiero* from the soap operas. I had taken to watching *novelas*, or Mexican soap operas, with the live-in maid, Flora, in the afternoons. I only knew enough Spanish to exchange pleasantries with the family, but when I watched television with Flora, I didn't feel like I needed to say anything. I laughed when she laughed, even if I didn't get the joke. And she would smile at me, making me feel like I really did understand. She would recline with her swollen feet propped up on the table, but as soon as she heard a car pull into the courtyard, she pulled her feet off the table and shoved them back into her house shoes.

I looked at the note again, but I was so tired the words started to blur on the page. *Te quiero* didn't mean "I want you." It meant "I love you." Could that be true? I fell into bed and went to sleep.

When I met David a few hours later at the bus station, he said, "I knew you would come. I'm so happy you're here."

Because I'd surprised myself by meeting him there, I thought maybe he was able to understand me in a way I couldn't yet figure out myself. I felt understood. Was that love? I thought maybe it was.

"I'll see you again," I said.

"Promise?" he asked and kissed me.

I said I did. A promise I didn't know how to keep.

David told me, "Te quiero." I smiled and nodded, and he walked to the bus. I waved good-bye.

Rather than going back to my homestay, I boarded another bus headed to Tepoztlán, an artist community near the ruins of a temple built three thousand years ago by the Tlahulca Aztecs. The temple is known for its carvings, depicting offerings and sacrifices to the Aztec *pulque* gods for fermentation, drunkenness, and fertility. The ruins of the Temple of Tepozteco were a mile and a half up a steep, rocky trail. David and I had been there together a few days before, but we had gotten a late start, and we hadn't made it to the top.

I wasn't sure what led me to take the bus to Tepoztlán that morning. I hadn't even planned on going to say good-bye to David until I found myself setting out for the station. The rules of my life had failed me; I had done a lot of unplanned things already, and maybe what I needed wasn't a rule book but a compass. I was learning to follow an impulse I didn't understand. And maybe I needed to practice the detachment I would need to survive the coming years when the life I had created would unravel.

I got off the bus and walked along the cobbled streets of Tepoztlán, looking at the colorful stalls—fruits and vegetables, candy and paintings, ceramics and other handicrafts. I bought a small ceramic turtle with a bobble neck for my mother, and for myself, I purchased a tiny carved replica of the Pirámide de Tepozteco. I headed for the trail to the ruins, knowing only I wanted to complete the hike David and I had started together, to see what was there. This, at least, was something I could finish.

The day was clear—a blue sky stretched tight across the morning. It was a Saturday, and the trail was crowded, so I had to stop many times to let people pass on the narrow stone steps. I was so tired my bones hurt, and my eyes felt like they were full of sand. The locked gate where David and I had turned around was open, so I passed through it and kept hiking the rocky path.

When I reached the top, I realized that David and I hadn't even made it halfway to the ruins that day. I couldn't have known that this one-night stand would lead to a messy eighteen-month affair. Nor could I have predicted all the broken hearts left in my wake, including my own. Or that shattering and reassembling my heart many times over would help me find a truer version of myself, a woman who would learn how to be happy alone and live—finally—on her own terms.

I only looked out, past the ruins and over the green valley, and thought that there had been so much farther to go.

Loving the Lie

San Jose, Costa Rica, July 2004

The ex-pat showed me the kissing parks.

"The what?" I asked him and squinted into the rain.

"The kissing parks. Young ticos live with their parents, so at night, they come here to make out. Once it's dark, every bench fills with amantes."

I stared at him, and he explained: "Lovers." I already knew the Spanish word *amante*, and I hadn't been looking at him in that strange way because I was confused. It was that he was more handsome than I had initially thought. "Some sightseeing tour," I said, and he laughed.

I had arrived in Costa Rica that morning, but it was one of those travel days that feels more like a week. When I told the taxi driver the name of the San Jose hotel where I wanted to stay, he said, "That's a very bad hotel. I know a better one. The Hotel Inca Real."

I told him in my strained Spanish that I wanted to go to the one I had already picked out.

"It burned down," he tried.

"Really?" I was too tired for this, having just arrived on a red-eye.

"Or maybe it went out of business. It isn't there, but I know a very good one."

I told him I wanted to go to the address of the bad, burned down, out-of-business hotel. I told him I had a reservation.

"Listen," he told me. "The hotel where I'm taking you is only 25 dollars American. A very good price. Nada para ti." Nothing to you.

I tried one more time to tell him I wanted to go to the hotel in my guidebook, so he finally admitted if he brought me to this other hotel, he'd get a cut. And he needed it for his children. I agreed.

Tourists filled the lobby, smoking cigarette after cigarette, drinking Cuba libres. A near-empty fish tank bubbled in the corner. The hotel tried to improve the smell with lilac air freshener, making a sickening odor of fake flowers, rotting fish, and smoke. The manager showed me to a room with no windows. I paid him the $25, and a portion of it went to my taxi driver.

Before traveling to Central America, I had contacted my friend's brother, who was living in Costa Rica. This ex-pat had offered to help me find a place to stay, but I had insisted I could do it on my own. Maybe, I realized, I should have accepted his help.

I had agreed to meet him that afternoon at a bar called La Casa del Cerdo—The House of Pig—to watch the soccer match, and then he would show me around San Jose before I left for Quepos, where I would be taking Spanish language classes. I had met him a few times; he wasn't exactly a stranger, but he might as well have been. The only things I knew about him were that he was deeply religious, he had moved recently to Costa Rica, and he was a seemingly nice guy. I didn't think much else about him.

The bar was crowded with soccer fans in an uproar because Argentina was beating Costa Rica. I ordered rice and beans with—of course—*cerdo*. And coffee so strong my gums hurt.

The game ended with a win for Argentina, and he asked, "Okay, museums or parks?"

"Parks, definitely," I said. The bar started to clear out.

"You don't want to go to the Gold Museum?"

"No, not really."

"Parks, huh? Even in the rain?"

"I'd rather be outside. It'll keep me awake. I haven't slept for more than twenty-four hours. And I have an umbrella," I said, showing him. He smiled. We left the bar and weaved through the rain-soaked streets. He told me about the pickpockets who sliced the bottom of tourists' backpacks and stole whatever dropped out. We passed the colonial buildings of the Barrio Amón and walked by the national library and through the Parque Nacional, the Parque España, the Parque Central, and the Plaza de la Cultura, which the ex-pat called the kissing parks.

The rain turned to mist, the broad-leafed trees dripped with rainwater, and the air filled with a chorus of birdsong. "Listen to that," I said, "it's amazing."

Even though I was exhausted, I ran on fumes of novelty. I was determined to occupy each moment, so when the ex-pat wondered if I wanted to see the brothels, I didn't stop to think about whether or not this was strange—only that I wanted to see whatever there was to see. And whatever there was to do, I would do it.

"Kissing parks and brothels," I said. "This sure is some city tour."

"We can always go to the Gold Museum."

"I'm not complaining."

Looking back, I see what this sounds like—a tour of kissing parks and brothels—yet in the moment, it felt like part of the adventure of travel.

The Costa Rican brothels were not like the ones we have in Nevada, trailers hidden in the desert with women walking around in lingerie. Here, some of the hotel lobbies served as brothels; you just had to know which ones to go to. And like everyone who lived in San Jose, the ex-pat knew. We walked into the Hotel Rey, overflowing with middle-aged American men and young Costa Rican women. A giant man wearing Wranglers and a cowboy hat was flanked by two beautiful women; they were so young that really they were girls, dressed up to look like women. Dark rings of sweat circled the underarms of the man's button-down shirt, and his wide face glowed red like a beet.

I needed to get out of there. "Let's go," I said. "I need a nap."

We walked back to my hotel in the rain.

In the lilac-scented lobby, the hotel manager was talking to two American surfers. The manager cupped his hands over his chest, saying, "Grande, muy grande."

"What's he saying?" I asked.

"He's arranging a sale."

I nodded, understanding the exchange. We said good-bye and made plans to meet up for drinks later. I fell into a deep sleep in my windowless room and dreamed about sex with the ex-pat.

I woke up, startled by my explicit dreams. I showered and walked to the Dunn Hotel. Dusk had already fallen; men filled the street corners and stood in the shadows of the buildings' eaves. They whistled at me as I passed, calling out, "Guapita, bonita." I hurried by, looking at my shoes. I knew I shouldn't be on the streets of San Jose alone after dark, but I wished that wasn't true, so I walked alone, still shrinking at the catcalls of men. I tried to be brave, but it was exhausting.

I hugged the ex-pat hello, and then we ordered two small plates, a glass of wine each. When it came, it was obvious the bottle had been open for days if not weeks, more vinegar than wine. He told me about his life in San Jose, wondered if he would ever return to the States. "My parents are worried I won't come back," he said, "and to tell you the truth, I can't see it." He asked, "How are you able to do all this traveling?"

"I have summer off from teaching," I said, curating my story so that I didn't have to tell him about accruing a mountain of debt, my divorce, the long-distance love affair with the Spanish teacher from Illinois that had recently ended, or moving back in with my ex-husband, Craig, in order to pay my mortgage—I left out those glamorous details of my life. "And I need more Spanish for my doctoral degree requirements, so here I am."

"Since you're here," he said, "how about some Latin dancing at El Pueblo?"

"I'm up for whatever," I said. The sky was an inky black, and the birds sang to each other in the trees.

In the bathroom of the Cuban salsa club, I stared into the mirror. My face was sweaty and flushed from dancing. As it turned out, my ex-pat—I was now thinking in terms of "my" rather than "the"— was a very sexy dancer. I said this to the mirror: *Don't do it, don't do it, don't do it,* as if anyone ever talked herself out of something— especially this—in the mirror of a bathroom in a Costa Rican bar.

I went back and found him, and after one spin around the dance floor, my resolution shattered. I knew what I was about to do. I'd taken this time to travel alone, and I should have been working on myself, as they say, but desire was an intoxicating distraction from the mess of a life I'd created at home.

When we got into my ex-pat's car, he asked, "What do you want to do?"

It was 1:30 a.m. I was jetlagged and tired and a little bit woozy from the wine. I looked at my hotel key, which I already held in my hand, but still I asked, "What are our options?" I probably cocked my head in a way I thought would look alluring in the dark car. I probably made sure there was a lilt to my voice, that I emphasized the word "options." I was thirty-three, old enough that I should have seen this coy act for what it was: silly and more than a little bit sad. As a girl, and then a woman, I had been taught these small gestures, so I could lure a man. Make him want me. I learned this by watching my own mother. Nobody had ever told me to make sure that's what I wanted, to make sure the man was worth wanting. And I hadn't yet realized my own worth, separate from men.

"Well," he said, "we can go to another bar, go to your hotel lobby and talk, or go to my place for another drink."

"I'm too tired for another bar," I said.

"And your hotel lobby smells like fake flower perfume, right?"

"It's gross."

"Then to my place for a drink?"

Of course, we both knew it wasn't a drink we were after. We had both switched to water hours earlier, and he admitted that the only thing he had to drink at home was cheap whiskey.

"I can't drink that straight," I said when we got to his apartment.

"Well, we can mix it with milk or pink lemonade. Your choice."

"Yum. Milk and whiskey."

He poured himself a shot of whiskey and mixed mine with lemonade. I can't report what this mixture tasted like because before I took a sip, we were tangled on the couch. I remember being embarrassed because my sandals had cut indented stripes across the tops of my swollen feet. But after the shoes came off, the clothes followed, making me forget about my puffy feet. We made it to the bedroom, clothes scattered across the dark hallway in a clichéd trail, and I said, "I wasn't expecting this."

That, of course, was a lie.

In bed, he told me he had been a pastor, a virgin until twenty-nine. He said, "I can't stop touching you." Then he switched to Spanish, and I had no idea what he was saying. I loved not knowing.

I loved the lie more than the truth.

At the time, I didn't realize the real lie was the one I told myself: I shaped myself to reflect the male gaze.

We stayed up all night, knotted in the sweaty bedsheets; the streetlamps glowed through barred windows, casting shadows like teeth.

The taxi blared its horn through dawn rain. "There's still time," he said, reaching for me as I rose from the mattress on the floor.

"No," I said. "My taxi's already here." I gathered my things, dressed in the dark. He walked me down the stairs to the door. The rain was a yellow spray, caught in the taxi's headlights. The streets were beginning to fill with the *madrugadores*, early morning workers. There is no word in English for *madrugada*—that time between midnight and morning, the grayish blue of nearly dawn that hovers in the sky during the small hours.

He followed me barefoot into the street, handed me my bag, kissed my cheek, and I said, "¡Hasta pronto!" meaning "soon."

Meaning "I won't see you again."

The San Jose bus station coursed with tourists and locals, carrying huge satchels, babies, plastic bags full of things bought in the city. Because I ended up missing the earlier bus, I was trying to figure out how to get to Quepos on another one that was *directo*, meaning I wouldn't have to change buses. Two women approached me. One stood behind me and the other in front, asking me for change. I said I didn't have any, trying to get the Spanish right, and then I remembered what my ex-pat had told me about the pickpockets. I twirled around, and the other woman backed away. I pulled my backpack to the front, and the pocket was open. Both women hurried off. An empty sunglasses case and lipstick were both gone. "I hope it's your color," I shouted to them in Spanish and felt the pressure behind my eyes, but I would not allow myself to cry. *It's just lipstick*, I told myself. *Who needs lipstick in the jungle?*

I figured out which bus to board and chose a seat near a window. The city fell away, replaced by a greenscape of fern, teak, bamboo, and orchids. I worried about what I had just done: a one-night stand in a foreign city. It wasn't that I minded how it sounded, at least for somebody else. I wanted to go where my desire led me, to inhabit my own body, but I didn't know how to do that without being a body in relation to another body. I had been looking to feel adventurous and sexy, but replaying the previous hours in my mind only intensified my aloneness, my anxiety about where my life was going. And if I was being honest with myself, I was looking for a flicker of love in each brief encounter.

Outside the window, a man stood at the edge of the highway, where the jungle encroached onto the potholed asphalt; he leaned on a roadside cross, hiding his head in the crook of his elbow. A waterfall trickled down the green mountainside, pooling at his feet. A bicycle lay off to the side. His pants were rolled up to his knees, and a river ran over his bare feet. He was sobbing and didn't look up as our bus rattled by. I watched him as we passed. The cost of great love, I thought, is the terrible beauty of grief.

We rounded a curve, leaving the man and his tears. I looked ahead. "Jesus está en mi corazón" was painted on the windshield. A crowned Jesus clasped his hands in prayer. The eyes had been scratched out, and the canyon walls and a ribbon of highway twisted through them.

The Call of the Coquí

Rincón, Puerto Rico, December 2004

"I crossed the ocean and then the island for you," Sancho said when he found me at the bar in Rincón, his white teeth shining like the keys of a piano. His small blue backpack was slung over his shoulder. He pushed back his long dreadlocks and kissed my cheek. "And it wasn't easy," he said. "I had to take the ferry, and then the guagua, and finally hitch a ride to Rincón. So here I am."

"Here you are." I smiled. We stood on the deck of the small, noisy bar. The band had just taken a break, and my friend Tracy was inside talking to the guitarist.

"You called me, and I knew I had to come," he said.

"How did you know I'd be at the Tamboo Bar?" I asked.

"I knew," he said, smiling. "This is the place to be."

"And I'm always in the place to be."

"You are," he said with a seriousness that made me laugh.

I felt giddy at the idea of a man crossing an ocean and then an island for me, even as small as Puerto Rico was. I slipped off my sandals, and we walked from the deck into the sand; we watched the waves unfold and retreat, leaving a lacy curtain on the shore. The night filled with the sounds of palm fronds, crickets, and coquíes, the tiny singing frogs, and the smells of salt and seaweed. Each wave shone blue-green; the crashing caused the bioluminescence, the same flash we'd seen while kayaking a few days earlier in Mosquito Bay, also known as the "Bio Bay" of Vieques. The glow zippered across the sand with each wave, the foam a patchwork of neon.

That's when Sancho kissed me, and his broad mouth and soft lips took me by surprise, even though I'd been waiting two days, or maybe a lifetime, for a kiss to happen like that, on the edge of an island, between two palms, under a sky canvassed with stars. My toes splayed out onto the sand, the ground below me shifting.

Tracy and I were at the end of our two-week tour of Puerto Rico, a mostly rambling unplanned-out trip over holiday break from teaching. We traipsed across the island, then out to Culebra and Vieques, the smaller Spanish Virgin Islands, ending our trip with two days in Rincón. We had no reservations, no real expectations—no thoughts of the future aside from being husbandless and free.

Except I was living with my ex-husband, so technically I was not husbandless, nor free. But I had become good at lying to myself on these points. And travel gave me a way to escape.

Two days earlier, Sancho had been our guide on a kayaking tour of Mosquito Bay, the brightest bioluminescent bay in the world. With our towering long-haired island man extraordinaire, we kayaked through the dark mangroves and then jumped into the black waters, where our bodies lit up. Tracy and I twirled, sparks flying. When we lifted our arms from the water, tiny stars of light rolled off. Although I knew there was a scientific explanation—that millions of one-celled microorganisms were responsible for the blue-green flashes of light as a way to scare off predators—it seemed like fairy dust, nothing short of magic.

Later in a bar called Bananas, Sancho bought me a drink (or maybe he knew the bartender and got it for free) and said, "Why don't you girls come on my snorkeling tour tomorrow to Red, Blue, and García Beaches? I'll give you a good deal."

"I think we're leaving for Rincón tomorrow," I said, trying to ignore that he called us girls and not women, even though we were in our thirties.

"How about you come for free? On me?" he asked.

"That's awfully nice of you," I said. "Really. But we're leaving tomorrow. Tracy wants to try surfing. Or at least boogie boarding. The waves are supposed to be good in Rincón."

"The surf's big for you girls this time of year."

"How do you know?" I asked, probably trying for a demure smile. The ocean outside rolled onto the shore behind me.

"I know," he said, smiling. "Listen, I want to spend the night with you."

"You're asking me to have a one-night stand with you?" I laughed and took a sip of my drink. I wasn't offended by the offer because I was flattered.

"No, I want to spend two nights with you." He put his arm around me. The bioluminescent bay had made me feel like I was swimming through a fairy tale, a magical place where a stranger asking me to have sex with him turned him into an island prince.

"I don't know about that," I said. A princess should always be coy; my beauty queen mother had taught me that. In her economy, being wanted by a man determined self-worth. And I couldn't escape my upbringing.

At some point in the evening, Sancho wandered away, and Tracy and I decided it was time to head back to our hostel. I liked flirting with Sancho. Like usual, being pursued was intoxicating. But I wasn't sure I wanted to spend two nights with him. Or even one. I knew only that I wanted to be wanted.

Sancho spotted us the next morning, having breakfast at the picnic tables outside The Tiki House, and he came over to sit down with us. "You coming on my kayak tour today?" For the first time, I noticed how big his hands were, easily twice the size of mine, and I'm not exactly petite.

"No, we have to leave. I told you that last night." I took a sip from my mango smoothie.

"You disappeared from the bar. Where did you go?" Sancho shaded his eyes from the sun.

"We didn't disappear," I said. "You disappeared, and we left. It was late."

"But I told you, I want to spend two nights with you."

Tracy shot me a look. I shrugged my shoulders. We communicated whole sentences in this way, as girlfriends do. I told Sancho, "Then you'll have to come to Rincón." I knew Rincón was across an ocean and then an island—difficult for someone like Sancho, a tour guide without a car, to navigate. Tracy and I had decided to rent a car from the ferry dock, and even so, it would take all day to get there.

"Take my number," he said. "Call and tell me where you are."

When we arrived at the dock on the mainland, I left a message for Sancho from a payphone, telling him we were headed to Rincón. I didn't think he would really show up.

Sancho had been right about the waves in Rincón being too big for us to surf. We settled for a turbulent swim in the white water, fighting the ocean's strong undertow until it shoved us under, our limbs akimbo in the surf. The woman who checked us into our studio apartment told us that a band was playing later that night at the Tamboo Bar, so we stopped there for a drink. When we arrived, the band was on break, and the guitarist, an American ex-pat named Patrick, headed straight over to Tracy. He flirted with her and bought us both drinks. I told Tracy I thought he had weird eyes, but she said, "He's fine, Suzanne. Stop worrying." I had inherited my mother's propensity to worry, to be afraid, though I did everything I could to counter it, which sometimes included recklessness.

Because I was famous among my friends for worrying about the wrong things, I nodded at Tracy and tried not to think about Patrick's ice-blue eyes. I told myself that worrying is living in the future. I reminded myself to live in the present.

And that's when Sancho, his little backpack slung over a shoulder, walked into the Tamboo Bar. "There you are. I finally found you," he said as if he had been following the rainbow and had finally reached the pot of gold. This was the kind of surprise made possible only in the days before everyone carried a phone.

Tracy and I both hugged Sancho and introduced him to Patrick, who then bought us all another round of drinks, though I suspect as a member of the band, he was getting them for free. The band started up again, which meant more dancing and then another round of free drinks. The rest of the evening, except for that first kiss on the beach, is a blurry memory, like it happened underwater, or on a film reel that keeps catching.

I invited Sancho back to the studio apartment Tracy and I had rented. Patrick told Tracy, "I think we should have sex, don't you?" She didn't think so, so she sent him on his way. Meanwhile, Sancho and I dragged the futon mattress onto the balcony, while Tracy slept on one of the double beds inside.

I don't remember the sex as much as I remember how it made me feel. For the moment, drunk on tropical drinks and an island man, I lived in the present tense of my life. Or at least that's how it seemed. In my memory, the sex was the blue flash of the ocean and the call of crickets and coquíes. It was the way the palm fronds rustled in the moonlight, the static of the sea. It was the fine shadow of a banana spider as it trellised up a stucco wall. It was an escape into place, as well as an attempt at fearlessness—to be bold without apology.

Afterward, I listened for the call of coquíes on the pleats of wind. Coquí is the common name for several species of small frogs endemic to Puerto Rico. They are characterized by the direct development from egg to small frog; the tadpole stage happens inside the egg, so when the egg hatches, little frogs crawl out, emerging fully formed, hidden during their evolution, their becoming. Critical habitat has been designated, as coquíes are in danger of extinction.

The mating call sounds like *koh-kee*, hence their name. Only males call during courtship: the first part of the call establishes territory; the second syllable is meant to attract a mate. The females travel long distances to answer. We heard the call of the coquíes nightly in Puerto Rico. We looked for them but never saw one.

At dawn, with Sancho's long limbs draped over me, I felt hungover and, worse, stifled and ashamed. I untangled myself, got up, pulled on my pajamas, went into our studio apartment, walked past my bed, and crawled into Tracy's with her.

"Hi," she said. "Did you have fun?"

"I'm sore," I said. "And I have a headache."

Tracy laughed. "Ay, chica."

Sancho came in, went to the sink, splashed water on his face, and examined himself in the mirror. I watched as he pulled out vials of lotions from his backpack and started smearing the various creams on different parts of his face.

"What's that stuff?" I asked.

"These are my face emollients," he said. "The sea water is hard on the skin." He smiled his big, toothy grin. "How do you think I stay so good looking?"

"Is he for real?" Tracy asked.

Sancho turned from the mirror and smiled at us again, and we all laughed. Then Sancho peered back into the mirror and said, "Shit. I don't believe this."

"What?" Tracy asked.

"I think I have a pimple," he said touching his chin. Tracy and I were still laughing, but Sancho was serious now, inspecting his blemish.

Patrick arrived at our open door, shouting, "Hello! Who wants to go to the beach?"

We changed into our swimsuits and piled into Patrick's car. On the way, we stopped at the market to get snacks.

"Can you buy mine?" Sancho asked. "I don't have any money."

"What do you mean you don't have any money? You came here without money?" I'm not sure if I was surprised or just pretending to be.

"I spent it all trying to get here. I came all the way here for you."

I bought our beach snacks, plus two ice cream bars for Sancho. I watched as he stuck out his long tongue, scooping up a little bit of ice cream with each lick. I had wanted him to be part of my experience, like the moon shadows or the call of the coquíes. It was now clearer than ever that I didn't want to keep him.

Certainly, Sancho hadn't followed me across the island so he could have a meaningful relationship. He'd stated exactly what he'd wanted: two nights with me. At least he had been up-front. If I had used him for sex, we would be even. But I began to see that Sancho fulfilled some sort of island fantasy, and something about that made me feel even worse. I had used him in an attempt to reach a part of myself that I wasn't sure how to access without seeing myself through a man's desire—the same as it always was.

I felt as if I had been turned inside out. I knew I wasn't special or sexy or interesting. Let's face it: a young woman can have sex with nearly any young man of her choosing. I wish someone had told me this then. No matter how I tried to frame it, I was a conquest, the loose American woman. We didn't differ in our intentions that much, except for one important way: Sancho wanted to spend two nights with me, but I only wanted him for one.

Once we got to Corcega Beach, Sancho and Patrick went swimming. Tracy and I sat on our towels. She turned to me and said, "You're acting *so* weird."

"Weird how?"

"I don't know. Just weird. What's going on?" A seagull landed next to us.

"It was fine last night," I said. "I mean I was caught up in the moment. And the sex was good, actually. But now, I just want to get away from him." I looked out at the ocean where Patrick and Sancho were bobbing around in the giant waves.

"Next day regrets?" Tracy asked.

"Totally."

"You're just hungover," she said and rolled over onto her stomach.

"No, it's more than that. I don't want to be with him." I brushed the sand from my thighs.

"Then tell him to leave," Tracy said.

"He has no money."

"Not your problem." The gull took off and swooped above in the wind, the morning light reflecting off its wings.

"It feels like my problem."

A little boy with a box of beads hanging from his neck asked us if we wanted him to make us earrings. Tracy waved him away and then said to me, "It's not like you invited him here."

"But I sort of did. And I don't want to sleep with him again."

"So don't." Tracy told me she would sleep on the balcony and give us the apartment. That way I could make Sancho sleep on the other bed. Looking back, I wish I had asked him to leave. But I was used to putting men's feelings above my own. So even though I was determined not to give him what he wanted, I would still let him stay in our apartment. Hadn't it been my fault for luring him across the island?

"I'm sorry," I told Tracy. I knew I was putting her out. I could not stop apologizing.

"Don't worry about it. It's all part of the adventure. And I want to sleep on the balcony anyway, to the sound of the waves," she said. "Maybe you should go for a walk? You'll feel better."

I looked out at the water. Sancho and Patrick were still splashing around, trying to body surf, but it was clear that the waves were too big. "Okay. A walk," I said. "Are you okay here alone?"

"I'm fine. And don't beat yourself up too much. You're on vacation."

I got up and walked down the long stretch of beach until I could no longer see Sancho, Patrick, and Tracy. What I really wanted was to walk away from myself. I couldn't understand why I did the things I did. I wanted to get away from Sancho but felt like that made me an awful person—the kind who would rather have a one-night stand than a two-night stand. I knew what my mother would say about a woman like that: she had let things "go too far." According to my mother's logic, she could make amends by feeling guilt and shame—in other words, if you felt badly enough, you might have a chance at redemption and regaining your "good woman" status. For my mother, guilt was a very useful emotion. But I knew that just as worrying was living in the future, guilt meant living in the past.

I wanted to claim my own desire but without guilt, to be carefree, wild even, without having to down tropical drinks to erase my shame. I wanted to wake up with the clear-eyed acceptance that perhaps I was someone who wanted to have a one-night stand with a handsome stranger without it meaning anything at all, and I could still be a good woman. What I didn't realize at the time was that my self-worth shouldn't have depended on whether I was a good woman or not.

I walked back along the shore and decided I would forgive myself if I made this promise: I would not have sex with Sancho again. Not because it was wrong but because I didn't want to. And that would have to be enough. A pelican dove into the ocean, came back to the surface, and gulped down a fish. The boy with a box of beads asked me if I would like a necklace. I answered him in Spanish: "No, thank you, not today."

I knew it would take a lot less explaining to just go along with the sex, telling myself I had already been with him, so what was one more night? But this time I knew I couldn't. This was no longer about Sancho. This was about me. It seemed pretty straightforward—what I wanted for my body was more important to me than what he wanted. Yet that would mean I had to tell him I didn't want him, and that seemed difficult.

I started searching for an excuse, a convenient lie.

We left the beach and drove to a small outdoor bar. The bartender asked us how we were doing. Sancho put his arm around me and said, "I'm doing great, especially after last night. What a night. Wow." He smiled his big, toothy grin at the bartender and squeezed my shoulder.

There it was, my excuse. I pulled away from him and whispered, "How dare you."

"What's the matter, sweetheart?" He looked genuinely surprised. "What's wrong? It was just a joke."

"Well, it wasn't a funny one. I'm embarrassed." I made more of a fuss over the comment than was called for, hoping I could hang my rejection of him on that boastful remark, making it easier than trying to explain my real feelings.

"I didn't mean to embarrass you," he said.

"Well you did."

Sancho had wanted to spend two nights with me. And he would— one on his terms, the other on mine. It didn't seem like much, but at least it was something: a way to start breaking free from my pattern of fucking followed by self-flagellation. A way to stop depending on men to feel interesting.

Patrick bought Sancho's drinks, and they smoked cigars. By then, Sancho and Patrick acted like old friends. Patrick still hoped Tracy would change her mind, so he approached her from every angle possible. He didn't realize what a bad wingman Sancho made. And Tracy didn't need Patrick to complete her island experience, so she said no without apology.

"Didn't you say you had friends here to stay with?" I asked Sancho.

"I do."

"Where are they?"

"I don't know. I'll see them later."

Sancho stood at the edge of my bed and said, "But I want to make love to you."

"I said no." I turned to face the other wall.

"But I don't understand. What did I do?"

"You made that comment at the bar, bragging about your conquest." The palm fronds shook against the window, their shadows flowing like hair across the white sheet. I pretended to be asleep and thought about how if Sancho tried to force me, I could call for Tracy, who slept on the balcony, but I wasn't sure she would be much help against a man nearly seven feet tall. Also, I could hear my mother's voice, blaming me for getting myself into this situation to begin with. I was lucky that Sancho wasn't the type of man who would force me, but he did plead.

He stood there at the side of the bed in the blue shadows and begged, "Please?"

"Sancho, no." I tried to sound half-asleep.

"Can I sleep in the same bed with you?" He hovered over me.

"No," I said without turning to him.

"Please? I don't understand."

"I can't explain it. You hurt my feelings." I put the sheet over my head. It was true, and it wasn't true. I knew I had been the one to hurt my own feelings first, and this seemed like the only way to redeem myself.

Sancho went back to the other bed, but every couple hours, I caught him trying to sneak into bed with me. I kept telling him, "No. I'm not going to change my mind. Go away."

I waited for the pink break of day and listened for the call of the coquíes, the crickets, the ocean. And there it was: no meant no. My needs were more important than his. Something broke free inside of me. I could feel it.

In the morning, we drove Sancho back to San Juan so he could catch the *guagua*, or the small bus, to the ferry station. I had to give him $10 for the bus and ferry. "Are you sure the bus is only $5?" I asked.

"Yep," he said, "they charge tourists more."

"Is that how everything here works?" Tracy asked. We had paid $25 and only after an argument. The driver wanted to charge us $50.

"Yeah. I mean I charge different rates for my tours depending on where people are staying. You were at the Tradewinds; it's a cheap place, so that would be one rate. But the people at the spendy hotels, I charge them at least double. Why not? They can afford it. And they pay it."

At the bus terminal Sancho asked, "Are you still mad at me?"

"Not mad," I said. A taxi blared its horn.

"Good," he said. "I hope I can see you again. Can I have your address?"

"Why don't you write yours here, in my journal?" I handed him my small notebook and a pen. When he finished, I noticed he had written a different name. "Who's that?" I pointed to the name.

"That's me. That's my name." He gestured to himself. "Sancho's just a nickname." He pulled his small blue backpack onto his shoulder.

"I didn't even know your name?"

"Sancho's enough," he said. He walked away, then stopped and turned to wave.

I waved and then got back into the car and turned to Tracy. "I didn't even know his name."

"Not surprised," Tracy said, looking into the rearview mirror as she pulled out into traffic.

"I had a one-night stand with someone whose name I didn't know."

"So what? What difference does it make? Why do you care?"

She was right. What difference did it make? I could revise the story to make myself feel even worse—now I wasn't just a woman who'd had a one-night stand with a stranger; I also didn't know his name. But I was too tired for that. And didn't I know his name now? I looked out the window. The American and Puerto Rican flags flew together, each on its own silver pole. We drove for a while, past a Texaco and a McDonald's, and I said, "You know, we never did see a coquí."

Tracy nodded, as if she had never expected to see the frog we heard nightly. She tended to accept the world the way it was. I said, "They say that when a coquí is removed from Puerto Rico, it will never sing again."

"Who's they?" Tracy asked.

"I don't know. I probably read it in the guidebook. But I like the metaphor."

"You know, Suzanne, something isn't always something else."

I would never see Sancho again, though that's probably obvious enough. But later I would google his name—the nickname he went by—and find a Tripadvisor review saying he was a great guide and had a fantastic sense of humor. The reviewer said that Sancho had told his guests he was actually 150 years old, that the bioluminescent bay was responsible for his youthful appearance.

I thought of him standing in front of the mirror in the morning light, and I smiled. All these years later, this image makes me love them—the man at the mirror and the two young women curled up together in the bed. And there it is—not the transgression nor moral failing nor the morning-after anxiety. Just what it was—the final calls of the nocturnal coquíes, three young people laughing in a cheap rented room, and the early morning light tumbling onto shore.

Fourteen One-Night Stands

Nicaragua, December 2005

I woke up with that not-sure-where-you-are feeling, and I turned over to face the back of a man I didn't know—or at least that's how it seemed to me. I was in a Managua hotel room. And the man wasn't a stranger.

Dawn brightened the room: pink stucco walls, a painting of a brightly colored fishing village, an unlocked safe, a stained flowered bedspread crumpled on the floor. The broken wooden shutters rattled against the window. Through the slats, electrical wires cut the balmy sky in half. Palm fronds hesitated against uneven wind, a slate-gray sky. Rain followed the light, scattering water across the tile floor. When Tom woke up, we dressed, packed our bags, and walked to the bus station to catch a bus to Granada. Yellow-uniformed guards holding military-grade weapons sat watch on the street corners.

Tom and I didn't talk about what had just happened between us. The new sights outside the bus windows gave us plenty of other things to notice and to say. Vendors sold bright cotton hammocks. A pig snuffled through a smoldering pile of garbage, tore at the black feathers of a dead pigeon, ripped off a stiff wing, ate the soft body. A group of boys formed a circle around a smaller boy, who dropped to the dirt. The others took turns kicking him in the side, the back, the face. As we passed, they became smaller and smaller on a backdrop of tropical green, red earth, corrugated tin, and blue tarps. Farther down the road, a boy in orange plastic flip-flops carried shovelfuls of clay, filling potholes.

As we stepped off the bus in Granada, a girl on a bicycle handed us a flyer for a hostel as she rode by. "Might as well check it out," Tom said, so we walked through the town square, past the vendors selling ceramics and the horse-drawn carriages. When we got to the hostel, the only private room had just one bed. Did it matter now? How long did we need to pretend we were just *amigos*?

We had once been colleagues at the college where I still taught; we had decided to meet in Central America, sharing rooms to cut costs but sleeping in separate beds. My ex-husband, Craig, had moved back in with me, and though we had both had various affairs by then, Tom was our mutual friend, had in fact attended our wedding, so taking him as my lover would complicate things considerably. I liked and trusted Tom and didn't want to lose his friendship. We were young and naive enough to believe that this kind of travel arrangement would work.

A young boy at the front desk greeted us with a friendly smile, and he let us hold the baby bunnies he kept in a box. The hostel room smelled like SeaWorld, but it was $10 a night and included breakfast, so we agreed.

The next morning, the boy knocked on our door, asking us if we wanted to eat. He held up a meat scramble in a pan.

"What is it?" I asked.

"Conejitos," he smiled.

"No, thanks," I said, but Tom said he would try some.

"Do you know what conejitos are?" I asked him in English.

"No, but it looks really good."

"Remember those bunnies from yesterday?" I asked, and Tom nodded. "Conejitos are bunnies." The boy from the front desk smiled at us, ready to dish them onto a plate.

"I think I'll pass," Tom said, and I translated, thanking the boy but telling him we weren't hungry.

We set off on a boat tour of the isletas. The driver, Victor, didn't speak English, so Tom said to me, "I want to discontinue our physical relationship. I don't feel right about it."

"Because of Craig?"

"Not just that, but that's part of it."

"Okay." I felt both relieved and annoyed. Couldn't we continue on without talking about my live-in ex-husband? And then came the feelings of rejection. I sat in the boat, nodding and smiling as Victor named the various birds and trees. I made small talk with him in Spanish. But mostly, I wondered if I should try to get away from Tom and travel on my own.

On our way back to the plaza, we passed a school. When the schoolgirls saw us, they ran to the chain-link fencing, stuffing their hands through and shouting, "¡Hola, hola!" Some of the little girls climbed onto the fence in their uniform dresses and hung onto it, their fingers and toes gripping the wire. We shouted "hola" back, and they giggled. In the square, tired carriage horses strained against their ropes and into the shade. Older girls yelled to us, "Cerámica," asking us to shop their wares.

We ate a dinner of *tostones y frijoles* on a balcony overlooking the plaza. We laughed about the *conejitos*, and I thought maybe I hadn't made a mistake traveling with him. Maybe we could enjoy traveling together as friends?

After dinner we walked around the plaza, and girls no older than twelve or thirteen teetered across the cobblestones in silver platforms, pink halters, sequined dresses. They fluttered false eyelashes, asked, "You want girl tonight? You want me?" They gathered on the corner across from the church, shouting, "¡Chicas!" A gray-haired tourist passed them, slowed his pace. He was dressed in the standard gringo outfit—zip-off rain pants, light-weight button-down, and Teva sandals. I willed him to pass them by.

The girls tried harder, calling to him, "Have me tonight?" They were young enough to be his granddaughters, dressed in their mothers' ill-fitting evening wear, their faces painted with eye-liner, blue shadow, red lipstick—I wished it was just an innocent game of dress-up.

As the man moved in to choose, he noticed me watching. He turned to me and said, "I wasn't going to. It's not my thing. It's one night, but then the next thing you know, you're taking care of the family. You're buying Grandpa his teeth. For these girls, it's hitting the jackpot."

I felt my face flare with hot anger. "The jackpot?" I whispered to Tom. "What the fuck?" I wanted to gather the girls and bring them home with me and wash the makeup from their faces, erase the gringo men with their zip-off rain pants and replace them with sand castles and Chutes and Ladders.

The man crossed the street but circled back around under the streetlamps, passing the church and the school where smaller girls had climbed the chain-link fence that morning; their shouts of "hola, hola" still seemed to echo off the cobblestones. "That makes me so mad," I told Tom. "I want to do something to help those girls."

"Like what?" he asked.

"I'm not sure. But something." How could Tom understand? I knew I didn't fully understand, either, but I did know how hard being a girl in the world can be.

I was angry with Tom for what I saw as his apathy; now I see the savior complex in my response. Thinking that I could swoop in to save these girls was misinformed by my own privileged place in the world. I am ashamed to admit how many times I have been traveling and thought that there must be something I could do, as if my sympathy could solve the world's big problems. I wished the world was a different place in that moment, as I often do now, but I also realize I must deeply consider my desire to "help" or "save" others, especially when I'm traveling, and channel these impulses into something meaningful, something useful, instead.

We rode the local bus to Revas, then took a taxi to San Jorge, where we caught a small cargo boat to Lago de Ometepe. Wind and rain churned up the lake, creating towering swells that tossed the small craft. We held onto the wooden rafters above our heads, swayed with the boat and wind, leaned against cargo—frozen chickens, children's toys. Water rolled in past a blue tarp, seeped the floors, draped over my sandaled feet. I noticed the only other tourists in the back of the boat: two men and a young woman. All the other tourists had waited for the more comfortable, larger ferry.

A man leaned over the side; a ribbon of vomit spiraled into the gray lake. The young woman beside him held a baby in a basket. She handed the man a cloth, and he wiped his face. The infant was new—age in days. I wondered if she had just had the baby and was returning home to the island. I watched the woman as she held a tiny hand, unfolded the fingers to study them. She didn't notice me at first. She held out her own hand, spread the fingers, compared her hand to the tiny one reaching for her. Then she looked from the hand, down to my feet with the red polished toenails, and up to my face. I held her gaze until the boat hit a big swell, and we nearly toppled onto the floor, the water splashing over us.

We arrived at the dock in Ometepe but still had to cross the small island. The tourists from the back of the boat paid for a ride in the back of someone's pickup, but Tom and I agreed to take the chicken bus because it was the cheaper option. We were the only tourists on the old school bus. We sat on the wheel well, so every time the bus hit a pothole, we flew from our seats and back down onto the curved metal. I asked Tom, "Do you want to make sure we have two beds in the hotel room? Or would two rooms be better?"

"Can we talk about this later?"

"Why?" I asked. "No one speaks English. And even if they do, it's not like we know anyone here."

"I just feel like it's getting in the way."

"What is?"

"The physical relationship." He rubbed his bald head.

"In the way of what?"

"I feel like I'm being used." When he looked at me, I noticed that his eyes were the color of moss. He continued, "I feel like we're here, having fourteen one-night stands, and it's getting in the way of us having a real relationship."

We hit another pothole, flew into the air, and landed back on the hard wheel well. I wasn't sure what Tom meant by a real relationship. He lived in Florida, nearly three thousand miles away from me.

At our hotel in Santo Domingo, we were shown to a room with two beds. The three Americans from the boat were already drinking at the open-air bar. Tom joined the other tourists, but I wanted only to sit alone and think and write. I didn't want to make small talk about where we had been, where we were going. I sat at a bistro table on the small tile patio outside our room. Magpies clung to the tree branches overhead. Their curled head feathers made them look like nobles wearing feathered caps. They were beautiful and mean. I took out my guidebook and my journal. I wondered at the possibilities that the world held for me if only I could find the courage to leave Tom and set out alone.

A waiter came over with a Toña, a local Nicaraguan beer. He told me that Tomás sent it for me. I looked at the napkin-wrapped beer and wondered if it meant, *Come to the bar*. Or maybe, *Don't wait for me*. Or maybe Tom just thought I would like a beer? Maybe it didn't contain hidden messages or secret agendas, the way it would have had I sent it. The lake went a charcoal gray in the dusk. The mist crawled across the shore, shrouding the water in white. I thanked the waiter and then went inside to take a shower.

When I got out of the shower, Tom came into the bathroom and tried to kiss me. He smelled like beer and tobacco. "Have you been smoking?" I held my towel around me, my hair still dripping.

"Those guys had Cubans."

"Yuck. You stink." I wouldn't let him kiss me, but I let him fuck me, there in the bathroom, up against the sink. My half-finished beer sweated on the counter.

And then I cried.

"What is it now?" Tom asked.

"I just think I deserve more," I said. "I deserve for you to like me more than you do." I wrapped the towel back around me.

"You have missed it completely." He wrapped a towel around his waist and sat on the edge of the bathtub.

"You say one thing, and I get ready for that—no more sex. And then you do another. What am I supposed to think?"

"I'm sorry. I know I'm sending mixed signals."

"I just want you to like me." I realized I wasn't saying what I thought I should say. I was travel-weary—too tired to be guarded. I was telling the truth. And I immediately felt the shame of that and wished I could take it back.

"You're missing it."

"Missing what?" I squinted at myself in the steamy mirror. My wet curls stuck to my pink face.

"You shouldn't fuck around anymore." Tom stood up. "It's not good for you."

"You started it this time," I said without turning to look at him.

"I know. I'm sorry. But I don't mean with me." He came up behind me, close enough that he was almost touching me but not quite.

"Why are you so special?" I looked at him in the foggy mirror.

"You need to trust yourself more." He started to lean into me.

"Enough with the advice," I said and walked into the bedroom to get dressed.

"I'm not special. You shouldn't fuck around with me either. It's not like a relationship could work."

"No," I shouted from the other room. "Probably not."

"And I couldn't fit in with your lineup," he called over the sound of the shower.

I put on my pajamas, a formality I had not yet bothered with, toweled off my hair, and walked back into the bathroom. "What's that supposed to mean?"

"Aren't there others?" He shut off the water, pulled back the curtain, and wrapped the towel back around his waist. "That guy in Mexico, the ex-pat in Costa Rica, the Puerto Rican tour guide. Wasn't there a poet? I don't know who else."

He was using the secrets I had shared with him against me. It was true I had engaged in a string of brief love affairs, even though they never seemed to give me what I was looking for. I felt like a character in a novel I was reading, and I was sitting back, watching her make mistakes. I said, "I'll never see any of them again. That's all over now." I couldn't say how I knew this was true; I only thought it was.

"Your ex?" He toweled off and then asked, "Do you have any lotion?"

"I guess I'm a little screwed up." I handed Tom a small bottle of lotion from my bag.

"A little?" He looked at me through the mirror.

"Okay, a lot. So why are you here with me? What does that make you?"

"Traveling with fucked up."

"More like fucking fucked up."

"Very funny," Tom said.

"Or a challenge?" I asked. Tom had told me that even though he was in his midthirties and had never been married he didn't have commitment issues. He said he had been looking for a woman who challenged him.

He looked at me again through the foggy mirror. "That's *not* what I meant by a challenge."

"What did you mean?"

"I don't know, but definitely not this."

Tom didn't feel well that night, maybe because of the cigar, so we ended up sleeping in separate beds after all. I looked out the window, wishing I knew the name of the pink-flamed palms. Frogs and cicadas sang in a chorus. The lightning bugs sparked like miniature shooting stars against the trees, and the moths circled the porch light. I listened for the crackle of the burnt bodies flying too close to the light. Each one fizzled into a coffin of flame.

Time slid into shadows. Window blinds cut latticed moonlight onto the wall. The stiff sheets smelled of bleach. I thought about getting up to look for my journal but didn't want to wake Tom. I wondered if we could go back to being friends. That way I could make a break from Craig without having anyone else involved. I thought about the trajectory of my life, knew I couldn't go back and change the decisions I had made. I resolved to leave Craig once and for all, even if I couldn't afford my mortgage.

I watched the rays of the moon turn into the light-blue hour of dawn.

Our hike up Volcán Madera began at Finca Magdalena, a coffee plantation and hostel where gringos lazed away the morning in two-dollar-a-night hammocks. We joined our guide and walked through a dripping forest of frogs, termite nests, and ant mounds. The jungle filled with the echo of mantled howler monkeys, and the white-faced capuchins swung from the branches above, knocking leaves and twigs into the muddy path. Stacy, one of the tourists

Tom had met the night before in the bar, joined us. She was traveling alone and told us, "I'm here to look at the agribusiness of plantains. Bananas and plantains are my passion."

Stacy was soon out of breath and said, "Sorry you guys," and stopped. I shared my water with her. "I'm not used to hiking," she said. We started again, but as the trail became muddier, Stacy had more trouble keeping up.

At a scenic overlook, we stopped for a snack and took pictures of the hourglass-shaped isthmus with active Volcán Concepción in the distance. Smoke hid the volcano's apex. Our guide told us it was more active than usual and had caused an earthquake just months earlier that rated 6.2 on the Richter scale. It was closed to hiking because of the recent activity. "It's going to get muddier," our guide said, pointing to our trail, "as we enter the clouds."

"Muddier than this?" Stacy asked. Mud coated our shoes and splattered up our legs. At first, I tried to avoid the mud by stepping on branches, sticks, and rocks as our guide had done but soon gave up. "If there're no more views, there's no point in going on," Stacy said.

"Isn't there a lake in a crater?" I asked. "Don't we want to see that?"

The guide nodded, but he looked at Stacy and said, "It's still a long way off."

I translated, and Stacy said, "Let's turn around then."

"Maybe some of us can go on, and some of us can turn around?" I asked.

"We should stick together," Tom said. "We can't go on without the guide."

"Stacy can find her way down. We haven't come that far, and it's just back down the way we came up."

"She can't go down alone." I was glad that Tom was so kind, looking after this stranger. But at the same time, I was annoyed. I had never felt so many mixed emotions about someone, ever.

The guide watched us, and I could tell that even though he didn't understand our conversation in English, he was hoping his work-day would end early.

We turned around, and on our way back down, Stacy asked me, "So what's the story with you two?" She pointed to Tom, who walked ahead with the guide.

"We're friends." What should I have said? *We're friends, and though we are trying not to, we're fucking every chance we get. That is until one of us decides it's a bad idea, and we have a fight. And it is a bad idea, in fact, on account of my live-in ex-husband.*

"Oh, come on," she said. Monkeys issued their guttural calls from the trees above us.

"Do you hear that?" I asked. "Howler monkeys."

"But you guys seem to have fun. Why aren't you together?"

"I live in California. He lives in Florida. We're just friends. Really."

"But I saw you two laughing on that boat ride. You look like a couple."

"We're not." I realized I sounded defensive. We were now below the low ceiling of clouds, the jungle glistening green in the fil-tered light.

"But you should be," she said.

"We live too far apart." Then I asked her about growing plan-tains, which she was more than happy to talk about.

The other tourists with whom Tom had smoked cigars at the hotel bar offered us a ride to San Juan del Sur. Rob and John were in Nicaragua to check on the progress of the beach house Rob was building with his Nicaraguan brother-in-law. Tom and I didn't have a schedule, so we figured that this was as good a plan as any. I still wasn't sure I wanted to keep traveling with him, but I knew it would be easier to set off on my own from San Juan del Sur, a solid stop on the Gringo Trail.

We went to Rob's brother-in-law's house on the way, a mansion in the middle of a plantation. White stucco archways separated the courtyards from a number of open-air living rooms, all decorated with Persian rugs. A maid brought us coffee and cookies on a gold tray, and I couldn't help but think of Carolyn Forché's poem that takes place in El Salvador, "The Colonel," where the maid brings in a rack of lamb and fine wine though the country is in shambles. Rob's brother-in-law did not spill a sack of human ears onto the table like the colonel did in Forché's poem. But being there, after driving past the shacks made from corrugated sheet metal and blue tarps, reminded me that the way some lived—the way I lived back at home—was in such sharp contrast to so many others across the world. My tiny cabin in the woods was, in fact, a luxury.

Rob drove us up to his lot in San Juan del Sur to have a look. His house had been framed, but that was about all. "Not as far along as I'd hoped," he said.

"Pretty view." I looked out at the sea.

"Land is cheap here," he said. "I could never afford to buy a view like this in the States."

I had that feeling again—so many people around the world struggle just to live. And we rode chicken buses and called it a holiday, but if we were deprived of our cars and needed to ride these buses to work every day, we would have a different perspective. It wouldn't be an adventure, and it wouldn't be fun—it would just be hard.

Tom and I found a $10 room. Corn husks smoldered below the window. A small bed sat in the middle of the room. I looked at Tom, and he said, "It's fine. Don't you think?" I nodded and told the innkeeper, "Está bien." There had been a recent outbreak of dengue fever in San Jun del Sur, and I thought the smoke billowing outside the window might drive mosquitoes away. Beyond that, I didn't know what to think.

On the beach, Tom walked ahead of me, just far enough that it looked like we weren't together. I decided not to worry anymore about whether or not Tom liked me or what would become of us after the trip. I couldn't do anything to change him into what I wanted, and I wasn't even sure what that would be. I knew I could only concentrate on what I wanted to be, and I was still so far from it.

The late afternoon light glared off the waves. Two girls played in the foamy surf. One girl splashed the other, and they both laughed. I wondered if they were sisters or friends. In that moment, I wished I was traveling with one of my girlfriends.

Tom waited for me, and when I caught up to him, he said, "We should buy property here."

I was stunned. "What do you mean? Like together?"

"Sure, why not? It would be a great investment. Rob said land here's cheap."

I could think of plenty of reasons why not. I wondered how I was going to pay for this trip. Even if I had money and wanted to buy land in Nicaragua, why would I buy property with Tom? I said, "Because that's the craziest thing I have ever heard you say. That's why."

We walked back to our hotel. The bedsheets were like canvas, and smoke from the corn husks drifted in through the window.

Tom stopped telling me we shouldn't have sex.

We took a minibus back to Managua. We rode by the row of hammock stands we had passed on our way out of Managua. Under the banyan trees, next to the aluminum roofs and the hammocks soaked with rain, the small boy we had seen before filled the same potholes. He wore the same orange sandals. Tom and I both stared out the window, and I wished he would hold my hand, but he didn't.

We flew to Big Corn Island in a plane painted to look like a Jersey cow, which did nothing to instill my confidence in the airworthiness of the tiny plane. Then we bobbed across the rough seas in a small boat, finally arriving at Little Corn Island. Two boys met us with red wheelbarrows to carry our bags. No cars were allowed on Little Corn; sandy footpaths crisscrossed the island. I knew from the moment I stepped onto the sand that I would love it there. We followed the boys along a dirt path to the other side of the island, where they deposited us in front of our hotel. The casitas were painted in pastels like Easter eggs, and they sat on top of the sandy bluff, overlooking the Caribbean Sea. We were told about the honor bar and the no-shoe policy in the restaurant. "There's a rack here for your flip-flops," the owner said.

We checked into our casita—it had a bed and a futon, and I wondered if we were going to go through the just-friends two-bed charade again.

We dropped off our stuff and went out onto the beach. It was getting dark, and no one was around, so we skinny-dipped in the ocean. Our swim was so spontaneous that I had forgotten I was wearing my glasses and lost them in the sea. Without my glasses or my contacts, I couldn't see well enough to walk back on my own. "You'll have to lead me," I said to Tom, and he grabbed my hand. We walked back down the beach, under the rustling palms, holding hands. I tried to ignore the feeling that bloomed at the base of my rib cage: I wanted to be more of an "us" than we were. Not just friends. Not just fourteen one-night stands.

At the family-style dinner, we sat with a single mother and her son, Jake. He was twelve years old but seemed much younger. He talked about snorkeling, and I kept asking him questions about it. What did the fish look like? Did he see turtles or sharks? With every question, the boy became more excited and animated. He flapped his hands.

Tom kept giving me looks that I knew meant, *Stop*. But I didn't. Tom wasn't my boyfriend. What did I care if he was getting annoyed with me? When I asked Jake if the fish blew bubbles at him, he got so excited that he jumped up and knocked all of our drinks off the table. His mother apologized, and Tom said, "It's not *his* fault."

By the time we got back to our casita, we were both half-drunk and full-angry with each other. He said, "Why did you do that, Suzanne?"

"Do what?"

"Get that kid all riled up. You could see it happening, and you just kept at it."

"I don't know what you mean," I said, even though I did.

"Let's just go to bed."

"Should I sleep on the futon?"

"Come on, Suzanne."

"You keep going back and forth with this. It's not fair. I feel like I'm the one being used."

"How so?" Tom asked.

"Because I'm the one who's falling in love with you." I didn't realize it was true until I said it. And it made me mad—that definitely wasn't supposed to happen. It was the voice behind my voice, the one I started to recognize as my truth, but I was angry that I had allowed it to speak aloud, so I tried to ignore it and said, "And you don't deserve it."

"Why not?"

"Because you should be the one falling in love with me." I believed that the most important thing was to be wanted. Not the other way around.

"Let's just go to bed," Tom said. "We'll talk about it tomorrow."

I lay next to him, careful not to touch him, and listened to the rain on the tin roof. I didn't want to discuss it the next day. I didn't want to talk about it ever. I wanted to escape from him and from myself. I felt raw and vulnerable, like I had shed my skin.

As soon as the sky turned from black to gray, I grabbed a towel and my journal and snuck out of the casita. Everything seemed darker because I was too tired to put my contacts in and was wearing my prescription sunglasses. I walked along the beach and sat down on the wet sand, and I wrote in my journal. Why did I say I was falling in love with Tom? Was it true? I didn't know, but I knew a thing eventually became whatever you named it.

The sky shifted from purple to a pinkish yellow and then a pale blue. Raindrops clung to the sand. Seaweed rotted in the sun—the smell of decay and death and ordinary uncertainty. But I knew one thing for certain: I needed to be alone, not in another relationship. A magnificent frigatebird screeched its *kack-ka-ack* above. A translucent crab scurried sideways, popping into a hole in the sand, seeming to disappear, which was exactly what I wanted to do. But there was no escaping myself no matter how many countries I crossed or how many men I fucked. A coconut rolled with the waves. Up and back down the shoreline. Never getting anywhere. I thought about getting up to kick it into the ocean.

A teenaged boy hauled a large plastic trash can across the sand. The storm brought piles of seaweed onto the beach and, with it, an array of trash. The boy started sifting through the mounds of seaweed with a rake. He threw plastic spoons, water bottles and caps, pens, and toothbrushes into the bin, tidying up the storm-strewn beach for us—the tourists. I stopped writing in my journal and watched him, then I offered to help. He asked if I was sure. I nodded. He smiled and said, "Claro."

I put down my pen and journal and started sifting through the seaweed with him. We introduced ourselves, and he told me his name was Ebner. Then we worked in silence, sorting through coconuts and seeds, pulling out torn flip-flops, straws, traffic pylons, Penzoil containers, disposable razors, syringes, an IV bag. I kept an eye out for my glasses amid the piles of seaweed and garbage, but they were gone for good, lost to the sea.

My scream surprised me: a drowned rat, the fur matted with salt and sand. The claws curled and the head reached up, as if swimming through death's rigidity. The eyes were open wide, the sharp yellow teeth biting the air. Ebner left the rat in the sand, working around it. Then he told me it was time to carry the garbage to the boat and that it was nice meeting me. We shook hands. He hoisted the bin to his shoulder, took the path through the jungle, and disappeared.

I returned to my towel and watched the same coconut wobble up shore with the rising tide, up and back down like Sisyphus's rock, returning sea to sand to sea. I finally got up, walked over to it, and tossed it into the water. I went back to the casita, and it was empty. I changed into my bathing suit, grabbed my sun block and beach hat, and as I was about to head out again, Tom returned with coffee. "You're up early," he said.

I nodded and said, "Listen, I know I got that boy excited; I could see it happening, and I could see you trying to stop me, but it made me want to do it even more. But I'm sorry, and I'll apologize to his mother."

"Why did it make you want to do it more when I tried to stop you?"

"Because I hate being told what to do, that's why."

"I never tell you what to do. That's your own stuff." I nodded, and Tom asked, "Did you mean what you said?"

"Which thing?" I hoped he didn't mean the thing I knew he meant.

"About your feelings toward me? What you said last night?"

I felt like I was being dissected under a microscope. I couldn't say yes or no because I didn't know what was true, so I stayed silent. But maybe that was an answer, too.

"Well, I'm moved," he said.

We swam out toward a shipwreck, moored just past the breakers. The waves pushed me back, and I was afraid of scraping my stomach and knees on the coral. Tom grabbed my hand to pull me against the current. I let go of his hand and said, "You go." He nodded, and I turned around and swam back to shore.

I saw Jake's mother on the beach, and I told her I was sorry for getting her son so excited. "Don't worry about that," she said. "I'm so used to people giving me looks for his behavior that I was just glad you engaged with him." He played in the sand next to her, intent on his castle.

"No," I said. "It was my fault he spilled the drinks."

"Are you kidding? That happens nearly every night. I'm happy you were nice to him. Most people aren't."

I said good-bye and walked to the end of the island, which wasn't far. I thought about Jake and his mother and realized there was always more than one way to look at a thing. I passed many of the small hotels and thatched cabañas and reached a dwelling that was part blue tarp, part corrugated tin. I wondered how they survived hurricane season. A little girl emerged from the tent, and she made a motion of taking a picture. I asked her what she wanted, and she did the camera charade again; I realized she took pictures for tourists who then gave her a tip. "I don't have a camera," I said in Spanish, "or money."

A pregnant woman stepped out of the tent and smiled. The sun glinted off the gold veneers on her teeth. She took her little girl's hand, and she waved at me with her other hand. The girl did the same. I smiled and waved back at them and then turned around and walked back down the beach.

I found Tom sitting on his towel. I sat down next to him, and he said, "I missed you."

"You what?"

Then he said, "I'm yours for the rest of the trip."

I didn't know what he meant. And I did. But I was still thinking about the mother and daughter, so I just nodded. Clouds crowded the sky, and the wind carried rain. By the time we gathered our things, we had to run back to our casita in the pouring rain.

We took the boat back to Big Corn Island and sat under the tin roof of the hotel restaurant; the rain gutters made from plastic cups filled with water and overflowed. A stray dog begged for food; a bullfrog hopped by. The fake Christmas tree with gold tinsel and the Phil Collins holiday rock songs crackling over the speakers depressed me. We ordered chicken, then heard the wringing of its neck in the back. The smell of garbage burning hung in a sky slung with clouds. Two men on horseback pulled a reluctant cow down the dirt road with a rope tied around its horns. In our hotel's courtyard sat a little monkey named Irma who had been chained to a pole. Irma pulled the chain behind her every time she moved, but she could not get out from the rain, so she sat squint-eyed, her arms crossed over her shivering belly.

There was a short break in the rain, and we went for a walk. A group of men crowded around something near the edge of the water. I leaned in to see what it was. They were slicing meat from the body of a sea turtle. One fisherman told me it worked as an aphrodisiac. "Good for love," he told me and grabbed his share of the meat. Another fisherman said that in the neglected place, you will find the turtle. Or at least that's how I translated what he said from Spanish to English for Tom.

The rain started again, so we ran back to our casita, where we toweled off and then drank beers on our small patio, talking late into the night. Tom knew about my affairs, but I told him the deeper secrets—my alcoholic father who shouted at me and the regrets and grief I carried in my own neglected place. Tom suggested the ways I looked for love might be connected to my childhood. Through the flickering porch light, he nodded at me. He held my gaze. It made me uncomfortable, so I looked away and laughed.

"What?" he asked. "What is it?"

I took a sip of my beer and shook my head.

"You don't have to tell me," he said, but I guessed that he already knew what I was thinking.

Eating and Drinking

~~~~~~

Drink heavily with the locals
whenever possible.

ANTHONY BOURDAIN

Gone Missing

Acapulco, Mexico, July 2002

The Spanish language school was like summer camp with *cerveza*. The first weekend, my new friends and I traveled from Cuernavaca to Acapulco to see the sights, meaning the beach by day and the discos at night. Because most of the students were twenty-something, this was one of the more popular excursions arranged by the school.

I shared a hotel room with Mina and Anna—both younger than I was. They were in their midtwenties; I was thirty-one, which seemed much older at the time. Anna was quiet, often standing off to the side, observing the scene around her. Mina was married like me but seemed like more of a party girl, someone who was always up for anything. Her Spanish was even worse than mine.

Our Acapulco hotel room had purple and fuchsia black-out shades, a rattling window air conditioner unit, and a balcony with a view of a yellow wall. But if you stood out on the corner of the tiny balcony, you could see a wedge of the sea; Mina, Anna, and I took turns standing there for pictures, wearing the clothes we had picked out for the disco that night. Mina and I both wore short black skirts, slinky red tanks (which we called hoochie tops), and strappy sandals. We posed together and joked; with our long dark hair and matching outfits, we were like *gemelas*, twins.

The disco's expensive cover charge included free drinks for the ladies. I was careful to order bottled beer since we had been warned about tainted drinks. A week earlier, one of our classmates had been drugged. Luckily, she had been with a group of friends, and they made sure she got home okay. The next day she didn't remember anything, and she couldn't see. Her vision returned, but her memory of the evening never did. I entered the information into the Rolodex of my mind and thought of my mother's warning: *watch your drink*.

Within minutes of walking into the club, Mina met a Mexican named Angel, a man young enough that I thought of him as a boyman—he couldn't have been older than twenty. She danced off with him into the crowd. Anna danced with another classmate, and I found myself sitting at a table with Jimmy, a beefy college student from Ohio. As I sipped my Tecate, Jimmy told me, "I decided while I was here, I'd go off my meds." Then he told me he had just found out his girlfriend was cheating on him. "I'm really angry." He clenched his fists. I took another sip of my beer, trying to think of something reassuring to say, something like, "She's not worth it anyway," or, "There are other fish in the sea"—something cliché and encouraging and untrue.

The Mexican house music vibrated through the club. It had been at least an hour since I last saw Mina. I told Jimmy I had to go find her, that I was worried about her. He grabbed me with his giant man hand, the gym-sculpted forearm bulging. "She's fine," he said through his teeth and took another swallow of tequila. I needed to get out of there, with or without Mina.

"I have to go to the bathroom," I lied. Jimmy still gripped my wrist. "Female trouble," I said, pointing with my free hand to the general area of my uterus and making a circling motion. I mouthed the words "down there," implying the mysteries of the not-to-be-messed-with female woes. At that, Jimmy let go of my wrist. The blood returned to my hand, and I headed toward the restrooms. I looked around, hoping Jimmy didn't see me, and then I searched for the door—the exits are obscured in Mexican discos the same way they are in casinos, to discourage leaving before dawn.

On the way out, I found Anna on the dance floor, and I shouted to her over the music, "Where's Mina?"

"Don't know," she said. "Last I saw her she was dancing with a Mexican guy."

Over the giant speakers, Eminem sang "Without Me." I scanned the hundreds of people on the strobing dance floor but couldn't spot Mina. Had she left?

"We'll never find her," Anna said, motioning with her hand. "Let's go."

I agreed. It was 3 a.m. and the men, huddled in groups around their bottles of rum and tequila, no longer tried to act like they weren't staring at us, no longer tried to hide the fact that while we may not have been their first pick, we were better than nothing. As young women, we were accustomed to these looks, even believed that the male gaze gave us power.

We left the club—a line of beautiful people still waiting to get in—and caught an unlicensed cab and headed back to our hotel through the rain. We had been cautioned to take the radio taxis with antennas on the back. But the unlicensed taxis were cheaper, and we had been in Mexico for a week and already felt invincible.

Anna fell asleep next to me in the backseat, and the taxi driver asked me in Spanish if I believed in God. The lights of the city glistened through the rain-spotted windshield.

"No lo sé," I answered.

"What?" he asked. He clutched the steering wheel with both hands and held my gaze in the rearview mirror. From his tone, I could see that "I don't know" hadn't been the right answer. "You have beautiful blue eyes," he said, "a beautiful girl, but how could you not believe in God? What's the meaning of that?"

"Oh, you're going to ask me about God?" I messed up the verb tenses on purpose. "My Spanish wasn't very good, and I am misunderstanding you. God? I *love* God. Of course I believe in God."

"Your Spanish is sufficient," he said, looking back at me in the rearview mirror, the rosary with a cross swinging with each curve in the road.

I nudged Anna awake. "We're close to the hotel," I said in Spanish, though I wasn't sure where we were. The moonless night glimmered wet from the storm. The falling rain flickered in the headlights—the city a multicolored blur in the distance. Had the club been this far from our hotel? I felt the terror of being at the mercy of a strange man. "We are close, no?" I asked the driver.

He held my eyes in the rearview mirror and said, "Close enough." He knew he scared me, and perhaps that was enough. I was a "rich" gringa but also a defenseless woman. My fear meant he had won.

After a few more turns, the landscape started to look familiar, and the taxi pulled up in front of our dilapidated hotel. I didn't argue when the driver charged us double his original quote. I already knew he would say that his estimate had been per person or that it was more expensive late at night or in the rain. I gave him what he asked for. Anna and I walked through the courtyard, past the small, green-lit pool, and upstairs to our shabby room.

Sometime in the early morning, I turned to look at the other double bed, figuring Mina had snuck into bed with Anna. Without my glasses in the dark room, I convinced myself Mina was there. I fell back asleep.

Our wake-up call rang at 10 a.m. Our bus back to Cuernavaca was leaving in an hour. "Mina?" I asked.

"I thought she was in your bed," Anna said.

We both sat up. This was in the days before everyone carried phones, so we had no way to reach her. "She'll be back before the bus," I said. "If not, we'll worry then."

I felt relieved to have a plan, though I couldn't help but fret. What else could we do? Calling the local police would just turn us into a joke: *We're looking for our drunk friend who was flirting with one of your super sexy young men even though she's married. She was last seen in a disco. And now she has gone missing. Can you help us?*

I imagined the authorities laughing at us. Another drunk gringa. Another loose American girl. We had no idea where Mina was or with whom she might have left, aside from the young man she had been dancing with, someone we knew only as Angel.

We knew how it would sound. It sounded that way to us, too.

The woman from our school who had been drugged the week before was saved by her friends, but Mina's friends, including me, had left her at the disco. I may not have made the best lover or wife, but I had always been a good friend, so I knew I had failed her. I felt terrible.

We showered and packed up. I pushed Mina's things into her bag, wondering if I should leave it at the front desk or bring it with me back to Cuernavaca.

We headed to the lobby breakfast buffet, where watermelon rotted under the hum of flies. I sat with both bags, and I couldn't eat. Every time the door opened, I hoped it would be Mina walking through. Our chartered tour bus pulled up outside, and I wondered if I should get on. Should I stay in Acapulco until I found Mina? I told myself she was a grown woman. She could take care of herself. I also knew friends should look out for each other, especially women in a foreign disco in the small hours of the morning.

Anna and I found Jimmy on the sidewalk, waiting to board the bus. His backpack was unzipped, and things were falling out of it onto the sidewalk. "Your bag's unzipped," I told him.

"Thanks." He reached for his stuff, then said, "Hey, did I get weird last night? I'm afraid I might have gotten weird."

"You were fine," I said.

"I'm sorry if I got weird." He stuffed his deodorant and toothpaste into his backpack. "I turned around, and you were gone."

"It's okay. You're fine."

I wish I would have told him that he should continue taking whatever drugs were prescribed to him. I should have said he deserved to be left in the bar. And that I had a bruise on my wrist, and he had no right to act like such a brute. And yes, he was weird. But here I was trying to console him, reassuring an asshole for his bad behavior and pretending everything was okay. My response was automatic; it was the way that I had learned to react to men. Even still, it left me feeling bothered, but at the time I couldn't articulate why. Young women are taught to reassure men, to apologize for them. This follows an unwritten code that even if you don't particularly like a man, it's important to be liked. I should have been able to crack the code, but because I wasn't confident in myself, I went along with what I had learned, the expectation of how I should act around men—saying it was okay and fine when it clearly wasn't. This was before women spoke out about these things, so I thought I was more alone in this than I was.

"Where's Mina?" Jimmy looked around.

"She never came home," Anna said and shrugged.

"What?" Jimmy started to clench his fists again, a flash of the anger I had seen the night before, and I started to back away. "Where is she?"

"I wish I knew," I said.

Then he looked past us, and he shouted, "There she is! Why, look what the cat dragged in."

I turned around, and there she was. And indeed, she looked like something a cat or some other sort of animal-dragging creature would be carrying in its jaws. Her hair fell wet on her shoulders, her disco-going clothes rumpled. She smiled and stage-whispered to me, "What a night."

"I was really worried," I said. "I didn't know if I should leave or what."

"I know. Sorry." She was still smiling.

"Here's your bag." I handed it to her and boarded the old school bus. I chose the seat with the wheel bump, hoping no one would sit next to me. Just like that, I had had enough of my summer camp friends. I had gone from scared to angry. I came to Mexico to think about my failing marriage and to learn some Spanish. Instead I let myself get distracted by drama.

On the bus, Mina squeezed in next to me, excited to have someone to share her adventures with. "I'm not going home to my husband," she said. And then, "Stay in Mexico with me. We'll get an
apartment. It'll be so fun."

"Are you still drunk?"

"Suzanne, I'm *serious*."

"So am I, Mina. I can't. I have to go home to my husband. I have
to be a grown-up." I looked out the window at the palm trees, bill-
boards, and sagging electrical wires. High-rise office buildings
and hotels climbed the hillside. I didn't know what that meant—
being a grown-up. But it felt like the right thing to say.

"And I'm not?" Mina crossed her arms.

"I didn't say that." I reached into my backpack and pulled out
my sunglasses. Wearing them felt like protection I needed.

"It was implied."

I turned to her and said, "Look, I didn't mean to hurt your feelings. And quite frankly, neither of us is acting like a grown-up."

Mina laughed and admitted it was true. "So what? Why *not* have
some fun?"

"I was really scared. What if something happened to you?" I
looked out at the Pacific Ocean, glistening greenish-blue in the
late morning.

"Sorry you were scared," she said. "But I'm serious about moving here."

Mina ended up calling her husband and telling him she wasn't
coming home—and she didn't. After it was settled, Mina's husband
got to keep the cat and the dog, the house and the Range Rover. And
Mina got her apartment in Mexico and a succession of Mexican
lovers. At the time, I thought she was crazy, but also something—a
big something—in me envied her. I didn't admit it to her, but it
was Mina's spontaneity that drew me to her; I too wanted to quit
my life, to leave home behind. I was in awe that she could spend

one night in Acapulco, hours really, with a boy-man and then leave her unhappy marriage. That she could be so sure of herself.

In the days before, I had written the following into my journal: *I want to live alone in a flat with red tile floors, a ceiling fan, and flowers. I want to sit on my balcony wearing a white linen dress and drink agua de limón.*

Like Mina, I was looking for something, but I couldn't name it, and it certainly didn't answer to Angel—all I had for my longing was an image of a woman in a white linen dress, a woman who wasn't really me but who was also me in the most profound sense of the word. What I wanted was the feeling I got from imagining that woman on the balcony alone, but I knew moving to Mexico with Mina wouldn't give me that. Yet what Mina had done created a crack that let some truth in—what was possible seemed to shift, though I didn't want to fall for a beautiful man with liquid brown eyes who whispered Spanish into my ear while we made love. I wanted only for everything to have its place. I wanted to be able to make decisions. To say good-bye to my marriage as easily as I'd said hello, maybe even go missing for a while, traveling until I found the life—and the version of myself—I had been too afraid to imagine.

One Degree of Separation

New Delhi, India, January 2007

"Stop being so silly," the dinner-party guests said. "It's a driver's job to wait." While we ate chana masala and palak paneer and drank imported red wine, I tried not to think about our driver, Sharma, waiting outside in his threadbare double-breasted coat, and the January smog spinning around the Ambassador car like a web.

I had wanted to ask Sharma to drop us off, but Sholeh said there was no way we were taking a taxi home late at night, and since we had hired a driver, we should use him.

"It's cold," I said. I felt like a character in *Driving Miss Daisy* or *A Passage to India*.

"It's his work," Sholeh said. "He'll be okay. He has a coat."

I bought Sharma a packet of apricot cigarillos—to make myself feel better, though it didn't work.

Our hosts were a well-known Indian poet and his wife, who was also a writer and an editor at an Indian publishing house. She was young and beautiful, gracious but silly—after dinner, she practiced the hula hoop in the small living room, avoiding the stacks of books climbing the walls. Her hips swayed, and when she extended her arms, her gold bracelets flickered in the candlelight. She asked, "Who wants to try the hula hoop next?"

It was impossible not to love her.

Everyone drank and laughed, and some even tried their turn at the hula hoop, though none were as graceful in their movements as our hostess.

One of the guests was a famous British Indian novelist who said his wife never read his books, said he enjoyed the company of

93

Bill Clinton as much as the Queen of England, said you might not know it, but Margaret Thatcher is *such* a touchy person. Mostly, he wanted to talk about the new Harry Potter book. He asked me where I was from and then ignored my answer, more intrigued by our hostess and her hula hoop. Who could blame him?

At 3 a.m., we said our good-byes to the other guests, thanked our hosts, and walked out of the gated apartment complex and into the foggy night. We knocked on the car window and woke Sharma. He opened the doors for us, and we slid into the backseat. The smell of apricot cigarillos filled the Ambassador car.

I turned to Sholeh and said, "There's only one degree of separation between us and the Queen of England now. And Margaret Thatcher. And Bill Clinton. Probably Oprah, too. Imagine that!"

"Yes," Sholeh said. "So that makes two degrees of separation between Sharma and the Queen."

Sharma smiled at Sholeh in the rearview mirror.

We stopped at a streetlight. A slice of the moon appeared, disappeared—a white cutout in the smog. Out of the smoky night came children, emerging from their roadside tents to knock on the windows of the car. Sharma looked into his rearview mirror at me and said, "So poor . . . so many poor. What is it we can do, ma'am? What can we do?" I shook my head. The children put their hands to their mouths, acting out their hunger. They rapped harder, and I was afraid they would shatter the glass. Sholeh said she wished she had a lollipop, something to give them. Sharma said, "It is better if you give nothing. Or they will get angry that you do not give more and break the windows."

"It makes me sad," I said. The light turned green, the weak smiles of the children fell, and we left them behind, still miming their hunger.

Sharma said, "Work is worship." I sat wondering at all the ways he may have meant that. Sholeh rubbed her temples. I turned around, watching the children disappear into the quilt of night, smoke, and distance. Later I would read in the Bhagavad Gita that work is a form of worshipping the creator, who dwells in every creature.

In very real ways, we are all separated by one degree.

The Peruvian Blackout

Cusco, Peru, March 2007

I blinked into the spilling light, turned away from the window, the tinny sounds of the announcer at the *fútbol* game across town, the street dogs fighting below. Sometimes when I traveled, I couldn't remember where I was when I woke up. I had learned to let go of the panic and wait. Eventually, the desk, the narrow bed, the stuffed animals on the shelf, the curtainless window, and the locked door would make sense.

I waited, but still I couldn't figure out where I was or, more frightening, who I was. The panic flooded into my throat like bile. My tongue stuck to the roof of my mouth, and pounding hammered between my eyes. Maybe I was hungover? But where had I been? What had I done the night before? There was nothing—a cutout where there should have been memory. I waited, hoping for the shadowy images from the night before to form.

But they didn't.

I sat up on the bed. I was in the homestay the language school in Cusco had arranged for me. I still wore my clothes from the night before, jeans and even my sandals. I hadn't gone to bed without changing out of my clothes since college, and I had never before slept in my shoes. How did I manage to drink so much? I reached into the pockets of my jeans and found the crumpled bills. I knew how much money I had brought out with me. It was all there. Nothing made sense. How could I have gotten drunk enough not to remember, yet I hadn't spent any money?

I went into the bathroom and looked in the mirror. Mascara smeared down my cheeks. I hadn't even washed my face—no matter how much I drank, I had always managed to wash my face.

I tried the faucet, but the water was out again. Someone had gone to the bathroom, and a brown turd floated in the toilet. I sat down to pee, trying not to look in the bowl. I went back to my room, took off my jeans and shoes, and crawled back into bed. I wouldn't make it to class. I tried to retrieve something from the day before; I ran through the morning and afternoon and into the blank space where there should have been night.

I tried to piece together where my memory had stopped the day before. I had eaten breakfast as usual, the seventeen-year-old maid, Juana, serving me cereal and bananas, instant coffee, and bread. She told me she had been working for the family ever since her mama married her new papa, and he didn't want her. The family called her lucky because they had enough money to take her in. In exchange, she cooked and cleaned for them, fed their children and their host students. I asked her to sit down and eat with me, but she said she wasn't permitted, so she stood there, leaning on her mop, waiting for me and the "real" daughter to finish so she could eat.

The real daughter asked me if I had ever been to New York.

I told her I was born in New York, and she gasped and clutched at her chest. "Really?"

I felt a little bit famous myself and said, "Yes, why?"

"It's just that I've always wanted to go."

"Why?"

"Because of *Sex and the City*. I love that show."

"Most of the women in New York aren't really like that," I told her in my elementary Spanish. The direct translation of what I actually said was probably something like this: "That's only pretend."

"What?" she asked.

"It's just a TV show. The women in New York aren't all like Carrie Bradshaw and Samantha Jones."

At this, the real daughter stood up and said, "Forget it. I'm not asking you anymore questions." She walked away, leaving her dishes for Juana to clear.

Juana took her plate to the sink and began washing it. She turned to me and said, "I'm glad."

"Glad?" I asked.

"That the women in America aren't really like that. I had believed the same thing. That all the women in New York are glamorous and have fancy clothes and high heels." Then she told me, "I've lost one of my sisters."

"What do you mean?" I wondered if I had misunderstood.

"We don't know where she is," Juana said.

"I'm sorry."

"Me too," she said. And then, "It's so hard to be the oldest."

I nodded, thanked her for breakfast, and left for school. I walked along, and men in the streets called to me in both Spanish and English: "Hola, guapa. Dame un beso. Hey, babyyy. I looove you and I want to kisss you." I learned to stare ahead, ignore them. My host sister told me that only a prostitute—or a North American— would dare to meet their eyes.

I stared up at the ceiling and concentrated on what I remembered: the pack of dogs that came after me, and a little girl with a rock who scared them away. I thanked her, and she told me it was nothing. I was glad she was already so tough. I remembered walking past the Incan walls, the stones smooth like pillows, fitting together like the pieces of a puzzle. We studied the subjunctive tense in class, and then I went to the orphanage where I volunteered. I read books to badly broken children, and one boy begged me to take him home when I left, making me feel like I swallowed my own heart.

I walked home and ate a dinner of Jell-O alone in the kitchen and then caught a taxi back to town and asked the driver how to say "hello" in Quechua. I arrived at the fondue restaurant to meet my friends and ordered a glass of red wine. I remembered everything before the Cuba libre. The rest of the night was like a hole punched from my memory.

There had been fuzzy nights in college, the kind where you don't remember until someone says something, and then all the embarrassing details rush back. I had only had one true blackout in college, when I discovered hard alcohol and passed out in the hallway of my dormitory. According to what I was told, I had to be carried outside by my friend Jason to throw up and then back to my room, where I passed out in my clothes. But still, these were only patches of memory missing, not a whole night. This was something else entirely, as if there had been nothing—straight from dancing to dreamworld, though I couldn't even remember my dreams.

Like I did every time I had ever woken up with a hangover, I tried to count my drinks. I ordered a glass of red wine at the fondue place. My friend Marcela said, "I'll pay for your wine. You bought mine last time." We then left and walked to a nearby bar on the plaza because they had a DJ and *dos por una*. I went up to the bar with Marcela and Louis, another language school friend. "Do you want a Cuba libre?" Louis asked me. "Two for one."

"Sure," I said, digging into my pocket for the money. Unlike in Mexico, you could order *dos por una* with a friend and each have one drink.

"I'll get these; you get the next two." He handed me a Cuba libre, more Coke than rum.

"Deal," I shouted over the music.

One small glass of wine, one Cuba libre. Two drinks. That's all I remembered drinking. Nothing made sense.

We brought our drinks over to a table and sat down with our Swedish friends, Lena and Gus. A group of Peruvian men came to our table, and one of them said, "We want to practice our English. Can we sit with you?" We all wanted to practice our Spanish, so we agreed, even though the loud dance club wasn't exactly conducive to conversation.

One of the men turned to me and said, "Do you like to dance?" I nodded.

"Then let's go," he said. "And your friend," he pointed at Lena, "she can dance with my friend Gustavo."

Lena and I agreed and followed them onto the dance floor. I brought my drink with me, but it was nearly full, so Gustavo took it and set it on a table behind us, so I wouldn't spill it. He took Lena's and did the same. After a little while, our dance partners seemed to multiply. I left the group and went over to Marcela and asked her to join us. On my way back to dance, I walked past the table where we'd left our drinks, and I took a sip before joining the party on the dance floor.

I remembered someone saying another dance club would be more fun, and the group of us walking down the narrow street and around the corner to another bar. My legs felt heavy, and I leaned on Marcela while we walked because the cobblestones seemed more slippery than usual. I remembered being tired and sitting down on a couch next to a young man from Israel, talking to him about something—maybe birthright and how I was now too old and had missed my chance. The next hour or so was a little blurry.

And then there was nothing at all.

I rubbed my pounding temples and then fell back asleep until the afternoon; I still felt horrible, and it was as if my brain wasn't working. I couldn't think in Spanish or in English. But I dragged myself out to meet my friends for dinner that night because I wasn't sure what had happened during the hours I lost, and I needed to find out.

At the restaurant, I slid into a seat next to Marcela and asked, "What happened last night?"

"You were in rare form," she said in her Dutch accent.

"What do you mean? I remember dancing with the Peruvian guys, and then I can't remember anything else."

"It was so strange," Marcela said. "It was like one minute you were fine, and the next you were slurring your words, stumbling around, and hanging on Louis."

"What do you mean hanging on Louis?"

"I don't know," she said. "Like flirting."

"What? I was flirting with Louis?" He was eighteen—exactly half my age. The term "cougar" hadn't even been invented yet, or if it had, I didn't know it.

"Or maybe," Marcela said, "you just couldn't walk and needed help. You were pretty messed up."

"How many drinks did I have?"

"I don't know. I only saw you with the one at the first place. It was like one second you were sober, the next you were wasted drunk. I've never seen you like that."

"Did someone buy me drinks?" I asked. "I didn't spend any of my own money."

"I don't know."

"What happened after the second club?"

"You were slurring and falling down, so we put you in a taxi. We paid the driver and told him where to take you."

I realized these new friends, most of them much younger than me, had saved me. "Where's Lena?" I asked, my drunkenness still a mystery.

"No one has seen her all day," Marcela said. "She didn't come to school, either. She got drunk really quickly, too. We sent her home in a taxi as well."

"So weird." My head still felt like it was clenched in a vice.

I started to apologize for getting drunk and having to be taken care of. Marcela interrupted me, asking, "Do you think maybe someone slipped something in your drink?"

"What do you mean—" I started to ask and then realized what had happened.

Suddenly the evening made sense, along with my grinding headache and loss of memory. I was mortified I had been so stupid; I had allowed myself to be in the way of danger. The what ifs, the possibilities of what might have happened even without my ever knowing it, scared the hell out of me. Between the poundings in my head, I remembered the woman I knew who had been drugged in Mexico, her memory and her sight both gone; I could hear my mother's warning again. For my mother, there was always someone to blame. Certainly it was the fault of those who had put the poison into my drink, but the men remained faceless, so I blamed myself. Shouldn't I have watched my drink?

I had been stupid but also lucky. I had a group of new friends— people who were the same age as my college students back home— who saw I was in trouble, even if they didn't know why. Between them and dumb luck, I was okay and was grateful, even if I felt like shit. I was angry at myself for being careless, for letting this happen to me when I knew better.

Lena eventually turned up at the restaurant. Same story as mine. I realized I wasn't critical of her in the way I judged myself. I needed to shift the blame to where it belonged: to men who drug women. I also needed to focus on the happy ending: our friends took care of us. It could have been so much worse.

The strangest part of the ordeal was later seeing the digital images of me before I went home but after my mind stopped recording memory. There I was, dancing with Louis, and I had to admit, it did look like flirting. In other photographs, I had my arms around Lena and Marcela; I recognized myself, but I also wasn't there. The mind had gone elsewhere, yet the body still smiled for the camera, the mouth maybe even saying "gringo" as the shutter opened and closed.

One Hundred Boyfriends

Somewhere along the Arabian Sea, January 2007

After many hours bouncing over potholes along a dirt road, Sholeh and I arrived at the small thatched cabin on the edge of the Arabian Sea. It was hot and humid, so we changed into our bathing suits and headed out for a swim. Aside from a few tourists sitting at the open-air restaurant and fishing boats pulled onto the sand, we had the beach to ourselves. We knew that in India it was against decorum to frolic around in our bikinis, so we sat on the beach in our tops and our skirts until the coast seemed clear, and then we pulled off our clothes and ran for the sea, laughing in the way you do when it feels like you're getting away with something. But we hadn't been sneaky enough, because by the time we reached the water, the fishermen had quit fiddling with their nets and boats and the waiters and patrons at the restaurant had stopped what they were doing to stare in our direction.

We floated in the salty sea, and Sholeh said, "We have to get out again, you know?" I nodded but didn't care. The southern sun hung low in the sky, and beads of light bounced off the waves. Children played with coconuts along the palm-fringed beach. We swam until our skin pruned.

When we emerged from the water, breathless and happy, everyone again stopped what they were doing to watch. We toweled off, hurried our clothes back on, and took a long walk along the beach. On our way back up to the restaurant, we passed a couple. The man wore shorts, a tank top, and sandals. He said, "Nice day for a swim. It's very hot." The woman wore a full black burka; only her eyes showed through.

"It is." I couldn't help myself from adding, "Humid, too."

A big group at the restaurant was finishing up. The men sat at one table, making merry with many bottles of beer. The women and children sat at another table, drinking sodas. I watched as a man, having left the beer table, unsuccessfully tried to climb into a hammock. The slant of afternoon light rode the sea to shore on each wave.

Sholeh and I sat at a table, ordered beers, and watched the sun set over the Arabian Sea. We squinted into the light, breathed in the salty spray. The warm night fell around us.

An Indian couple sat across from us, and I could feel them eyeing us, especially the wife. Maybe she felt some sort of camaraderie with us. After a couple of glasses of rum, they worked up the courage to walk over to our table. "May we have a picture?" the husband asked.

"Sure," I said, reaching for his camera. "Do you want the sea in the background?"

"My wife would like a picture with you."

"Okay. Sure." Sholeh and I posed with the woman in the middle, our arms draped around her shoulders. We were all wearing little tops, flowing skirts, and flip-flops. We looked like three girlfriends, not strangers from different countries. We giggled and smiled.

"Why don't you join us?" Sholeh asked them.

By the time we had drunk the restaurant out of its supply of beer, Padmesh and Badra were our new friends. They were on holiday from Mumbai, and they wanted to know as much about our lives as we wanted to know about theirs. Badra was a beautiful woman with long black hair and large, curious eyes. Padmesh, a business entrepreneur, was soft in the belly and quick to laugh. They showed us pictures of their two children on their phones, and they both seemed pleased when we commented on how beautiful they were. I didn't yet have a phone that could take pictures and was impressed by this new technology. This was six months before the first iPhone was released.

I asked them if their marriage had been arranged. Whenever I did this—ask locals too-personal questions—Sholeh shot me a look, meaning I had crossed the line into poor cultural etiquette. But I ignored Sholeh and her good advice because I'd had a few too many drinks. Plus, I was curious and wanted to know.

Padmesh didn't seem put off by my question; he said their marriage was arranged through the internet, which he said had become an increasingly popular way for parents to find spouses for their children.

"How do they choose?" I asked.

"By horoscope," Badra said. "They find the astrological match."

"But what if your horoscopes don't match?" Sholeh asked.

"Then no marriage. Or you must go to the temple and pray to see if you can overcome the bad match," Padmesh said.

"I do have friends who have love marriages," Badra said. "It's becoming more common. And they are happy, I think."

I tried to imagine whom my parents would have picked for me. My father would have chosen a smart, sensitive Jewish man, one with whom he could talk literature, politics, and baseball. My mother would have picked out a rich older man, one in a position of power who liked to spend his money not only on me but on her. Neither would have been as poor a choice as I had made for myself with my own love marriage, my ex-husband, who was a walking mirror of my insecurities.

By now, dusk had become true dark, and the first stars blinked in the sky. We were the only patrons left in the restaurant.

Sholeh and I excused ourselves to find the restroom. Badra followed.

Sholeh was married, so she avoided most of the questioning. Badra was more interested in a creature like me, a woman in her midthirties who had a boyfriend but remained unmarried. I didn't tell her I had been previously married—that seemed too complicated, too difficult to explain after drinking three Kingfishers, but really, I was embarrassed.

"Have you had boyfriends before this current one?" Badra asked me.

"Yeah." I attempted to fix my wild sea-blown hair in the mirror.

"Many?" She moved in closer.

"Sure." I looked at Badra through the mirror.

"How many?"

"I don't know. One hundred?"

"What? One hundred?" Badra turned me around to face her.

"I don't know. Give or take." I realized one hundred boyfriends might be a lot in any culture, but I felt self-conscious, so I said, "It's different in the United States."

"Did you sleep with any of them?" Badra now had me up against the sink, the fluorescent lights flickering above us. She stood so close I could smell the Kingfisher on her breath. If I could ask her if her marriage was arranged, it was only fair for her to ask me if I had slept around, which of course I had. A lot.

"You sound like my mother," Sholeh laughed. Badra ignored her and looked at me, waiting for an answer.

"Uh-huh," I said, then added, "a few," hoping that my diminished number of paramours might satisfy her.

"Oh God. Does your boyfriend know about this?"

"Yes. I mean, I guess so."

"How many?" she asked.

"How many what?" I knew what she was asking, but I couldn't tell the truth. Not because of what Badra would say but because I wasn't sure. My friend Kortney once asked me how many men I had slept with, and I admitted I had never counted. Did people really keep track?

"How many previous boyfriends did you sleep with?" Badra asked this between hiccups.

"Not sure. Fewer than one hundred." I laughed to make light of what seemed a weighty subject for my new friend.

"Oh my God. Will he ever marry you? How could he?"

"He would be crazy not to," Sholeh said, and I smiled at her, hoping that was true.

I said, "I'm not sure, but maybe you're right. Maybe he can't."

"He knows?" Badra asked and put her palm to her forehead as if she wanted to block the words from entering her mind.

"Well, I suppose he assumes."

"Have you told him? I mean, you haven't, have you?"

"Not explicitly," I said, even though Tom, who had started as a friend before his promotion to boyfriend status, knew about all of my exploits and was a very practical person.

"You have." Badra nodded.

"No. I don't know. I'm not sure." I began to feel dizzy. And more than a little worried. I looked into the mirror and tried to see myself though Badra's eyes. Could it be that, from the outside, she understood more about my life than I did?

"Don't tell him." She looked very serious, then asked, "Is he a virgin?"

"What? God no."

"And you don't mind?"

"I've never thought about it that way." I tried to imagine Tom as a forty-year-old virgin. I started to laugh.

"Why are you laughing?" She looked to Sholeh for help. She was looking in the mirror, putting on lip gloss. "Did *you* have boyfriends before you were married?" Badra asked her.

More private than I was, and therefore less likely to discuss her sex life with a stranger in a ladies' room somewhere along the Arabian Sea, Sholeh said, "I was very young when I married."

This seemed to satisfy Badra, so she turned her attention back to me.

Padmesh called into the ladies' room, "Are you all right in there? What are you doing? Didn't fall in, did you?" He laughed, as if he didn't really want to know what we were doing, but it was his duty to get his wife out of the bathroom. By this time, Sholeh was also losing her patience, but I didn't know how to answer questions the way she did—so that the answer gave nothing away but also satisfactorily closed the discussion.

Badra called back, "Everything's fine, Padmesh. Go away." She then turned to Sholeh and asked, "Can I borrow your lipstick?" Sholeh handed it over, and Badra applied it to her lips, as if that were reason enough for spending twenty minutes in the ladies' room with two Americans.

We all left the bathroom, but Badra followed Sholeh and me back to our cottage, came inside, and continued with the questioning. Mostly she repeated, "One hundred boyfriends, are you sure? You can't be serious. Oh God, you are serious," which made me wish I hadn't gone into detail. But more than that, I was now sure Tom would decide he didn't want me, after all.

Although I hadn't slept with anywhere close to one hundred men, I was pretty sure I had kissed that many, maybe more. And what counted as a boyfriend?

Badra looked at me and said in a serious woman-to-woman tone, "You must follow this advice. You must not relay this information to your boyfriend. If you do, he will never marry you." Padmesh called to her from outside our cottage, and Badra gave each of us a long hug good-bye and placed a glossy kiss on our cheeks. She wished me luck and said, "Don't forget. Listen to me."

She retreated into the dark and salty air, waving. I promised I would consider her sound advice but knew it was already too late.

Spas and Beauty Treatments

~~~~~~

Travel is only glamorous in retrospect.

PAUL THEROUX

Prague and the Unbearable
Lousiness of the Tourist

Prague, Czech Republic, July 2011

Before visiting Prague, I had heard it was the most beautiful city in Europe. Friends most often used the word "magical." And in my first couple of days, I saw Prague the way they did—the cobblestoned streets, the ornate centuries-old buildings, the charming red streetcars, the looming Baroque clock towers, the Gothic cathedral spires jutting into the roof of the cloud-quilted sky. Yet after a couple of weeks of wandering around, bumping into people because I wasn't watching where I was going, the magic wore off. I noticed the posters advertising Darlings, a cabaret famous for the dwarf prostitute who dressed up like Chewbacca or maybe an Ewok. The smell of urine drifted through the old town square. Though the castles of Disneyland were modeled after those of Prague, the city wasn't a Disneyland, and the denizens were not paid to smile and say "Dobrý den" if you wandered within a magical meter of them. Even the beggars started to seem fake humble to me.

I started to see how the locals were tired of the tourists. After four weeks there, I was sick of the tourists, too. I was in Prague at a summer writing program, but to the locals, I was no different than the Germans with their pink ice cream cones, the Americans shouting their twangy English, or the tour bus passengers waving video cameras from the windows, filming the Starbucks tucked into a Baroque building or the KFC sign in front of Kafka's birthplace. I hoped that if Kafka himself could somehow see this from beyond the grave, he would appreciate the irony.

A man with an audio headset around his neck shouted and pointed at the woman in the deli. "I want this sandwich cut into four pieces." He was in a hurry because there was a tour guide with a giant yellow umbrella outside waiting for him.

"I cannot cut four ways. Just two pieces. You do it yourself," the woman helping him said.

"May I please have tap water?"

"We don't have tap water here."

"No tap here? What do you mean?"

"Bottled, still or with gas."

"All right, to go."

"Take away?"

"To go. To Go. TO GO."

Even though she was rude, I found myself siding with the woman behind the counter—so smug was I with my ten-Czech-word repertoire. The Velvet Revolution may have freed Prague from the communist regime, but the city seemed to have passed hands directly to the tourist regime.

I had been living out of my suitcase in a Soviet Bloc dorm room for a month, and the filters I carefully placed to hide my sense of entitlement were scratched thin by exhaustion. I told myself I needed a pedicure. I figured I could read for my workshop, do some writing and editing, and get my toes done all at the same time. The perfect way to multitask. Plus, it was raining. Again.

Let me be clear: you cannot sit there while someone rubs your feet, picks at your toes, and polishes your nails unless you have developed a sense of entitlement. This is coming from someone who gets regular pedicures, understands this, but also knows she should be grateful and that the words "need" and "pedicure" do not belong in the same sentence.

The man at the salon said he had been in Prague for three years, and he spoke a little Czech and about as much English as I knew

Czech. With some back and forth, we settled on a price of 500 crowns for the pedicure.

He cut my nails too short and then picked at the skin around the nails with his mean metal tool until each toe bled. As I put my feet back into the grubby water tub, I hoped my hepatitis shots were current. There was no salt scrub, no calf and foot massage. He must have wondered why I had hiked my pants up past my knees. *This is a different place*, I reasoned, determined not to be the typical tourist who expects to get everything just like at home. I tried to be grateful that I had the means to sit there while he worked on my feet.

When he was finished, he said, "You got paint with your French pedicure. That's an extra cost. 600 crowns."

"Paint comes with a French pedicure," I said. "It isn't a French pedicure without the paint."

He shook his head. "600 crowns plus tip."

I reached for his calculator and divided 600 by 16, which was the exchange rate at the time. "That's 37 dollars. I'm not paying 37 dollars for that."

"Extra for paint."

"A French pedicure is *defined* by the paint."

"Extra for paint."

"Do you know the word for 'thief'?" I asked.

He shook his head.

"'Robber'?"

More head shaking.

"What about 'stealing'? How about 'swindler'?" Now I was reaching. Thankfully, those words were not in my Czech repertoire.

"600. Plus tip."

"Listen," I said, "I have 500. That's what we agreed on. And here is your tip—50. 550, that's plenty. That's a lot. Too much, even. And it's all I have."

He shook his head, crossed his arms, and "tsk, tsk, tsked."

What was he going to do? Run after me? Call the police? It was true—that was all the money I had brought with me, so I turned on my 550-crown toes and headed for the door. Another ugly American, another bad tourist. I wanted so badly not to be this thing I couldn't help myself from becoming. Yet this man had swindled me, hadn't he?

Walking back to my dorm room in the rain, the metallic ring of the streetcars sounded more like a whine than the song I had heard when I first arrived in Prague. But the pitter-patter of the rain and the cooing of the pigeons soon fell into harmony, and I realized I had met wonderful Czech people. The in-country staff of the writing program couldn't be more lovely. Yet there was that Disneyland feeling again: were they nice to me because they were paid to be? The people pushing by me on the streets were not nice to me, but then again, most of them were fellow tourists.

Sandra was coming to visit me in Prague as soon as my writing fellowship ended. I had told her about the city's historic architecture, the beautiful parks, the graceful Vltava River. When she arrived, we decided to visit Vyšehrad Castle. We wandered the grounds, relieved to be away from more of ourselves, the dreaded tourists, but also the waiters telling us there was no tap water, that the stale pretzel on our table that we thought was complimentary and had taken a bite from would be 50 crowns.

On our way back, we walked past the river, the swans preening and wagging their tails. Baby ducks swam after their mother. The water refracted the evening light. We both wanted to extend this feeling of peace before heading back to the touristy center of town. We followed a maze of streets through a quiet neighborhood and came to a crowd overflowing from a small shop. They were all holding glasses filled with white, pink, and red wines.

"Should we go in?" I asked.

"It looks like a local place," Sandra said. "I'm sure they don't speak English. But I think it's a wine tasting. Czech or no Czech, we can do a wine tasting." This was our turf, our *terroir*. If wine couldn't break down the language and culture barriers, I wasn't sure anything could. We at least had to try.

"Listen," I said, "I know how to say 'hello,' 'please,' 'thank you,' 'red wine,' 'white wine,' and 'sparkling wine' in Czech. We can do this, right?"

"Right." Sandra looked determined. We headed straight for the wine bar, and I didn't stop to wonder what it said about me that I could order wine in about ten languages but hold a basic conversation in only two.

The rotund, bald man poured wine from barrels behind the wooden bar. He looked at us from the corner of his eye but didn't speak to us. I bumped into a man next to me, and when I said, "Sorry, I mean, Promiňte," he turned to look at me, and I recognized him. How did I know him? My mind's directory flipped through the possibilities. Who would I know at a small local wine shop in Prague?

"I know you," I said. "You're um, um, um . . ."

He smiled and mimicked me: "Um, um, um."

My mind flipped to the right entry, and I blurted out, "Miloš. Miloš, the guide." He had led a walking tour I had taken on my first day in Prague.

"Yes, so nice to see you." He offered his hand, and I shook it.

"I'm in the Prague Summer Program. The writing program." Miloš specialized in the arts, specifically music, which was the theme for that year's program.

"Welcome. How did you get here? You have found the best wine shop in Prague. This is my second home. Do you want to try the wine?"

Sandra and I both nodded. Miloš told Roman, the bartender, that we would like to taste.

"He says you have only half an hour; I am afraid they close at six."

"That's okay. Tell him we'll be quick."

Four hours later we were still at the bar, trying every wine on tap. Roman also started opening bottles from the shelves, and eventually we all switched to beer. I made friends with a woman called Eva. Miloš translated. Though I couldn't talk to her directly, I felt the harmony of female friendship through the clinking of glasses, the laughing at wordless jokes. Roman introduced us to his son, invited us to come back again. "I am honored to have you here," he said through Miloš. We took photographs arm in arm, all hugged good-bye.

"You have found the soul of the city," Miloš said. "You are true Praguers."

I looked down at my French pedicure, smiled, and I wished it were true.

Stretching the Thigh Fat

Alleppey, India, February 2007

I noticed a sign at our hotel offering yoga lessons and told Sholeh, "Let's sign up." I had been practicing at home and was determined to take yoga in India, the place where it all began.

We changed into our sweats and went to meet our instructor, a young man in his early twenties, lanky and big-eyed. He led us to a room that looked like a dining hall, but the tables and chairs had been pushed against the walls. He instructed us to lie down on the concrete floor. The air outside was hot and thick, but inside, the air conditioner hummed from a wall unit in the corner, circulating cold air with a hint of cardamom, lemon polish, and mop water.

We were his only students.

"Do we get mats?" I asked.

"This is real yoga. No mats."

Determined to do *real* yoga, I followed his instructions.

"The floor's a little cold," Sholeh said.

"You will become warm," our teacher told us. He went over to turn off the air conditioner and opened the window. The brackish, humid air pushed into the dining-hall yoga studio.

Our instructor then came back over, kneeled down on the floor between us, and yanked on my leg. "I must pull your leg this way," he told me, "to stretch it."

"What about the asanas?" I asked. "Don't we do the poses ourselves?"

"Don't you want to do Indian yoga?" He left me and edged over to Sholeh. He sat down cross-legged next to her, rubbing her arm.

"It just seems strange," I said. "It's not like at home. Not even a little bit."

"Have you done yoga in India before?" he asked. He had me there. I admitted that I had not.

"Well, this is *real* yoga." He progressed from massaging Sholeh's arm to tugging on it, as if trying to dislodge the arm from its socket so he could bring it home with him.

"Ouch," Sholeh said, so he went back to a slow caress.

"My teacher at home studied in India," I tried. "And we don't do it this way. What about sun salutations?"

"But this *is* India, a twenty-five-thousand-year tradition. Do you argue with that? Things are very different in India." He reluctantly left Sholeh's arm and instructed her to lie in Savasana until he could return to her. He then came over to me and wrenched my leg with vigor.

"That's too hard."

"You have children?" He continued his stretching work.

"No. Ouch. Why?"

"And your friend?" He pointed to Sholeh.

"I have two children," she said, still in corpse pose.

"Well, the reason you are inflexible," our teacher told me as he jerked at my leg, "is that you have too much thigh fat."

"Thigh fat?"

"Yes. You have thigh fat and that's why you don't stretch. And no children?" He shook his head with disdain. "Your friend, she has an excuse—two children. But you . . . ?" He wagged his finger at me. "You have no reason and even more thigh fat than your friend with the two children. You have no excuse whatsoever." He yanked on my leg, nearly succeeding in popping it from the cradle of my hip.

Our instructor finally left me and my thigh fat and walked back over to Sholeh, who looked like she might have gone to sleep. He called to me, "You can do your sun salutations now if you want."

I got busy with my sun salutations, thinking about how I knew this wasn't right, knew that just because this was India, that didn't make it *real* yoga. Then I thought about how during yoga, I should notice my thoughts and let them go rather than engage in internal arguments. I tried to concentrate on my breathing, wondering what would come next and if my ideas about yoga had been wrong all along. Maybe after years of practicing at home, I didn't know what yoga really was. I tried, without success, to still my mind.

A couple weeks earlier, Sholeh and I had arrived at the Jagat Palace in Pushkar, a marble-domed hotel overlooking the Thar Desert, Snake Mountain, and a scattering of tents in the field where the drivers stayed. I looked out the window of my marble palace, knowing our driver Sharma was camped out there somewhere. I turned from that window and made our spa appointments for Ayurvedic massage. And I would get exactly what I deserved.

Two Indian women, one stout, the other spindly as the stem of a daisy, arrived at our room with a male translator. He explained to us that we would follow the women to the spa, where we would enjoy Ayurvedic massage. "Do you think they have a steam room at the spa?" I asked Sholeh. "Or a Jacuzzi?"

The translator left us, and we followed the two women. They were both dressed in simple saris with their black hair in tight buns. They knew two English words between them, which was two more than the number of Hindi words I knew.

Sholeh disappeared into a room with the willowy masseuse, and I followed the stout one into a dimly lit closet that held brooms and cleaning supplies. A wooden table, covered with a plastic tarp, stood in the corner. The drafty space smelled of ammonia and moth balls. My therapist pointed to the table, and I hesitated for a minute before I began to disrobe. Then through the thin walls, I heard Sholeh's voice: "Oh my God. I can't. I'm sorry. I just can't. Really, I'm very sorry."

Within seconds, Sholeh pushed open the door to my "treatment room" and blew in, her skinny masseuse trailing her. My therapist's face squeezed into a wrinkle when she saw them. Sholeh said, "She brought me to a restroom. A *men's* bathroom. She wanted me to lie down on the *floor*. Under the *urinal*."

"I'll switch with you," I said. "You can have my broom closet."

"No, no. I'm not doing this. There was a bug this big," Sholeh showed me with her thumb and index finger. "It crawled right over the mat on the floor. Right where she wanted me to lie down. On the *floor*. You're not going in there either."

Sholeh stuffed a few rupees in the palm of the confused woman, saying, "Here's your tip. I'm very sorry, but I just can't." Sholeh turned and left, disappearing into the misty courtyard. The two Indian massage therapists conferred with one another. My woman looked angry and said something I imagined went like this: "Spoiled princesses." She then looked at me, and I gave her a look of resolution; I was more determined than ever to have the massage. Ayurveda had been around for five thousand years—who was I to complain because my treatment was happening in a supply closet?

Sholeh's masseuse walked out the door into the dark, and that's when mine pointed to my panties and insisted, "Off, off, off." She tugged at the corner of my underwear and then motioned toward the wooden table.

I did as I was told.

Later Sholeh would ask me, "Why didn't you just say no?" and the only answer I could come up with was that I was too embarrassed not to take them off. I put myself in this situation, after all. Here I was, across the world, standing naked in a cold broom closet with a woman I could not talk to. Maybe this was standard fare. How did I know? I didn't have the words to ask. And it wasn't this woman's fault, so rather than decline, I disrobed.

I lay face down on the hard tarp-covered wooden table, and the masseuse made a motion with her index finger to flip over, face up like an egg. I anticipated some sort of privacy towel, but none appeared. I motioned to the women with my arms that I was freezing. "Brrrr," I said, hoping this was the international word for "cold," and I crossed my arms over my breasts in an attempt to hide something. Of course, my crotch remained exposed, sunny-side up.

She disappeared for a minute and then returned with a small space heater, which she plugged in next to my feet. Within a minute, my feet began to blister while the rest of me shivered. The woman got to work. First, a healthy dose of oil was poured onto my entire body, and the woman rubbed me up and down like she was pushing a rolling pin over raw dough. She went up over my pubic bones and breasts, as if they were bubbles in dough in serious need of flattening. Then she set about cracking my toes with one loud pop after another, which was even worse than it sounds. When she was satisfied that I was fully slickened with oil, she motioned for me to turn over. This seemed like a blessing, but really it meant more oil, more steamrolling over the body. I glistened like a seal.

I prayed it would be over quickly.

At last she motioned for me to stand up. Just when I thought my treatment had finally—mercifully—ended, she pulled a metal folding chair into the center of the room and pushed me onto it. The other word in her English-language repertoire was "sit."

There I was, following directions, my naked butt against the cold metal, my bare feet on the concrete. She stood behind me and poured more oil into my hair until it dripped down into my ears. I closed my eyes, letting it slide past them and over my nose and lips. Once I was doused, she scratched the oil into my scalp with vigorous glee.

And at last, the grand finale: karate chops to the head, the hard edges of her palms pounding my skull. I sat there, trying to touch the cold floor with only the tips of my toes while enduring a jarring assault from above.

My masseuse finally motioned for me to put my clothes back onto my oil-slicked body. Once again, I did as I was told, and I followed her out of the broom closet. She put out her hand, and into it I folded her generous tip and uttered the commonly used Sanskrit word "Namaste."

I would later learn I had received Abhyanga, the Cadillac of Ayurvedic massage, the ultimate spa experience.

And perhaps this was *real* yoga. What did I know? After ten sun salutations, I practiced my *ujjayi pranayama* breathing in downward-facing dog. I stared at my thigh fat, mad at myself for not lying to the instructor about having children. Maybe I could tell him that I had three or four at home that I'd forgotten about. Three children would be enough to justify my thigh fat, wouldn't they?

Our yoga instructor continued to pull at Sholeh's arm while she rested in corpse pose. She opened her eyes and said, "I think I've done enough Indian yoga for now."

As we were leaving, he said, "I can come to your room for private lessons. For yoga. Or for massage. And I'll give you a very good discount."

We told him we'd already had our Indian massages, tipped him, and waved good-bye.

"That was strange," I told Sholeh as we followed the grassy path back to our room. "I mean, have you ever done yoga like that?"

"I've told you before," she said. "To enjoy India, you must let go of your expectations."

Was I annoyed that Sholeh was always right?

I wasn't. Instead I congratulated myself for choosing such a smart and sensible travel partner once again—a girlfriend who never let me down and helped me navigate the way. I couldn't deny that my three imaginary children and I needed her.

Bellagio People

Your lover's family doesn't like that you're from California, that you're only half Jewish (and the wrong half), but most of all that you're still married. While the family doesn't seem to question your lover's decision to have an affair with a married woman he met in Mexico, they do wonder about your lack of scruples. When you meet his sister in the lobby of the Bellagio, the first thing she says to you is, "Are you divorced yet?"

You tell her that in California, it takes six months.

"Well, I can't see what's taking so long," she says.

"I've moved out. We're separated. I filed for divorce."

"But not divorced. I mean, technically, you're married to someone else."

According to your lover's mother, a prim woman who wears tailored outfits and a healthy dollop of makeup, the family agrees that if he loves you, which he claims he does, you will be invited on the Annual Family Las Vegas Trip. Even if you are (unfortunately) still married. "We're very accepting," she says.

You will meet the entire family in Las Vegas, including the grandmother, who says, "We're Bellagio people."

The men carry golf clubs; the women wheel enormous suitcases. The father remarks on how small yours is and says to his wife, "Look at that bag! Why can't you bring a suitcase that small?"

The mother makes a face that says, *Oh please.* And when you say, "It's just a weekend, right?" the mother looks at you like you have personally insulted her and her giant matching Louis Vuitton suitcase and carry-on, like you have no real appreciation for the Annual Family Las Vegas Trip.

You will soon find out that everything is preplanned to the minute, from drinks and dinner, to shopping excursions (for the ladies) and gambling (for the men), to the rental of the cabaña at the pool, and most importantly, golf (for the men) and spa day (for the ladies). An appointment for a massage has already been made for you. You will wonder if you can go golfing with the men instead, and you will find out that no, you may not.

The women meet in the ladies' lounge, where you are to relax in your fluffy bathrobes and then follow a spa attendant to a room for a fifty-minute massage. Then you are to meet back at the ladies' lounge for a sauna, steam room, or Jacuzzi. Your choice.

The first part goes well enough, most of the women flipping through magazines, the older ladies perusing *Good Housekeeping* or *Martha Stewart Living*, the younger ones looking at *Marie Claire*. You have brought along an eighteenth-century Gothic novel, Matthew Lewis's *The Monk*.

One of the younger cousins asks you what you're reading, and you are glad to talk about books, but maybe looking back, you were a little too enthusiastic. "This is the greatest book." You hold up a cover that features a naked monk being flown across a black sky by the claws of a demon. You should have taken the cousin's strange smirk as a sign to stop talking, but you are nervous, so without much thought to the words spilling from your mouth, you say: "It's about this monk everyone admires, but he is full of lust, and he has sex with this woman who turns out to be a demon. He ends up making a pact with the devil, and he unknowingly rapes his sister and kills his mother. All the while, he's responsible for a pregnant nun being tortured in the catacombs of the dungeon." This is when you notice the cousin's face drain of color, so you end your little book summary with, "But the nun lives, even though the baby dies . . . and the monk, well, he gets . . ." Because the look on her face tells you to stop talking, *right now*, you hold up the book with its graphic cover to show her.

You never thought much about the naked monk on the book's cover. Until now.

"Sounds . . . interesting," she says in that way where the word "interesting" doesn't really mean interesting.

"It is. I'm teaching it," you say, as if that somehow would excuse you from reading something so scandalous.

"You're teaching *that*?"

"Uh-huh. In freshman comp."

"I never read anything like that in college."

"No," you say, "I imagine you didn't."

The cousin is about to ask you what you mean when you are saved by the attendant, calling your name.

After the massage, you meet, as planned, to go into the family-sized Jacuzzi together. You are naked under your robe—it is a women-only Jacuzzi, so you thought naked was the appropriate choice.

By the time you hang up your robe and glance into the tub, you realize the mistake you have made. Not only are you the adulterous half-Jew from California, you are the only naked person, and to top it off, you are sporting a Brazilian bikini wax (special for your lover). The whole family—mother, sister, aunts, cousins, and grandma—stops talking when you submerge your naked, hairless body into the frothy tub. The sister glares at you and shakes her head.

You wish you had chosen the steam room, where the cloud of eucalyptus vapor might have hidden your hairless body.

"How was your massage?" you ask another cousin, this one a little older and very pregnant; she is sitting across from you on the edge of the hot tub with her feet dangling in.

"It was just average," she says as if she gets a massage every day of her life.

"Mine was really nice," you say and then turn to the mother, who is wearing a navy one-piece with little sailor buttons. "Thanks again for making the reservations."

"We're glad you could come," she says through a stiff smile, though she's not looking in your direction, saving herself from seeing her son's lover's boobs bobbing about in the spa.

"The girl who massaged me acted like I was going to break," the pregnant cousin complains, "but worse than that, she had these eyebrows that hadn't been plucked for a *really* long time, so she had stray hairs everywhere. It looked *so* gross."

Rather than asking her if she is serious (because you can already tell she is), you nod, trying to look sympathetic—not with the gentle masseuse, who maybe didn't have the time or the money to get spa treatments herself, but with the pregnant cousin.

Then you realize that you yourself have not had much time lately, and though you have tidied up your bikini area, you can't remember the last time you plucked your own eyebrows. You know that if you reach up to touch them and check, it will seem obvious, so you just sit there with your arms crossed over your breasts, wondering if your sweat smells like sauvignon blanc.

You hope you have spent enough quality time with the lady folk so you can get back up to the hotel room, where there's someone waiting (if the golf day is over) who will appreciate your new wax job.

After a couple of the women head to shower, you convince yourself it is appropriate for you to leave, so you rush over to your towel and robe and head straight for the mirror in the bathroom. Sure enough, your brows are wild with itinerant hairs. Even the middle section above your nose.

You do not know that your lover's family will soon plan an intervention (mostly successful). That they will drive over to his house late in the night and beg him to quit you like you are a drug he has become addicted to.

For the moment, you are living under the belief that because you have divorced your husband, your lover will travel the world with you indefinitely.

Sometime later, you will find out he has been working under another assumption. In his version of you, you will be happy living on a suburban midwestern lake, baking your children Jack-o-Lantern cupcakes for Halloween. He does not yet know that operating an oven is not among your talents, nor that you do not want children for whom to bake orange treats.

All of this will come later.

All you know right now is that you are not Bellagio people.

Knowing the Words by Heart

Napa Valley, United States, May 2008

The note read: *Room 214. Door is Open.*

They must have slipped it under the door after they came by the night before. I had been wearing a nightie, one of those slips Kortney referred to as a "number." The boys had come by, bottle of Silver Oak in hand, asking us if we wanted to "keep partying."

At the moment, Kortney was busy in the bathroom. "My friend," I said over the sounds of retching, "is a little sick."

"Can *you* come over?" More gagging from the bathroom.

"I don't think so," I said. "I better get back in there and hold Kortney's hair out of the way." As I said this, I knew I had given out too much information, though by the sounds coming from the bathroom, they could probably guess what was going on.

They shrugged and nodded. I think of them as Number One and Number Two—the dudes from the bar. It's not that I don't remember their names—it's that I never caught them in the first place. Let's just call them Billy and Ted. Number One will be Billy. He was the one who undoubtedly thought of me as "his." Number Two will be Ted.

Kortney and I met in Napa Valley to spend a relaxing weekend together. We had made massage appointments, imagining a day at the spa, some poolside lounging, a little wine tasting. She had recently been let go from her corporate job, and she claimed that she wanted to write a book. Or rather, she wanted me to write her story, because writing a book wasn't among her many talents. "It's the story of this recession," she had said. I told her I had enough ideas of my own, too many in fact, but she said, "We'll meet in Napa and talk about my book."

I didn't want to write her book, but I loved her. And besides, I wanted to go to Napa, so I agreed. My first marriage had ended, and I had begun dating Tom long-distance, but neither of us was ready for a commitment. I craved some girlfriend time, some time to process things. Even more than that, we were nearly thirty-eight, at the edge of something we knew was coming but couldn't exactly define. Or maybe we did know what it was—namely, middle age—and we wanted to keep pretending we were the same girls we had always been. Wasn't that what longtime friends were for?

As soon as we arrived at the hotel, we changed into our bikinis and headed for the pool. Many women our age had already transitioned to modest one-piece bathing suits, but not us. We were—and still are—holding out as long as possible, as if our choice of swimwear could stave off the inevitability of aging. We sat at the pool, and Kortney said, "We need some service. Where's our pool boy?"

You must understand something about Kortney: she has a $4,000 purse she named Duchess. She was not willing to accept that the Westin didn't employ pool boys, so I said, "I'll go to the restaurant. What do you want?"

"Sauvignon blanc," she said, still looking around for our pool boy.

"What about lunch?"

"That is lunch," she said, laughing.

"Right," I said and then returned with the wine. We raised our glasses and toasted to our twenty-year friendship.

You should also know this about me: I have a $20 page boy bag from Ross Dress for Less that I have named Butch. If Duchess and Butch sat on a shelf together for twenty years, they would be friends, no matter how different they were. That's how it is with Kortney and me. We don't need to have anything in common aside from our long-standing friendship.

"I think for my fortieth," Kortney said, "I would like to rent a private jet and take my friends to Tokyo for a long weekend." I couldn't agree more. That sounded like a most excellent plan, especially since I would be at the top of the invitation list. Then she said, "But my husband doesn't make enough money, so we'll just have to go to Puerto Vallarta or something."

"That will still be fun," I said, thinking Mexico would be an extravagant birthday celebration, one that Kortney would help me get to with her airline miles (which was exactly how it ended up happening).

"Not as fun as Japan," she said with a wistful little sigh.

"But still fun."

Before we knew it, we were out of wine, and the sun dropped beneath the building, leaving us in the shade. "Ready to go up?" Kortney asked.

On our way back to our room, we discovered the lobby was hosting a wine tasting. "Fabulous," Kortney said. "We're thirsty." We tried a few wines and then went up to get ready for dinner.

We walked to ZuZu, a tapas place in Napa, and ordered a beet salad and tortilla to share. And more wine. When Kortney was in the bathroom, I told the bartender she was going through a divorce, even though it wasn't true. I told him she needed some extra special attention.

"I'll sleep with her if you want," he said.

I told him that was a generous offer but I thought flirting would be enough, which he paired with complimentary drinks.

Kortney wasn't going through a divorce then, but ironically (or maybe not so ironically), when we met again five years later in this very restaurant, she was. At the time, though, she was happy, or so we thought. But I can't help myself from telling a story. Especially if I have had a glass of wine. Or three.

We walked back to our hotel, and Kortney said, "I think that bartender was flirting with you."

"What? He was supposed to flirt with you."

"What do you mean?" she asked. We rambled along the dark sidewalk and across the river, toward our hotel.

"I told him you were going through a divorce."

"You did not," she said, flipping her long red hair. Then without waiting for an answer, she asked, "Why would you do that?"

"For fun."

And Kortney laughed.

I did tell the bartender that story for fun, but even more than that—and what we don't talk about enough—is when you are a woman, there is a line between being young and cute and old and invisible. Kortney and I were hovering that line. As much as I wish there were no line or pretend I don't care about such a line, it's what we grow up with; I still see it in young women acting in certain ways because they know they are being noticed. Becoming invisible can be an unsettling thing. It's as if one day people see you, and the next day, they don't. The ways we have always mattered as girls and women don't count anymore. Reinventing ourselves on our own terms is hard but necessary.

"I guess he *was* flirting with me," Kortney said and smiled in the fuzzy light of the streetlamps.

Let me tell you something else about my friendship with Kortney. We were set up on a friend blind date when we were eighteen. She was about to turn nineteen, and my only job was to keep her occupied so that our mutual friends could put together a fabulous surprise birthday party for her—everyone loved Kortney! To accomplish this, I took her to the grocery store and bought us each two Foster's forty-ounce beers with my fake ID.

Kortney and I finished our beers, drank some more Budweiser from the keg at a fraternity TGIF party, and lost track of time. By the time I delivered Kortney to her party, we were late, and we had a very drunk birthday girl and chaperone on our hands. Our mutual friends were unhappy with me at the time, but it was the beginning of a lifelong friendship.

As we reached our Napa hotel, we noticed a large bus with tinted windows parked in front. In the lobby, Kortney asked, "Are you tired?"

"Not really," I said, not wanting the night to end. "Should we have dessert?"

And that's how we ended up at the lobby bar, splitting flourless chocolate cake. Two young men were seated next to us.

"Were you girls at the pool today?" one of them asked.

We said we were.

"Yeah," he said. "We saw you."

I whispered to Kortney, "Is that the best they can do?" I was kidding, not really thinking they were hitting on us because they looked like they were half our age.

She nodded and said, "I know. Seriously?"

"Can we sit with you?" the other one asked, and we agreed.

"What are you here for?" Billy asked.

"It's my friend's birthday," I said. Kortney just looked at me.

"How old are you?" Ted asked Kortney.

Before she could say anything, I answered for her because obviously. "Thirty-one. She's thirty-one," I said. Billy and Ted nodded and said Kortney looked good for being *that* old, so I asked, "How old are you guys?"

Billy said he was twenty-four and Ted was twenty-six. They both wore tight black t-shirts, Converse sneakers, tattoos, goatees, and small gold hoop earrings. Aside from Billy's horn-rimmed glasses and small potbelly, they are interchangeable in my memory.

"Thirty-one must seem so old to you," I said. Did I bat my almost forty-year-old eyelashes? Why yes, I most certainly did.

"I like older women," Billy said. If he only knew, I thought. Ted told the waiter we had a birthday, and so within a few minutes another piece of cake arrived, this one with candles, and we all sang to Kortney.

And I was very happy because I have a fondness for flourless chocolate cake.

Billy and Ted said how great it was that I was helping Kortney celebrate her birthday, cheering her up after her recent divorce. Kortney asked them what they were doing in Napa.

"We're here with Sugar Ray," Ted said.

"The band?" Kortney asked.

"We're playing the fair," Billy said.

"I don't think I know his music," I said, shoveling more cake into my mouth.

"Of course you know them," Kortney said, and she started singing "Every Morning." Among Kortney's many talents, she knows the lyrics by heart to more songs than anyone else I know. Don't challenge her to karaoke. She'll win. Once she sang the song, I agreed I had heard it before. In fact, it came out around the time we were the same age as Billy and Ted.

"Are you musicians?" Kortney asked. Now she was the one fluttering her eyelashes.

"Nah," said Ted. "We're band techs. Do you girls want to see the bus?"

Um, yeah.

We paid our bill and headed out to the front of the Westin with Billy and Ted. Billy fumbled with the keys and opened Sugar Ray's band bus. From the outside, it had looked like a regular bus with tinted windows. But on the inside, it was like an RV with a dining area, red velveteen couches, bunks for the band techs, and a suite for Sugar Ray.

"Does he have a four-post bed?" Kortney asked, and Billy and Ted acted like that was the funniest joke they had ever heard.

"Is he in there?" I whispered, still thinking Sugar Ray was one person.

"No. They're in the hotel."

"Can we see their suite?" I asked.

"We don't have the key," Ted said. "You want some wine?"

"What do you have?" Kortney asked, and Ted grabbed a bottle of Silver Oak cabernet. The glasses, though, were locked in Sugar Ray's quarters, so we ended up drinking the $100 wine straight from the bottle. Sorry, wine snobs, I can feel you cringe.

"How about some music?" Billy asked.

Kortney shouted, "Tiny Dancer!" which is one of her go-to songs. As soon as it began, she sang loudly enough to drown out Elton. Then she started doing interpretive dance, hanging from the bars of the bus while placing her hand on her heart. I drank Silver Oak from the bottle, and Billy squeezed in next to me on the red velveteen couch. Ted got up and started dancing with Kortney. She seemed oblivious to him—hiccupping and singing, asking for the same song again once it ended—but that didn't stop him from trying to put his hands all over her.

That's when I had a moment of clarity within my wine fog: I needed to get us the fuck off the band bus. "Time to go," I said, grabbing Kortney's hand on the way out, but the door wouldn't open.

"What?" Billy called. "We still have wine. Why are you leaving?" He sounded sad, indeed.

"Time to go." I pushed on the bus door. "How do you open this thing?"

"But it's her birthday," Ted said.

"Not anymore. It's after midnight. Her birthday is over."

"Oh," Kortney said between hiccups. "But I've just gotten a divorce. Or maybe I'm about to get one. Which is it, Suzanne?" she asked and laughed.

"It's time to go," I said again, and Billy pushed whatever button you press to open a bus door. "Thanks for the wine," I said, and we tumbled out into the dewy night air.

"We'll come with you," Ted called after us.

"No need. We're fine walking back on our own."

"We're staying in the hotel, too," Billy said.

"You aren't sleeping in the bunks?" Kortney asked.

"No, we only sleep there on the road. We have a hotel room. Sugar Ray has the suites."

We got into the elevator together, and as luck would have it, we were all on the second floor. Billy and Ted walked us to our room, and we said our good-byes.

"I have the hiccups," Kortney said, as if this wasn't obvious. Then she said, "I don't feel so well," and went into the bathroom. It was clear we wouldn't be making it to our massage appointments the next morning. I called the front desk and asked them to relay the message to the spa. Then I changed into my nightie.

"Look at that hot number!" Kortney pointed at my nightie. Then she shut herself into the bathroom, and the retching commenced. I went in to check on her, and that's when I heard the knock on the door.

The next morning, Kortney noticed the note on the floor. She asked, "What's this?"

"Oh that," I said. "It's evidence."

"Of what?" She didn't remember them coming by after we'd gotten home.

"Of cougars gone wild. It's like the men stay the same age, but we just keep getting older."

"Don't make me laugh," Kortney said. "It hurts my head." Then, as she often does, she busted into song: "Something's got me reeling . . ." That was when I realized those two decades separating the cute college co-eds sucking terrible beer from a fraternity keg and the cougars drinking Silver Oak from the bottle in the Sugar Ray band bus seemed like no time at all.

Activities

~~~~~~

We travel, some of us forever, to seek
other states, other lives, other souls.

ANAÏS NIN

Skiing the Fall Line

Carson Pass, United States, April 2002

We skied through a cliff band of "no fall zones," places where, if you fell, you might not survive—a fact I pushed out of my mind. I also tried not to think about something else: the Red Lake Peak chutes often slid, meaning an avalanche and a cold, dark burial.

Backcountry skiing is one of those activities where the benefits outweigh the risks, at least for me. It's one thing to ski at a resort with thousands of other people. It's a different thing entirely to hike up a mountain with friends and a dog, picnic at the summit, and then cut tracks in fresh winter powder or springtime corn snow, the mountain to ourselves.

Susan skied first, dropping off the cornice, cutting tight turns, pitching herself into gravity's net. I watched from above. She kept going, skiing the fall line, down the steep ravine; she fell and tumbled and righted herself and then kept on skiing.

I could tell my husband Craig and his friend John were impressed by Susan's fearlessness. I was, too, but watching her also scared me. It was like feeling vertigo at a cliff's edge—not a fear of falling, exactly, but of not being able to stop myself from flinging my body into the abyss. I wanted to ski the mountain as she did, without the usual hesitation. But I didn't dare. The benefit of doing that—if there was a benefit—definitely did not outweigh the risks. I knew skiing off a cornice in the backcountry could cause an avalanche, so I found the least scary place to enter the chute and chose each turn with caution.

We had met Susan that morning in the Carson Pass parking lot. We were getting ready to skin up Red Lake Peak, ski the chutes, and then traverse to ski the lower half of Stevens Peak. When she saw us with our backcountry gear, Susan asked, "Can I tag along with you?" She was petite, pretty, and wore her long brown hair in a thick braid. She took off her mirrored sunglasses, and the small lines crinkled around her blue eyes when she smiled showed that she'd spent a lot of time in the outdoors. She told us she was traveling alone. Her Subaru was packed full of ski equipment and camping gear. Like me, she used telemark skis, meaning that when she skied, her heel wouldn't be fixed into the binding. Right away, I saw her as the kind of woman I wanted to be—independent and sure of herself.

"Sure," we agreed to her joining us.

"Great. I wanted to go backcountry skiing but not alone." Susan pulled her equipment from her car, put her climbing skins on her skis, and pulled her pack on. When Craig and I went into the backcountry, other than discussing terrain and weather conditions, we hiked and skied in silence. And it was likely Craig and John would race up the mountain, leaving me to skin up alone. I was happy to have Susan along, this new friend to talk to.

Once we started hiking, Susan asked, "Should we do a beacon check?"

I hoped Craig wouldn't interject his favorite joke: *That's what she said*. Early on, I had found his sense of humor fun, like nearly everyone else did, but more and more, he seemed like a walking cliché.

Beacons are tracking devices worn in avalanche terrain so that if you are caught, your friends can find you and dig you out of the snow before you suffocate—which can happen within minutes. Often when Craig and I skied, I was scoffed at for asking to follow safety protocol. The snowpack in the Sierra is fairly stable, so he called me paranoid. But because Susan was new and cute, both men agreed, even though the avalanche danger was forecasted that day as low to moderate.

I couldn't help myself from saying, "Statistics will tell you, if you want to come back alive, bring a woman." Craig rolled his eyes. I gave him a side-eye glance in response. He may have given me that crooked smirk I once found so attractive, to lighten the mood. If he did at this point in our short marriage, I would have turned away.

Like I thought they would, Craig and John climbed the mountain as if they were in some sort of endurance contest, and Susan and I fell behind. To the rhythm of the slap and scrape of our skins on the snow, we chatted about skiing and the weather, and then about life and love, our mothers and our husbands. Something about Susan allowed me to open up to her; perhaps it was because I knew I wasn't likely to see her again.

We continued up the mountain, and the spring snow looked like wet sugar, glistening with tiny pinpricks of light. Susan told me she had come on this road trip alone in order to figure out how to leave her husband for good. She said she had outgrown him, that when the therapist asked him about his goals, he said he wanted to perfect his telemark ski turn. She said, "I love to ski, but I want more out of life, you know?"

"At least he went to counseling," I said.

"Craig won't go?" she asked.

"No." I stopped to take a sip of water and knock the snow that had accumulated on the bottom of my skis with my pole. "He says he's happy and that if I'm unhappy, well then, that's my own fault. He says I just don't know how to be happy. And maybe that's true."

Susan turned around and looked at me. "Seriously? You know that's fucked up, right?"

I started back up the skin track and said, "I'm just trying to focus on the other parts of my life that do make me happy—my friends, living in Tahoe, teaching."

"And how's that working for you?"

I admitted it wasn't, that there was a connection missing. I knew that sounded vague, and I wasn't sure exactly what I meant by it; I only knew it felt true. For a while, I believed that if I pretended things were fine, they would be. I had become good at pretending; this was the silent pact that my mother, father, and I had made when I was growing up—life was the story we told, hiding the real life that lurked beneath.

My father drank too much, and my mother, wanting to believe certain things about the way her life had turned out, covered up for him. When my older sisters came over for dinner, my parents both coached me, saying, "Remember, Daddy doesn't drink." I didn't know why Cathy and Cindy weren't supposed to know this about Daddy, but I had no choice but to go along with my parents. And maybe I even liked being in on this secret since there were so many others I was left out of.

I stopped and looked up the mountain for the guys. I spotted Craig's tall, lanky frame—he had reached the rocky ridgeline and looked down toward us, his arm shading his eyes from the sun. Our dog, Riva, trotted along above him, always in front. I knew I had loved him at one time, but my love, it seemed, had faded.

"Well," Susan said, "you shouldn't have to settle. How long have you been married?"

"September," I said. "We were married in September."

"This past September? Like six months ago?"

"Seven, I think." We were above the tree line, and a white contrail cut the blue sky in two.

"Listen," she said. "I'm not trying to give you advice, and Craig seems like a nice enough guy, but seven months in? You should be wildly happy. If not, there's probably something wrong."

At the summit, Susan pointed across the valley with her ski pole and said, "Look." The view collapsed in her mirrored sunglasses.

The mountains unfolded like white wings, notch after white notch. The blue tent of the sky seemed, for the moment, limitless. The mountainscape stretched to Sonora Pass, nearly all the way to Yosemite, more than fifty miles away as the crow flies. Times like this, I wanted to disappear into the mountains, become a shade in the landscape. "I want to burn this moment into memory," Susan said, and I nodded, knowing just what she meant.

We peeled our climbing skins from our skis and ate peanut butter sandwiches. I kept thinking about burning the moment into my own memory. Though I couldn't name it, I felt like I was at the edge of something, and not just the mountain. I had always wanted, more than anything, to be brave, to live an extraordinary life. Backcountry skiing and hiking adventures had become a way for me to *seem* brave without really *being* brave—a way of playing tourist to my own life. These adventures made me happy and, lately, were a way to flee the boring dysfunction of my marriage. I remembered a character in a James Salter novel who said the only thing she was afraid of were the two words "ordinary life." I had been living for some time with that same fear—my life would be ordinary.

I told myself I had created a sensible life for myself—I had just turned thirty, and I had a teaching career, a mortgage, a marriage, and a dog. I found a husband who would backcountry ski and backpack with me. Wasn't I living the life I had always imagined? From the outside, it looked like a very happy life indeed—young newlyweds and all that—and people had already started asking when the baby would be arriving. I smiled at these people, but the thought of a baby depressed me. I had painted a coat of shiny varnish over my life, but the finish was starting to crackle. I could hear the words beneath the words when I said, "We want to wait for a couple of years before starting a family."

I had not yet allowed myself to speak my truth: *I have made a big mistake here. I am unhappy, and I want to escape.* I did not say the words, *I have settled.* And it would take me a long time to say, *I don't want a baby at all.*

Saying things made them real, and I was terrified of losing what I had once so badly wanted. What if this was a passing thing? What if I was being unreasonable? I had a good life, so why did I always want more?

We made it down the chutes and traversed the frozen Crater Lake, crossing over to the lower section of Stevens Peak, which was not as steep as the chutes. Warmed by the sun, the spring snow formed pinwheels that rolled down the mountain, larger and larger, until they looked like giant white jelly rolls. Because of the wet snow, Susan suggested we ski one at a time for safety. She had just launched herself off a cornice and thrown herself down the mountain, so her mixed response to safety concerns didn't make sense to me, though I realized that so many times my own actions were also conflicting. But I agreed with her; the day had warmed up more quickly than had been forecasted, making the avalanche danger more significant.

I skied down first with Riva running alongside, followed by Craig and then John. We had hoped for corn snow, but the slushy snow felt more like mashed potatoes. Susan skied last, carving telemark turns into the heavy snow. We watched her from below, across a flat section where we had agreed to wait for each other, a spot that would be safe in case of an avalanche.

Susan must have felt some instability beneath her because she traversed the glade. The snow unfastened like a zipper, with a damp rumble and a guttural thump: a wet slab avalanche. We stood still, watching. I tried to keep my eyes on Susan. The words "last seen" from my avalanche safety courses echoed in my mind. I knew if we let her out of sight, we would have no idea where she was buried. It would take us longer to search for her with our beacons and probes, and every second mattered. Within minutes, she could suffocate. That is, if she wasn't killed on impact.

"Shit. Shit."

"Oh my God."

"There she is. There she is!"

I can't remember who said what. I stood there, shocked at witnessing something so singular and complete in its white, brilliant strength. A jagged crown ran across the top edge, with a crater etched below into the slope we had just crossed; the piles of snow at the bottom were like bubbling sea foam but crunchy and frozen.

I spotted Susan skiing through the trees on the far edge of the slide and then across the flat to join us. We were all safe now, but the avalanche left me breathless and reminded me how quickly things can change.

We didn't speak for a while after that. It was as if the tremendous power of snow and gravity gripped at our throats. We saw how thin the line was between a fun day of skiing and a disaster. Though the rest of the slope was at a lower, safer angle, we skied through the trees as quickly as possible; the spring sun made the snow more unstable each minute.

Once we had hitchhiked back to our cars, we joked and laughed the way people do on the other side of danger. "You skied out of an effing avalanche," Craig told Susan.

"It was a small one." She loaded her gear back into her car. She looked over at me, smiled, and added, "But probably big enough to have buried me. Good thing we checked our beacons, huh?"

I loved her for that.

And I hated that Craig said "effing." Why not just call it like it was?

Besides the snow, something else broke free that day. I'm not sure if it was because I had seen myself through Susan's eyes, but I knew I could no longer pretend. That moment seemed to mark the end of my marriage. Within the next few months, I would buy myself a plane ticket and travel to Mexico alone, setting off on a life of wanderlust. I would have love affairs, some suffocated by shame and regret; others felt as if they were carved out of water or electricity. I would forget to weigh the risks against the benefits. I would travel to escape and then to find myself; I would travel, finally, to come home.

We said our good-byes to Susan at the Carson Pass parking lot, and she drove off in her packed Subaru. I've never seen her again, though nearly twenty years later, I haven't stopped thinking about her and the extraordinary way she pitched herself down the mountain, narrowly escaping an avalanche, making safety seem like nothing more than superstition.

The Illuminations

Blackpool, England, September 2003

The innkeeper said, "Oh, love, I'm afraid your room's been rented."
She reached for the rose air spray and shot a little spurt into the
air, covering the smell of smoke and fish 'n' chips.

"But we called ahead. You don't have our reservation?" I asked.
It had taken an airplane, two trains, three taxis, and four days to
get here.

"No, sure don't, and with the illuminations going on, you'll have
a hard time of it if you try to find a room."

David and I just stood there, looking at her.

"Gotcha." She pointed both index fingers at us. "You Yankees
are *so* gullible. Fall for it every time. Welcome to the Silver Birch.
I'm Mary, at your service." She did a little bow and then said, "I
have your key right here." She held the room key, dangling from a
Blackpool Tower keychain, between her thumb and index finger.

We both laughed, not because we thought she was funny but
because we were both relieved and giddy from jetlag.

We dropped our backpacks in our frilly, rose-scented room.
From our tiny balcony, we could see the famous Blackpool illuminations, which were like Christmas lights on steroids. An autumn
tradition since 1912, the illuminations feature strings of more than
a million light bulbs that stretch over six miles of roadways, creating fanciful and eclectic images of everything from mermaids
to astronauts, Alice in Wonderland to warrior Indians.

Whenever someone British asks me where my mother is from
and I tell them Blackpool, the response is almost always, "My
God," the word "God" sounding like it's spelled with a *u* and not

an *o*. Or maybe they'll say, "Oh my. I'm terribly sorry," with a little hand-stifled laugh. Whenever I tell someone from anywhere else where my mother is from, I am met with a blank stare.

A seaside resort town on the Irish Sea, Blackpool is popular with tourists from Manchester, Liverpool, and Glasgow. Very few Americans vacation there, so the minute you open your mouth, the taxi driver or waitress will ask you if you know any movie stars. They will ask you this even if you live in Des Moines or Detroit. But tell them you are from California, or better yet Los Angeles, and they will assume your neighbors are Julia Roberts and Johnny Depp. To excite them further, tell them of any of your previous star sightings, which will set them off laughing and maybe even win you a "You don't say!"

Blackpool gained its fame in the days of tuberculosis, when doctors ordered sea air as a cure for consumption, and people traveled north from London to this spot to bathe in the Irish Sea. Aside from the train station and nearby Seed Street, Blackpool escaped heavy bombing in World War II because Adolf Hitler (who is now memorialized in the wax museum) earmarked the town to remain a place of leisure after his planned invasion. In addition to being cruel, it turns out that Hitler was also tacky. With its Golden Mile of peep shows, fortune tellers, chip shops, casinos, the 518-foot-tall Blackpool Tower (inspired by the Eiffel Tower), and of course the illuminations that light the night sky from September to November each year, it's an attempt at Vegas with some of the glitz and all of the kitsch.

Out on the streets that night, groups of women dressed as naughty school girls, police officers, sexy pirates, and French maids clamored by, giggling and shivering in the salty air. I bought some postcards and asked the shopkeeper if it was usual to dress up in costume during the illuminations. "Oh love, they're not dressed up for the illuminations. They're havin' themselves a hen party." Blackpool, in all its faded glory, draws stag and hen parties, or bachelor and bachelorette parties as we call them in the United States, and the city embraces them with drink deals, peep shows, naughty toys, and boob- and penis-shaped rock candy.

I bought a penis-shaped rock candy lollipop for my mother. I thought it was funny, though David didn't think so, which I should have taken as a sign. But I pushed it out of my mind because we were soon heading to Spain together, where I would be teaching for the fall term. After having a long-distance relationship for over a year, it would be our first time living together.

I had only been to Blackpool once before, as a child. Now I was here to see my ninety-year-old grandmother, but because like most Americans, David had never been to Blackpool, we visited some of the tourist attractions, too. I told him I wanted to go to the wax museum. I had visited it when I was a child, and it had given me nightmares.

"Why do you want to go someplace that gave you nightmares?" he asked.

"I was nine," I said. "I'm sure it isn't *that* scary."

As it turned out, I was wrong about that. After touring the rock 'n' roll rooms, featuring the likes of Michael Jackson, Elton John, Boy George, and of course the Beatles; the royalty rooms with Diana, Charles, and the Queen; the politician quarter with Margaret Thatcher and Winston Churchill; and rooms with the iconic Hollywood actors Marilyn Monroe, Elizabeth Taylor, Cary Grant, and James Dean, we headed down to the Chamber of Horrors.

I remembered the mechanical wax show featuring a crocodile biting off a girl's leg, which was the source of my nightmares so many years before, but I didn't remember the special section devoted to serial killers. The display featured both fictional killers like Frankenstein, Hannibal Lecter, and Freddy Kruger and real murderers, including a huge assortment of American serial killers—and their crimes, complete with axes, fake blood, body bags, and nooses.

I grew up with the dark humor of the British, with a mother who could make a joke out of the most serious illness or accident, but now that I had seen the Chamber of Horrors as an adult, I could say with confidence that allowing children to view these acts of death was more than a little sadistic. That may be why the Chamber of Horrors attraction was later removed.

I suggested we get murder off our minds by going to a drag show at the club Funny Girl, but David shook his head. A woman with a headscarf called to us, "Get your fortunes told!"

"Let's do it," I said. The red neon sign flashed: *Gypsy Petulengro*.

"Oh come on. Really?" David asked.

"Why not?"

"It's a waste of money. That's why."

"It'll be fun." We walked through the hanging beads to the anteroom of Gypsy Petulengro. "That's probably not her real name," I whispered to David. He rolled his eyes as if to say, *Really?* I ignored him and said, "My grandmother used to read tea leaves."

Gypsy Petulengro wore her dark hair in a bun and was shaped like a fire plug. I asked her, "Can we have our fortunes read together?"

"Put out your hands," she said. We did as we were told, facedown then face-up. "No, I cannot read you together. Absolutely not. One at a time."

"That's her way of getting us to pay double," David whispered to me. The gypsy heard him and told him it would be the same price, £10 each, whether we had our readings done together or separately. David was always generous with money, so it wasn't that—he really just didn't want to hear what a fortune teller had to say. "You go first," David said. "I'll wait outside."

I went into the gypsy's little room, sat down on a cushion, and she asked to see my hands again. I laid them face-up on the table between us. She focused past me, her gray eyes somewhere on the flowered wallpaper behind my head. Then she closed her eyes and spoke: "You have crossed this ocean before."

"My American accent has given me away."

She frowned and said, "You have been married, had an abortion, and a nervous breakdown."

"I've never had a nervous breakdown," I said.

"Well, trust me, you've come close, even if you won't admit it. You have stress marks all over your face."

I thought about the past year, teaching full-time at the community college and pursuing a doctorate, all while going through a divorce and carrying on this long-distance love affair. I thought about the poems I never seemed to find time to finish. And the student loans, the second mortgage, the debt piling up. "I've been a little stressed," I admitted.

"A little?" she asked. "I'll say."

"Okay. What else?" I asked. A vase next to her held fake red and white carnations. I started to wonder if this was a waste of money.

"You have never been good with money," she said as if on cue. I laughed. Then she said, "The man outside is not your husband." Her eyebrows had been shaved off, and in their place, two charcoal lines were drawn into perpetual surprise.

"True."

"Your husband, he has met someone else, but still, he wants you back, and I see that you still like him. You can't stick to your decisions, but you must. And you are unhappy in your current relationship."

"Ex-husband. And I'm happy now."

"No you're not. You aren't satisfied." She looked up at me and then said, "But he will ask you to live with him, this man outside the door, and you will say yes." At that she shook her head. "Any questions?" She interlaced her fingers, the nails sculpted and polished the color of bougainvillea.

Since she had pretty much covered everything, I asked, "How long will I live?"

Without pause she said, "Into your eighties. Anything more?"

"No, I don't think so." I handed her my £10, which it seemed to me she had earned. I got up and walked out to the smell of fish 'n' chips, cotton candy, beer, and the salty sea air. I found David out on the street trying on silly hats. He put on a plaid glengarry and asked, "How did it go? Did you get your money's worth?"

"I think so."

"What did she say?"

"She said I would live until I'm eighty." The tram trundled past.

"That's good news." Lights in the shape of a rabbit eating a carrot flashed on over David's head.

"Now you go," I said.

"You know I don't believe in that stuff."

"I want to see what she says."

While he was in with Gypsy Petulengro, I shopped around, looking at funny sunglasses, miniatures of the Blackpool Tower, and t-shirts. I bought a magnet that pictured the Pleasure Beach roller coaster with a double-decker bus in front.

When David came and found me, I asked, "What did she say?"

"Nothing much." He shook his head. "What a waste."

Even though I pressed, he wouldn't tell me anything else. I wondered if she had told him the same thing she told me. About us.

At Gaiety's Karaoke Bar, I sang my karaoke go-to, Joan Jett's "I Love Rock 'n' Roll"; it's a song you can shout rather than sing, and I have that kind of singing voice. David sang "Pretty Woman," which I thought was romantic because he picked the song for me. I didn't stop to think about how the song was most recently made famous by a film about a prostitute.

By ten o'clock, the streets were full of urine and vomit, and most of the hen and stag parties had stumbled off. The party had started early but also ended early. I began to understand why people apologized to me when I admitted that Blackpool was my mother's hometown.

When my cousin Debbie arrived in a taxi to pick us up the next morning, she said hello and then turned to me and asked, "You know about Richard, right?"

We splashed across the puddles in the street, and I told her I had heard something about that. My mother told me to never admit that I knew something fully because I might get more information that way. I already knew my ninety-year-old grandmother had a forty-five-year-old "friend" named Richard. My mother had heard from her sisters that he called her Aunt Sally, so no one at the pub would know what was going on, though everyone did. When I asked my mother about it, she just said, "You know."

Once we got into the taxi, I asked Debbie, "He's much younger than her, right?"

"He is," Debbie said. "She keeps him in beer and cigarettes, and if you want to know the truth, I think he's a bloody scoundrel." She put her finger in front of her lips as if to say, *Shh!* and motioned to the driver in case he was listening.

I nodded. I felt happy for Nanny. Wasn't it better than being alone?

My grandmother lived in a tract of low-income apartments. We knocked, and Richard opened the door. He wore a t-shirt and leather vest with jeans so tight there wasn't much left to the imagination. His shaggy black hair hung over his face; he was smoking a cigarette and drinking a beer. As my mother would have said, he was no oil painting.

"You want an ale?" He held up his beer. "This Black Sheep's a good one."

"No thanks," David said.

I wanted one, but as it was, David thought I drank too much, so I declined. Plus, it was still morning, and the last thing I wanted was for Debbie to tell the rest of the family how much I "liked the drink." One cousin had died already from "liking the drink" a little too much.

Richard led us to Nanny, who was sitting in the living room on a plastic-covered couch. She wore a flowered housedress, and her gray hair was piled into a bun. She rested one hand on a cane and the other on her knee. A set of keys was pinned to her dress.

"I'm here." She waved us over.

"Hi, Nanny." I walked over to hug her.

"Sit here with me, love. Is it really our Suzanne?"

"Yes, Nanny. It is. And this is my friend David."

"Come here, love." David did as she asked, and she felt his face. "Oh, you're a bonny lad, I can tell." Then she turned to me and asked, "What happened to your husband?"

"We got a divorce, Nanny."

"Oh, that's right. Our Sheila told me something about that." She nodded.

I wasn't surprised to witness my grandmother using one of my mother's signature moves, asking me something she already knew. "What are those for?" I pointed to the keys fastened to my grandmother's housedress.

"Oh, those are the keys to my room upstairs. I can't make it all that way up the stairs anymore, but it's where I keep my treasures." She looked around, and when she was satisfied that Richard was out of earshot, she said, "I've got a lot of nice clothes and jewelry, love. And I don't want anyone messing around with it."

I was about to ask Nanny if I could go up to see her treasures, but before I had the chance, Debbie said, "Nanny, isn't it great that Suzanne has come all this way from America?"

"It's lovely. Can you see your school pictures there?" She pointed with her cane to a wall that displayed photographs of the Queen, the Queen Mother, and Lady Diana. She also had pictures of her eight grandchildren, my grade school pictures sent by my mother among them.

"I see them, Nanny."

"Can I touch your face? It's a shame I can't see you very well. But I've made my bed, and now I've got to lie in it."

I wasn't sure what she meant, but I said, "Okay," and leaned closer to her.

"You're a bonny girl." She patted my face.

"What do you mean about lying in your bed?" I settled in next to her on the plastic-covered couch.

"I had one good eye, and I walked into a pointy plant, and now I can't see at all. I can't do me makeup anymore, so that means no more going to The Old England for me." Still touching my face, she said, "Oh, you're just like our Sheila. Such a shame she couldn't come."

I couldn't tell her I had tried to get my mother to come with us, but she wouldn't, that she routinely said she hadn't left England but that she'd escaped. Instead I said to Nanny, "You can still go to the pub."

"Oh, no, not without me face on, I can't. And without me sight, I can't do me face. Isn't that right, Richard?" She laughed and crossed her hands on her belly.

"Anyone want a beer?" Richard asked, standing in the doorway of the living room.

"Oh, we're fine in here," Nanny said. "Do you want anything, love?" she asked, turning to me.

"No, I'm fine."

"Oh, I know. How about a biscuit?" She patted around on her table and presented a tin of cookies to me. "Have one?"

I agreed and took one.

"Give one to your friend there. And some tea?"

"Sure," I said.

"Richard, put the kettle on, would you?" Nanny called, and Richard disappeared again. "And while you're at it, get me my purse."

"I'll go help him," Debbie said.

Debbie and Richard came back with tea and Nanny's purse. Nanny fumbled around in it and said, "Here it is. A gift for our Sheila." She opened a silver change purse and pulled out a string of rhinestones. "You will give it to her, won't you?"

I promised I would.

"Our Sheila and I were such good friends."

The stories I had heard were of my grandmother making my young mother drown kittens in a bucket in the kitchen. Or of being locked in the dark coal house with the spiders. But I couldn't connect these stories of cruelty to this old woman on the couch.

Behind my grandmother, a wisp of smoke rose from a nearby lampshade. I got up to have a look and found the light bulb pressed against the shade. I pulled the burning shade off and said, "Nanny, this doesn't fit the lamp. It's starting a fire."

"Is it?" she asked. "Oh well." She waved her hand at it as if she couldn't be bothered.

"I'll take it," David said, and he went into the kitchen to give the burning shade to Richard. I wondered if the offer still stood for a beer.

"Guess what we found out," Richard said, coming back in and lighting a new cigarette. "Here I've been calling Sally 'Auntie' all these years, and wouldn't you know it, but we really *are* related."

"What do you mean?" Debbie asked, the color draining from her face. "I don't understand."

"Well, Sally's second cousin is my grandmother, so that makes us second cousins or cousins twice removed. I can't remember how it goes. Do you, Sally?"

"No, I can't," Nanny said. "But isn't that a coincidence?"

"Is that really true, Nanny?" Debbie asked.

"It is." Nanny gave a solemn nod.

Debbie's face lost more color; her mouth now looked like a bright pink line of lipstick drawn on a white canvas. She said, "I'm not feeling well. I think I'll go out for a walk."

"Why don't you all go?" Nanny said. "I'm getting a bit tired, and besides, I have to wee."

Richard called us a taxi; we said our good-byes and then stood outside the small apartment, waiting. The light faded with passing clouds. Debbie said, "If Richard is her cousin, do you know what that means?" She clutched her stomach. I nodded, thinking she meant that Nanny might have been having sex with her own cousin. I wasn't sure whether that was better or worse than their forty-five-year age difference.

"It means," Debbie said, "that Richard is *our* cousin, too."

"I hadn't thought of that," I said.

"We're *related*. To *him*."

The taxi arrived, we left my grandmother's housing division, and Debbie asked the driver to take David and me to the house in Bispham where our mothers grew up. "My mother was born in that house," she said. "Yours was too." Mother always insisted she wasn't born at home. According to her, the version of the story that was true was the one you told.

The stone row houses on Bristol Avenue leaned against each other. The red paint was chipping, and dog droppings and weeds littered the cracked sidewalks. The yellow light and slant of drizzle made the street seem more like a memory. I thought about the stories my mother had told me—about her first kiss in that alleyway, and the woman who hobbled down the road on two sticks, and the woman's twenty-one kids, who all shit in the bathtub because one toilet wasn't enough. And the neighbor with the clubbed foot who, according to Mother, would do it with anyone for a packet of Woodbines. I wondered which house Jack Clare, who got his sister pregnant, lived in. And where the neighbor whose husband shot her for carrying on with the milkman had lived. I tried to imagine

Great-Grandma Smith, leaning on a bent elbow, shouting, "What? What's that?" No one paying her any mind.

I couldn't match the stories to the place, stories that always seemed to run the same reel as the grainy black-and-white pictures I had seen. Stories that were part memory, part imagination—both my mother's and my own. I loved the stories, asked my mother to tell them. The stories kept changing with each retelling, and maybe that's why I begged to hear them again and again.

I wanted my life to be like that—fluid, shape-shifting, something I could keep revising.

Once we were back at the hotel, David asked, "How long has it been since your mother has visited her mother?"

"A long time," I said.

"Why hasn't she been back?"

I could tell David that she didn't like to travel or that she didn't want to spend the money; both were true. Finally, I said, "Because she doesn't want to."

"But *why* doesn't she want to?" he asked. "Why wouldn't she want to see her mother?"

The why is always harder to explain than the what. Could I tell him that her mother drowned their kittens? That Nanny cooked my mother's pets, Peter Rabbit and Henrietta the chicken, for dinner? Would any of this seem unreasonable during the postwar years? Could I tell him that Nanny and Granddad went to the pub every weekend and made the kids cook dinner? Or that Nanny locked the front door from the outside, so they couldn't get out? This was a story that my mother had told me and then retracted, telling me, "I never said that about the door." Later, after she was gone, I would find that story written in her journal.

The truth, always up for revision.

But here are the stories Mother stood by: Nanny looked the other way when my granddad asked the two oldest daughters for a kiss on the lips on New Year's Eve—Mother was the oldest girl. Nanny also set up my teenaged mother with a fifty-year-old married man who showered my grandmother with dinners out and presents in return. I couldn't tell David this. I wasn't sure how to make sense of it myself. I knew only that these experiences shaped the way my mother saw men. For the first time, I wondered if her views of the world also shaped me, if her worldview had informed mine. To figure out who I was, who I wanted to be, I had to understand the connections. My mother didn't trust men, but her happiness was dependent on their adoration of her. Being a woman in the world involved a constant state of negotiation.

I wasn't ready to discuss this and certainly not with David, so I said, "She didn't have a happy childhood. She wants to leave the past in the past."

David nodded and said, "Your grandmother is sweet." I believed David's family seemed less complicated, more normal, and I wanted to believe mine was, too. Having a "sweet grandmother" felt good. In time, I would learn that David's family was more dysfunctional than my own.

But for now, we lived in our present tense, where we each revised the truth—and the past—in a way we could live with.

My last morning in Blackpool, I left our room and ran along the promenade north toward Bispham, where my mother grew up. I passed the pirates and the mermaids, the astronauts and the Indians. Seagulls struggled in flight, cackling to each other, wheeling unsteadily in the wind. The rain spotted my glasses, and I pulled my raincoat's hood over my head. It was a low tide, leaving rivers snaked through the sand. The air smelled of salt and the sea's sweet decay. I took the concrete ramp down to the beach, and everything except the coastline disappeared—the bars and the fortune tellers, the chip shops and rock candy stalls.

Sometimes it takes a long time to see a place.

The day before, the sea had splashed up against the concrete wall; now the water was farther than a mile out, a smudge on the distant horizon. I had never before seen such a dramatic tide. As I walked, each of my footprints filled with small puddles of water behind me, the watery evidence of my wandering. I turned toward the Irish Sea and looked out at the gray horizon. I pictured my young, beautiful mother standing on this beach forty years earlier, imagining what lay beyond the reach of her vision. I realized this place shaped both my grandmother and my mother: this city of artifice and kitsch but also the edge of an ever-changing sea, this landscape of natural beauty and of wildness.

Mating Season

Galápagos Islands, Ecuador, April 2007

While everyone else threw up off the sides of the boat or groaned from their beds, Sandra and I drank pisco sours and danced salsa with the crew. We laughed as the small boat pitched and rolled. The crew told us that the seas were always rough when approaching the equator. I asked why, and they said it had something to do with the meeting of the trade winds and that planes, too, experienced turbulence when passing over the equator. Since then, every time I've been on a plane crossing the equator, I brace for turbulence, and more often than not, the plane bounces and shakes.

The boards beneath our feet bowed and creaked. The first mate turned up the music, drowning out the sounds of sickness. The captain kept one eye on the black horizon and the other on Sandra's boobs. The cook's assistant, who also doubled as the bartender, tried to teach me to dance—impossible even on solid ground. He demonstrated, then laughed, "Debe haber algún problema con tus piernas." There must be some problem with your legs. When the boat rocked, we all grabbed onto the walls, the nailed-down table, and to the crew members' delight, each other.

The crew pretended they weren't married, didn't have four or six children each. Like the blue-footed boobies we'd seen earlier in the day, kicking up their webbed feet and showing off impressive wingspans, our small crew did their best to dance their way into our hearts, or—more accurately—our pants. And like the female birds, we acted demure, encouraging their dance but trying to stay one step ahead of them—the way we had been taught to do as girls and women.

At midnight, the boat shimmied across the equator—the line in the sea and the air separating one world from another. A little later Sandra went to bed, and I followed our nature guide, Mauricio, up to the deck. The rocking lessened to a slow roll, and the stars glittered like a million sequins in the night sky.

"I will tell you why I like you," Mauricio said. "It's because you're happy."

Then he tried to kiss me.

Sandra and I had chosen the least expensive Galápagos Islands tour, so we ended up on a small sailboat (which never actually sailed) with eight other passengers. Earlier in the day, our small group had hiked across the islands and snorkeled through the cold waters of the Pacific. I nearly climbed on top of Sandra's back when we saw the sharks. When Sandra had enough of the cold water and dealing with me, she went back to the boat, and I swam alongside Mauricio—not so much because he helpfully pointed out sergeant fish and sea turtles, starfish and penguins, trumpet fish and sea lions, but because I was too afraid to snorkel on my own near the sharks. Mauricio took this as flirting, though in truth, it was the sharks with whom I was flirting—a less familiar danger, one that felt more real and more pure. The sharks brooded below us, their movements primitive and predatory, their sharp faces atavistic. The flick of the dorsal fins unhinged me. Watching them filled me with a sublime fear—they were beautiful and terrifying.

"Galápagos sharks," Mauricio said when he saw that I was afraid, "they are vegetarians."

Later in the day, we motored past a starving sea lion cub, crying from her perch. Across the rocks below her, thousands of black iguanas sunned themselves, some draped on top of each other. "Will the mother come back?" I asked.

"Probably no," Mauricio said.

"Why not?"

"Maybe a shark."

"I thought you said they were vegetarian," I said, and Mauricio smiled.

When I climbed back onto the boat, Sandra and I claimed a spot at the front to sunbathe. A hatch at our feet opened, and I heard a click. When I sat up, the hatch slammed shut. We shaded our faces with our sun hats but kept one close eye on the hatch. We found the boat's cook popping his camera out, clicking pictures of us, and then disappearing back into the crammed kitchen. Sandra and I went down below, and he was surprised when I told him in Spanish that if he wanted our picture, he should have asked. He laughed and showed us the photographs in his digital camera. There were not only off-angle and blurry images of Sandra and me but of bikini-clad woman after woman—so many photos of unsuspecting tourists. Sandra and I offered to pose with him, and his assistant took a picture of the three of us. He laughed for a long time about that.

We went back to our towels, and the cook threw fish guts into the sea; soon a cloud of magnificent frigatebirds bobbed and weaved above us. The males grew big red-pouched throats for mating season—a testament to their virility and impressive gene pool. Across the islands, every species of male showed off for the females. The blue-footed boobies swaggered impressive dances, kicking their blue-webbed feet up in the air, unfolding their wings. The females acted coy, giving the males a sideways glance every now and again. On Española Island, the albatross, which spend most of their lives out at sea, had just settled down to nest. Male pelicans brought reeds and sticks to nesting females who brooded atop their eggs.

In the Galápagos, everyone, it seemed, wanted to mate, was mating, or had just mated. Everyone, that is, except Lonesome George, who lived at the Charles Darwin Research Center on Santa Cruz Island. He was the last living Pinta tortoise, found on the island in 1971. Goats had been introduced onto the island and devastated the foliage, leading to a mass die-off of the tortoise. Lonesome George was the only one of his kind left. And actually, maybe even he wanted to mate. Scientists hoped so, at least. George was kept in a pen with two females of a different subspecies. When we were there, George had not yet taken up with either of them. Later he would mate with one of his companions, but the eggs would not be viable.

None of George's mates were compatible—perhaps we had this in common, George and I? I had recently met someone I thought might be right for me, but I brought that optimism to many new relationships. The difference this time was that I realized the relationship that needed the most work was the one with myself.

Lonesome George would finally die of old age in 2010 and, with him, his gene pool, making the Pinta tortoise officially extinct. George's body was flown to New York to be preserved by taxidermists and then was returned to the research station on Santa Cruz Island.

"I can't kiss you," I told Mauricio. The Southern Cross hung in the sky before us. The air tasted like brine.

"But you say you're not married. Is that true?"

"I'm not married, that's true. But I have a boyfriend." I didn't know if what I had back at home could even be called a boyfriend, but that felt like the easiest thing to say. The truth was that I was tired of looking for love in so many places. Vacation love, or maybe more aptly travel flings, had become my specialty over the previous few years. I wanted, more than anything else, to claim my own desire. I wanted to feel the way I did in those few minutes between the wanting and the having—that dance. But what kept happening was that I repeatedly allowed myself to be the object of desire, rather than the subject of my own desire. I rarely did the choosing. If a man wanted me, I went along with it, flattered by the attention. I thought about how much time I'd spent in that mating dance.

Even the female blue-footed booby did the choosing; the males competed, but often the females waddled away, in search of a better mate. I was learning how to do that, too.

Mauricio tried to kiss me again, and I pulled away. He smiled and said, "He would have married you by now if he wanted to keep you from other men."

I laughed and agreed that could very well be true about my new boyfriend, who wasn't technically my boyfriend. But Mauricio was also right about something else: I *was* happy, and that meant I didn't need to sleep with him. Or even kiss him. In the past, I had used desire and sex as a way to distract myself from myself, but I finally realized it wasn't working. Once I stopped projecting what I wished I was onto myself and faced and accepted the current version of myself, I learned how to be happy in my own company.

Mauricio would have to wait and get his kisses from the next tour. The crew knew the dance well—next week would bring another boatload of tourists, more drinks and dancing. More bikini photographs. And more lonely ladies. Mauricio asked, "Did the crew tell you I'm married? Because I was, but I'm not anymore. They love to lie." He flashed a smile again.

"It isn't that. It's because I have someone else. That's the reason."

"Es mejor vivir en el presente," he said. It's better to live in the present. Then he added, "Plus he'll never know."

"But I'll know, and that's what matters."

What I had told him was true. But this time, I was the someone else who mattered. And that was reason enough. I looked at Mauricio's chiseled arms in the moonlight. I guessed he'd be good in bed, but I would never find out.

Jungle Love

Baños, Ecuador, June 2007

The farmer stood over us, wearing a Nixon mask and waving a machete above his head. Tom and I both laughed that special nervous laugh reserved for those times when you're about to be murdered, and you hope it won't hurt too much.

Perhaps, I thought, we shouldn't have accepted the invitation to tea.

We had been hiking the trail to Bellavista Cross in Baños, Ecuador. The trail hugged the side of the mountain, with views to town through the ferns, hydrangeas, and orchids. The volcano above rumbled. Tom and I passed a small cinder-block house, and a man peeked out the door. He was dressed like a farmer in suspenders and rubber boots. He started waving, calling us over. We approached, and he invited us in for tea. Tom looked at me, and I asked, "Why not?"

On one side of the single room sat a metal-framed bed and on the other, a small makeshift kitchen with propane burners. The farmer asked us to have a seat on his bed while he fixed us tea. When he brought the drink to us, he explained that he made it from a bush outside his house. I didn't translate the bit about the bush for Tom, and I started to worry that maybe we should have kept hiking.

I waited for the farmer to take a sip of his tea before I drank mine, like I had seen in the movies. I whispered to Tom, "Wait to drink your tea," but it was too late. Tom looked at me like I was crazy, a look he gave me a lot in the early days of our relationship, when the things I did or said were still a little shocking to him.

I hadn't yet told Tom that I'd been drugged in a nightclub in Peru some months earlier, so I knew he thought I was being paranoid. And maybe I was.

The farmer told us about his cows and his wife and children, though no evidence of a family existed in his tiny abode, nor of any cows on the side of the volcano. When I asked him his children's ages, he stammered. When I asked him their names, he pointed out the window at the volcano and said, "Can't you hear the rumbling?"

I translated for Tom, and we both agreed we could hear the volcano.

"But that doesn't scare me," the farmer said. "I had to be evacuated in 1997." Then he told us he had to get something outside and left. I assumed he went out to his bush for more "tea."

A few minutes later, he reappeared, wearing the Nixon mask. The farmer raised his machete in the air, Nixon's face frozen into a maniacal smile. That's when he said he wanted a tip for the tea service, though it was hard to make out his muffled words through the mask.

"What did he say?" Tom asked.

"I think he wants a little tip." I smiled up at Nixon.

"A little tip?"

"He said, 'Propinita.' It means 'little tip.' For his children." I kept smiling at Nixon, who had now lowered his machete to his side. "How much do you have?" I asked Tom.

"About ten dollars."

"Give him five."

When Tom handed over the cash, I told Nixon, "For your children. It's all we have." It was surreal and a little bit scary to hand over five dollars to a man who was wearing a Nixon mask and holding a machete. I also gave him my Spanish-English dictionary and said, "For when the next guests come."

I could only imagine how this transaction could have been translated by this small book. But this was my go-to whenever I thought someone was going to kill me. Act like everything was fine and be polite, give the person a gift, and maybe he would change his mind.

As we left, Tom asked, "Why did you give him the dictionary?"

Why did Tom think I gave it to him? I was annoyed. "I don't know, so he wouldn't kill us. And it worked."

"You have an active imagination," Tom said.

"Seriously? I couldn't have imagined that. I'm not sure anyone would even believe us if we told them. The Nixon mask?"

"He just wanted some money," Tom said, "and everyone in the jungle has a machete."

We walked on until we arrived at a little shack next to a pond. A woman called us over and said we could fish for our lunch. I explained the concept to Tom, who liked the idea. He kept catching small fish, but on the third try, he caught one big enough to share. The woman took the fish and prepared it for us. That and two bottles of water cost us five dollars. "The same as our tea," I told Tom.

"No, that was more expensive," he said. "That also cost you a dictionary."

When we passed a motorcycle rental shop on our way back into town, Tom said, "Let's rent one."

"I thought we were going to the hot springs."

"We can go later tonight."

"Have you ever even driven one?"

"I had a dirt bike as a kid."

We asked for helmets, but they didn't have any. I'm not sure why, but I tend to do things when I'm traveling that I would never do at home. Riding on feral horses? Sure. Rappelling down a waterfall? Sounds fun. Motorcycling without helmets over potholed roads with crazy truck drivers and rabid dogs? Yes, please.

Our first adventure was riding down a one-way street. The wrong way. Then we bumped along a dirt road (if you could even call it a road), and two German shepherd–looking mongrels chased after us, biting at our legs, as I yelled, "Faster, faster," which wasn't the word I imagined I would shout from the back of a motorcycle.

When we left the dogs barking in the dust, we entered the highway, where giant trucks barreled past. The road disappeared into dark tunnels, and all we could see were the headlights of approaching vehicles. We rode to the trailhead for a waterfall and hiked into the green hills. I was relieved to be off the bike. We crossed a rickety suspension bridge and took photographs of the eighty-meter waterfall, Pailón del Diablo, or the Devil's Cauldron.

We hiked back, and I hoped the motorcycle wouldn't be parked where we'd left it. Maybe someone would steal it? But there it was, so we got back on, and I tried not to be afraid. It didn't work; by the time we returned to the motorcycle shop, I was shaking.

"Wasn't that fun?" Tom asked. The man from the shop walked around the bike, inspecting it, making sure we hadn't added to the array of dents and scratches.

"No."

"Why not?"

"You couldn't tell I was terrified?" I held out my trembling hand as proof.

"I thought you were trying to get over your fears," Tom said. The man nodded that everything was fine, and we started walking back to our hotel.

"There's fearlessness, and then there's stupidity," I said. We passed the public baths, which the town of Baños was known for. Clouds of white steam lifted into the sky.

"We were safe."

"We weren't safe just because you say so." We weaved past colorful buildings, the green-clad mountains hunching above. Artisans lined the street, calling out their wares.

"We were fine," he said. Tom went to cross the street, and he reached for my hand.

"Just because everything's fine with you doesn't mean everything's fine. It's not fine if I'm not fine." I pulled my hand away and crossed my arms. We walked on, and I decided I had to let it go. I'd agreed to the ride, hadn't I? If I didn't want to go, I should have said so.

I don't remember how the fight started. We had traveled from Baños to a jungle lodge and had just finished tubing on the Napo River—another thing I would never have done at home. For some reason, this didn't feel as dangerous as the motorcycle ride, though it most certainly was. We kept getting stuck in weeds, our guides telling us to keep our legs out of the piranha-infested river. "Lift your feet!" they shouted as we swirled through the muddy waters in our little rubber inner tubes.

The argument began on the porch of the lodge, the brown Napo River now tumbling below us. I do know Tom shushed me, which always made me want to talk louder. We were still bickering when we went upstairs to our room, which was a screened-in area with two sets of bunk beds, making it look and feel like a treehouse. Tom got into one of the lower beds.

"Are we going to talk about this?" I asked.

"Not now."

"I think you should apologize."

"For what?"

"For what? For what!" I didn't know what else to say. I was so angry. This was another of my mother's signature moves. Rather than answer a question, repeat the question until it magically turns into a statement, tricking the person who initially asked it.

"Yeah, for what? I have nothing to apologize for," he said.

"Fuck you." As I said this, I knew I shouldn't have, but it was too late, so I went with it.

"You aren't allowed to say that to me," Tom said.

"Well, I just did."

"Fuck you, back. I would rather be alone than be with you." He pulled the ratty sheet over his head.

"That's what *I* was going to say," I told him, even though it wasn't true. I grabbed my journal and left the room, slamming the screen. I sat on the porch and wrote: *If you don't say you're sorry, en serio que me voy*. I'm seriously leaving. Spanish had bled into my rage. But where would I go? I looked over the balcony at the baby pineapples, into the dark river below.

I imagined an adjacent Suzanne, someone who was dramatic enough to fling herself from the balcony and into the water. If I threw myself over the edge, Tom would feel guilty, wishing he'd apologized. Then I remembered the drowned Zenobia from Hawthorne's *The Blithedale Romance*. The characters of the Gothic books I read for my doctoral work were always right there, in my imagination. I pictured Zenobia's hair streaming like seaweed across her bloated face, and I shuddered. Also, I realized Tom would get over it and go on with his life while adjacent Suzanne lost hers—there was no consolation even in my adolescent death fantasy. I walked down the wooden stairs to the bathroom, and a striated grasshopper sat on the mirror. I was mad at the insect for being so beautiful.

When I returned to the room, a drenched, dead yellow parakeet lay on the porch, the wings wet, useless with rain. It hadn't been there when I left, so it seemed like a sign—of what, I wasn't sure, but it couldn't be good. I stepped over the dead bird, went in, took a deep breath, and apologized. Or maybe I didn't exactly apologize, but I did say this: "I shouldn't have told you to fuck off."

"No, you shouldn't have."

I sat on Tom's bed and asked him if he wanted a midwestern wife.

"Where did you get that?"

"And kids. Do you want them?"

By now I was thirty-six and pretty sure I didn't want to have children. Accumulating passport stamps was more important to me than having babies. When I got together with Tom, my ex had told me it would never work out, that Tom wanted a midwestern wife, someone who would make a good mother; the implication, of course, was that I would not.

Tom said, "Only if I find the right woman."

"What's that supposed to mean?" I started to cry. I knew that by "the right woman," he didn't mean me. And how could I blame him? I'd just conjured a fantasy where I drowned myself, leaving him to a life of guilt. I'd abandoned my fantasy only when I realized he might not feel guilty enough. How was I the right woman for anyone?

"I was just kidding," he said. A chorus of frogs chirped outside.

"Well, it wasn't a very funny joke." I wiped my nose.

"I want you," he said. I lay down on the narrow bed with him, and he put his arm around me. "You aren't easy," he said, "but I love you."

Neither of us is easy, I thought, but I decided to keep that to myself.

We lived with a country between us, so our relationship had always been hitched to travel, but could that work long-term? I didn't know. What I did know was that I needed to stop thinking in terms of "real life." A life of travel, for me anyway, was real life. What we had was anything but ordinary, and wasn't that what I had always wanted? I looked through the green mesh screen at the dark sky, and I told Tom I loved him, too, even though he was already asleep. A canvas of clouds hid a galaxy. The stars were there, I thought, even if we couldn't see them.

Bargaining, or the Third Stage of Grief

Port Antonio, Jamaica, January 2017

The handicrafts, under a blue tarp at the back of the produce market, were easy to miss because, like everything else in Jamaica, there was no sign. An old woman with cloudy eyes and cropped white hair sat behind a table scattered with refrigerator magnets, shot glasses, key chains, and Rasta hats—red, yellow, and green. She waved her hand over her wares like a magician and then called to me, asking, "Are you a travel agent?"

I laughed. "No, do I look like one?"

She folded her hands over her belly and said, "I've been watching you and was admiring the way you wrote notes." She pointed to the journal in my hands. "You need another pen?" She showed me the pens on her table.

"I'm not a travel agent," I said. "I'm a writer. Or at least trying to be."

"Oh," she nodded, "then you *do* need a pen."

"I have a pen." I held up the one in my hand.

She nodded again. "But you *look* like a travel agent."

"Thanks," I said because looking like a travel agent seemed like a compliment, though I couldn't say why. I knew I was just another tourist, someone who might spend a few dollars on a Rasta hat or Bob Marley shot glass.

I introduced myself, and she told me she was Kathleen Henry. "Nice to meet you," I said, and we shook hands. She told me she was seventy-eight years old and that her photograph was in the Norman Manley International Airport in Kingston. Because she had been trying so hard to sell her handicrafts, I asked her if she had been paid for the photograph. She shook her head, and I said, "Selling the rights to your image might be worth something."

I could tell she wondered if maybe she ought to have been paid. I hadn't meant to upset her, so I told her that when I left Kingston, I would look for her photograph. She smiled.

I had traveled to Jamaica to teach a travel writing class and had taken my students on a field trip to the town of Port Antonio. I gave them a scavenger hunt of activities designed to help them get a story. I suggested they walk around alone. None of them did this, choosing instead to explore the town in small groups. I wanted to be on my own, but I was too distracted to do their assignment myself. I mostly wandered around, trying to pay attention to things—stray dogs following a man who fed them, the smell of jerk chicken, the vendors selling sugarcane or coconuts they would retrieve by climbing into the trees.

I also wanted to bring a gift home from Jamaica for my mother, something useful. We were between chemotherapy treatments. She had been given three months to live back in October. It was now January.

I fingered a green, yellow, and red knit cap. "Rasta colors," Kathleen said. "Fifteen dollars."

I nodded and then said, "My mom is seventy-eight next month. I'm thinking of buying this hat for her."

"Ten," she said.

I didn't mean to, but I told Kathleen that I wanted the hat because my mother no longer had her hair. When she looked at me in a strange way, my voice turned to scratch and squeak, but I managed to say, "Because chemotherapy."

I wanted to tell Kathleen I didn't want to bargain—that wasn't why I had shared this—but saying so would have sent me into a full cry. I put the hat back on the table. Kathleen Henry took a long look at me, and all I could offer her was a weak smile. "I'm sorry," I said.

I believed she really saw me, or maybe it was that, caught in her gaze, I finally saw myself and the reckoning of my grief. I started to cry and took off my glasses to wipe the tears away with the back of my hand as they came. I apologized again, but she looked at me in that way that said it was okay. I hoped my students wouldn't wander into the market then and see their teacher there, crying.

Kathleen put the hat in a plastic bag, looked around, checking that nobody would see, and handed it to me.

I pulled out my money. I didn't want the hat for free. I didn't want to cry. I didn't know what to do. I held three fives, and Kathleen Henry took one of them and said, "I hope your mother gets better. I'm very sorry."

It is always kindness that allows us our tears.

I nodded, thanked her, and walked out from the dark canopy and into the light, no longer just a tourist but a woman who was losing her mother.

Festivals and Special Events

If you find yourself drawn to an event
against all logic, go. The universe is telling
you something.

GLORIA STEINEM

Travel is about who we are; it can teach us,
it can surprise us, it can move us, but most
important: what it does is transform us.

KEITH BELLOWS

In Search of Genghis Khan

Outer Mongolia, July 2008

When I asked Rucker if he wanted to check out a Mongolian disco, he said, "Fuck yeah. But I have to go ask my granny first."

I had won a travel writing contest that bestowed me with the title "The Next Great Travel Writer," along with a two-week trip with the magazine's editor to Mongolia. The trip was run by a luxury tour company, so most of the other travelers were far older than me. I ended up spending a lot of time with Rucker, a wide-eyed twenty-four-year-old aspiring photographer who was brought along by his eighty-three-year-old grandmother Zu.

I had no idea what it meant to be a travel writer, so I felt like an imposter, which wasn't helped by my panic attack on the airplane. Keith, the magazine's editor-in-chief, looked at me and said, "Oh no. No, no, no. Don't tell me you're afraid of flying."

"Okay. I won't tell you that." I gripped the armrests and took deep breaths.

"You can't really live," Keith said, not looking up from his work, "if you're afraid to die."

The plane shook and dropped over the Gobi Desert, and I tried to look calm, like a real travel writer. The airline's name was Eznis, which I pronounced "Easy-Nice." That was probably incorrect, but I thought, an Easy-Nice plane couldn't crash, could it? Then I laughed, remembering irony. Of course it could.

I concentrated on trying to look unafraid in front of Keith, though he was busy typing on his laptop. The plane dropped again, and I clutched my little leather journal and thought that a real travel writer would have brought a computer.

When I told my mother I'd won a writing contest and would be going to China and Mongolia, she said, "What? Are you sure? You better be careful. That sounds like a sex slave scandal to me."

"Mom, I'm thirty-seven. I'm pretty sure I'm twenty years too old to be a sex slave."

"Just listen to me. I saw a show on it. If it sounds too good to be true, it is."

"Mom, it's *National Geographic*. You've heard of them, right?"

"That's what they tell you, and then boom!"

"Boom?"

"Boom. You're a sex slave."

Metropolis, a super chic discotheque in the capital city of Ulaanbaatar, was known for attracting the children of diplomats. A glowing neon bar sat at the center of the first room. Beyond the bar, a larger space opened with white leather couches, a dance floor, and a VIP-only balcony filled with women in booty shorts and stilettos who glittered with strobe lights and vibrated with the beat of trance music.

Rucker and I struck up a conversation with a Mongolian named Ivan. I wanted to earn my title, so I had my notebook and camera at the ready. I was intrigued by the Mongolian national hero, Chinggis Khaan, known to Westerners as Genghis Khan. I had read Jack Weatherford's *Genghis Khan and the Making of the Modern World* to prepare for my journey and learned that Genghis Khan was an early environmentalist; as was the custom of his tribe, he always offered a prayer of thanks to the mountains and the eternal blue sky. He also continued to live a life of simplicity even after he had achieved world domination. This aspect of him interested me most. Depending on whom you asked, Genghis Khan was either a great man, responsible for uniting the nomadic tribes and creating the largest continuous empire in history, or he was a rapist and murderer (early on, he even killed his own half-brother), responsible for large-scale massacres. According to our guide, Genghis Khan wasn't celebrated in Mongolia until the fall of socialism in the 1990s. She said, "They never even mentioned him in school." Since then, he has enjoyed a powerful revival. His face looms over Ulaanbaatar and graces everything from the currency and postage stamps to the beer and vodka. Hotels, restaurants, and the international airport are named for him.

In the flashing lights of the disco, I asked Ivan, "Do you come to this club often?"

"Yes," he said with a big grin.

"What are some of the other clubs you like to go to?" I asked him.

Ivan answered with another nod, but I was determined. "Where do you think Genghis Khan's grave is?"

"Yes." He smiled.

Genghis Khan died in Inner Mongolia, though legend has it that his body was returned to his birthplace in the Khentii Mountain Range. He had requested an unmarked grave, and for nearly eight hundred years, no one has been able to find it. I've heard two stories explaining why. The first claimed a stampede of horses covered the gravesite, and then the horse riders were killed so they couldn't betray the location. Then for good measure, the soldiers who murdered them were also killed. Folklore also has it that a river was diverted over the gravesite, forever obscuring it.

Rucker and I took a photograph with Ivan, and I moved on to find someone else to talk to about Genghis Khan. I started a conversation with Yaruunaa, a twenty-three-year-old woman who was clearly more interested in dancing with Rucker than in answering my questions. While Yaruunaa flirted with Rucker, I asked her about the country's reverence of Genghis Khan. I wanted to know what the younger generation of Mongolians thought about their national hero, but when I asked Yaruunaa, she said, "Omigod. That was like so long ago. Hello? I mean, it's embarrassing."

When I asked her about the possibility of their finding his burial site, she said, "Oh no. I mean, I'm a little superstitious. Maybe we shouldn't find it." Then Yaruunaa added, "Listen, we share his name and eat it for a hundred years." I didn't have a chance to ask what she meant because Rucker flashed his goofy twenty-something smile at her, and she grabbed his hand and skipped him off to the neon-flickering dance floor.

Like Yaruunaa, many of the Mongolians I spoke with were not in favor of finding the grave because it would be against Genghis Khan's wishes and therefore very bad luck, indeed. They did, however, hope that if the burial site was ever found, it would be in Mongolia and not in China. The Chinese have erected a mausoleum for him where he died, which is in current-day China, and many of the Chinese people I spoke to believed his burial site would be found in their country.

The hotel phone woke me at 8:30 in the morning. "Were you planning to come to Naadam or not?" Keith asked. "We're leaving right now." After my late night at the Mongolian disco, I had overslept. I was failing at being a travel writer. I flew out of bed, threw clothes on, and boarded the bus within five minutes. "Wow," Keith said, "I can't believe you made it." I smiled at him and pulled my wild hair into a bun.

The reason this trip had been planned for the month of July was because of the famous Naadam festival. Eriin Gurvan Naadam (Naadam for short) means "Three Manly Games" and is the most anticipated and important festival in Mongolia. Naadam consists of nomadic sports dating back to the days of Genghis Khan: horse racing, wrestling, and archery. Although they are considered "manly games," girls and women participate in all but the wrestling.

Before we entered the stadium, I wanted to take some photographs. That's what a travel writer would do. I offered a man in traditional dress some money for a picture of him with his horse. We negotiated the price with hand gestures, and we settled on 1,100 tugriks (about 1 U.S. dollar). When the man started pulling on Keith, I realized I had just paid for a horse ride. For Keith. The man kept tugging on Keith, who went along with it and mounted the horse.

Local people and tourists filled the stadium, and the ceremony began with a welcome from the president, followed by a colorful procession of soldiers, horse riders, archers, Olympic athletes, dancers, and singers. After traditional song and dance, five giant mechanical lotus flowers opened their petals, revealing brightly dressed contortionists. Then the wrestling began, which according to our guide, Oyunaa, could go on for hours if a pair of wrestlers were well-matched. She said, "Mongolia is a big country with lots of space, so we do not have time limits. No space limits. No time limits." The wrestlers wore tightly fitting shorts called *shuudag* and an open-fronted jacket called a *zodog*. Oyunaa told us that after a woman (dressed as a man) won the wrestling competition, they designed open-fronted jackets so this embarrassing episode would never happen again.

Smaller communities hosted their own mini-Naadam festivals, and we attended one a few days later in the Gobi Desert. In the Gobi version, we sat on plastic chairs, close enough that the crowd sometimes had to jump out of the way of the wrestlers. The early rounds eliminated those less-serious competitors wearing designer jeans, as well as the skinnier fellows. From my limited experience watching the sport, the biggest wrestlers usually won. Oyunaa whispered in my ear, "That's the one I like." She pointed to one of the wrestlers waiting for his turn. "He's hot." She giggled behind her hand. I told her I would get a picture for her. I zoomed in, and just as I snapped the photo, his finger disappeared into his nose. I told Oyunaa, "I got a picture of your boyfriend."

"Let me see, let me see." She grabbed my camera, looked at the digital image, and then fell off her chair laughing. She said, "I don't care. I still like him." Keith wandered over and asked what we were laughing at. "Show him," Oyunaa said, getting back into her chair. I wasn't sure what a travel writer would photograph, but I guessed it wasn't nose-picking. I handed over my camera, and Keith looked at the image. He shook his head and handed the camera back to me. I wasn't sure, but I thought I'd detected a smile.

We moved off to the horse races, which took place in the open desert. In Mongolian horse racing, it is the horse that competes and not the jockey, so a horse can cross the finish line without its rider and still win, though the winning horse in the Gobi race still carried its young jockey. The jockeys were children between the ages of five and thirteen. The nine-year-old boy who rode the winning horse had been competing for three years. When I asked his trainer how long he'd been riding, he said, "That's the same if I ask you when you first rode in a car. You were a baby. How can you know? Usually children can control their own horses by the time they are three or four, but they ride on them much earlier."

After the festival, I headed into the desert for a hike. In the distance, outcrops of rocky, black hills bubbled from the plains, the ancient inland sea. Crickets and geckos scurried out of my way. A shepherd zoomed past on the motorcycle he used to herd his flock. A couple of round, white gers with television satellite dishes dotted the otherwise empty landscape. The Mongolians are one of the last nomadic people in the world, and they still pack up their homes, or gers, on the backs of camels and relocate them season to season. As I walked, I thought about the stories I wanted to tell—stories about place. I didn't know much about travel writing, so I thought I was supposed to leave myself out of the story, but I didn't know how to do that.

I wanted to know more about Genghis Khan's lost burial site, but more than that, I imagined myself atop a horse, riding along the windy Mongolian steppes, meeting all kinds of interesting people.

I decided to pitch my idea to Keith. I felt like an imposter, but he had been kind to me. Keith and I had been blogging about this trip, and I spent hours in hotel business centers writing mine. When Keith found out, he let me borrow his laptop so I could write my dispatches without missing the planned excursions and spending a fortune on business center fees.

We headed for the Flaming Cliffs, named by Roy Chapman Andrews, the American explorer and alleged inspiration for Hollywood's Indiana Jones. In 1923 Andrews stumbled across dinosaur fossils and, more importantly, the first discovery of dinosaur eggs when he was in Mongolia looking for the animal that would link humans to apes. He led subsequent expeditions to recover dinosaur bones, including those of the previously unknown protoceratops and velociraptor. Now vendors sat on the clifftops selling fossils and dinosaur bones, which our guide, Dr. Niiden Ichinnorov, a pale-ontologist at the Mongolian Academy of Sciences, claimed were real. Determined not to be a bad tourist, I didn't dare buy dinosaur bones, but I went over to talk to some of the children who were selling them. One little girl said she wanted to be a paleontologist when she grew up, so I introduced her to Dr. Ichinnorov.

I walked along the cliffs, taking photographs of the red and orange rock formations. I found Keith standing at the edge, squint-ing into the afternoon sun. I said hello and then after a few min-utes, I asked, "What do you think about the story: 'In Search of Genghis Khan'?"

"Go on." He brushed his gray hair back from his eyes.

"I was thinking I could get a guide and a horse and ride around Mongolia, asking people where they think his burial site is."

"Uh-huh," Keith said.

"The story would be about his place in the collective conscious-ness, how the idea of him is connected to contemporary Mongo-lian identity."

"If scientists haven't found the grave in hundreds of years, why do you think you would find it?"

"I wouldn't find it," I said, "I would look for it. That's the story. The search is the important part. Besides, it's supposed to be bad luck to actually find it. I wouldn't want to find it."

"You're telling me you would go off looking for something you hope you wouldn't find? You're pitching a quest story, hoping you don't succeed?"

"Exactly." I was glad that he had gotten it. But then I realized how it sounded.

"How much riding experience do you have?" Keith asked. We had ridden along the steppes a few days earlier. Had it been obvious how inexperienced I was? I rode horses only when I traveled, which I realized sounded ridiculous. I thought about the time in Peru when my saddle slipped sideways, and nothing I could do would stop the galloping horse. Another time in Colorado, I couldn't get my horse to stop grazing; the animal sensed my weakness and took me under low braches, trying to knock me off. I told Keith, "I've ridden horses," and then, feeling self-conscious, I said, "I know, I probably sound like some quixotic wannabe. Maybe it's a crazy idea."

"No," he said, "I like it."

Early the next morning, we set out to hike into the gorge at Yolyn Am in the Zuun Saikhan Mountain Range. Pebbles crunched beneath our boots, and rocky cliffs climbed the sky above us. As we hiked, we spooked hundreds of jerboas, rodents that Mongolians called "ground mice." They looked like giant hamsters scattered across the grass. We passed *ovoos*, sacred rock piles meant to bring fortune and fulfill wishes. Vendors raced ahead of us on horseback to set up their wares. When we reached them, I bought a camel-hair hat because the temperature had dropped in the shade. We hiked up the narrow canyon to the blue-veined ice field. It was as if we had walked from summer to winter in the span of a morning.

One of the vendors sat behind a tableful of what looked like bones. I asked Oyunaa what he was selling. "Fortunes," she said, and when she could see I didn't understand, she explained: "He tells fortunes with the ankle bones of sheep. Do you want yours told?" I nodded and approached the table. The man rolled the bones like dice and then read them. He looked serious, and Oyunaa translated what he said: "He can tell you, but you must go after your work to have more attention."

I asked Oyunaa what that meant, and she said she wasn't sure. She suggested we circle one of the *ovoos*; I could make a wish, and then maybe I'd figure it out. I followed her up a small rocky hill. She instructed me to toss a stone on the cairn each time I circled it, and on the third revolution, I should make my wish.

Making a wish always feels overwhelming to me. I don't want to ask for too much, but I also don't want to blow my chance for something really great. I usually make a wish for someone else's health or happiness, so I don't seem like a jerk to the grantor of wishes. I circled the rock pile, and I couldn't make up my mind. When I completed my third time around, I settled on this: *I wish to return to Mongolia someday*.

Years later, I would berate myself for not using my sacred wish for Keith, though at the time, I couldn't have known what the future held. He died seven years after we took this trip together of what his obituary called "a long illness." I wondered if he had been sick when we were in Mongolia. If he was, he hadn't let on. He was, as he had said, too busy living to be afraid of dying.

On the way back down the gorge, Rucker caught up with me, gigantic camera in hand, and asked, "Is this awesome or what?"

I agreed that it was.

Odds Are

Number 13: Who's Your Momma? was an easy bet.

"What about Hello Darling, The Russian, or Where's Johnny?" Sandra asked. "Their odds are better." Bookmakers Michael O'Neill and Anthony Donning outshouted each other, asking people to place their wagers. We moved up in the line to make our own bets.

"Who's Your Momma? seems lucky," I told Sandra. "I love her name."

"Thirteen is lucky?" she asked.

"Why not?" We reached the man in the little glass booth, Michael O'Neill himself, and placed our bets.

"Who's Your Momma? is a long shot at 8–1," Michael said, and I told him I'd take my chances.

We were at the annual horse races in Dingle, Ireland, and everything seemed exciting. The horses ran on a grass track; the audience milled between the beer and wine tents outside of the track and the food vendors—Katie's Kitchen, The Dingle Crepe Van, and Sheehy's Ice Cream—on the inside. Sandra and I split an ice cream.

The crowd gathered at the track's edge. Green hills rolled into the distance. Gulls lifted into flight. Umbrellas popped bright colors against a gray sky. The rain cleared for the moment, and everyone was in a good mood. The horses pranced around the track, showing themselves off before the race. Though it was my first time at a horse track, and we had only just arrived, I turned to Sandra and said, "I love horse racing."

Sandra and I stood trackside as the race began. The horses galloped toward us, the ground rumbling as they passed. We were so close, we could smell their musty sweat and see their muscles working under their hides, the veins bulging in their faces, their nostrils flaring. A jockey in a pink-striped suit rode Who's Your Momma? He whipped her, and I wondered if it hurt. The announcer called, "Number 13, Who's Your Momma? takes the lead." I jumped up and down and shouted for her. The horses ran the curve, and Who's Your Momma? was in front, straining for the finish. She was going to win!

On the last straightaway, there was some kind of commotion, a confusing bunching of the horses on the track. A horse lost its jockey but ran on. Who's Your Momma? was no longer in the lead, but she raced on, her ankle flopping around as if her hoof was no longer attached to her leg. The jockey pulled on her reins to stop her, but still she ran.

"Don't look, don't look," Sandra said, but it was too late. I could not unsee the horse trying to run on her broken ankle.

Who's Your Momma? finally stopped and bucked; she flung back her head, her eyes straining from her skull. She shook the injured leg. A group of men came onto the track and surrounded her with a blue screen that looked like a giant shower curtain. A woman came over and briefly cried. Sandra said, "She must be the owner."

The men put the screen up around Who's Your Momma? and I went over and asked bookmaker Michael O'Neill what was going on even though I already knew, had already come to think of the men with the tarp as "the death squad." He said, "I've been around enough to know horses are replaceable, but people are not. Horses and cows are the same, and we like our steaks." I asked him if this was common in horse racing. He said it was, but only one had been lost that day, which wasn't bad considering the rain. And then he told me, "This is nothing compared to the steeplechase. They lose horses galore each day."

The dead horse was wrapped in the blue tarp. A yellow tractor trundled onto the track, lifted her with the giant shovel, and drove Who's Your Momma? away. I wondered where they were taking her. Would they bury her, or would she be transported to a dog food factory? With the track cleared, they got ready for the next race, and everything continued as if nothing ever happened.

I asked Sandra if she knew about the dangers of horse racing. She said she had never seen a horse go down but knew racing wasn't good for the animals. "Everyone knows that," she said.

I hadn't known it, but if I had thought about it long enough, this was a conclusion I could have come up with on my own. Though never could I have predicted the precision with which the death squad would come remove the horse from the track and the easy way everyone would return to their ciders and their crepes and their 8–1 bets.

My own bet made me complicit. "I want to leave," I told Sandra, and she nodded. The announcer shouted as another group of horses thundered past, but I couldn't watch. We walked back toward the shuttle buses, and the rain started again.

The Grand Elephant Festival

As we sped from the Cochin airport, two Indian strangers sat in the front seat of our car. Sholeh and I sat in the back, hanging onto each other as we weaved between other cars, trucks, camel carts, and cows. I clutched my noisemaker key chain (yes, I had such an implement, given to me by my practical boyfriend), just in case; in case of what, I didn't know. Pulling the chain would only omit a piercing siren that would surely result in a swerve off the road and a fiery crash, despite the Ganesh good luck charm dangling from the driver's rearview mirror.

"Do you like India?" Bijuraj turned around to face us. His giant white teeth gleamed. "Do you like my country?" Bijuraj had recently tracked down Sholeh on the internet and translated a few of her poems, and when he found out we would be traveling in India, he insisted we stay at his family's home. I kept asking Sholeh, "Are you sure we should stay with someone we don't *know*?"

"Don't be silly. It will be lovely to stay with a family. He invited us because we're poets," she said, as if that explained everything.

Sholeh and I originally planned to travel through the south of India from Mumbai, where we stayed with my friend Shalini's family—an actual friend, not someone I had met online. But Kochi worked out as a convenient stop on the way south to Alleppey, so Sholeh accepted the invitation to stay with Bijuraj and his family. I went along with it because I had learned Sholeh was usually right about these things. Plus, I had heard there would be a grand elephant parade, and I love elephants.

When we stepped off the plane, there was Bijuraj, grinning and waving his hands above his head. He had written to Sholeh, telling her he would hire a car and driver to fetch us from the airport. He had said: "Look for the tall and fat Indian." He was certainly tall but not at all fat, at least not by American standards.

Despite Bijuraj's large smile, I held my safety key chain until we pulled up to his house, a modest two-story home set behind a leafy patio. On the front porch waited Bijuraj's also smiling mother. She wore a beautiful maroon sari, a matching bindi on her forehead, and her black hair pulled into a tight bun. I didn't think a bigger smile than the one on Bijuraj's face was possible until I saw her.

"You see," Sholeh said. "They couldn't be more lovely."

I tucked my noisemaker away, feeling silly indeed.

When Bijuraj's mother heard I wasn't married, she began calling me daughter, which she pronounced "doughter." And she insisted I call her Amma, meaning "Mother." She also took it upon herself to make sure I was well fed, putting food into my mouth whenever I opened it. If I started to speak, which happened a lot, Amma would shove in half a banana. According to Amma, a well-fed child was the sign of a good mother, so she stood over me at mealtimes, replenishing my plate of rice, plantains, and chicken tikka masala as soon as I took a bite. She also made sure I used the proper dining etiquette; the right hand is for eating, while the left should be reserved for bathroom business. Because I have always had trouble keeping track of right and left, I could not keep my hands in order and received playful slaps to the wrist from Amma. I ended up sitting on my left hand at mealtimes.

Amma made her displeasure clear when I said I wanted to try *toddy*, a milky wine made from the fermented husk of a coconut. We stopped at a roadside "bar" on our way home from the tea plantations in Munnar, and Bijuraj had to go in for it because women were not welcome in such an establishment. He brought out a bottle of the whitish brew, though Amma stood with her arms crossed, shaking her head. Sholeh spit it out on the ground and said it tasted like someone had thrown up coconut milk. Amma looked vindicated, so I didn't tell her I didn't find *toddy* half bad.

For the most part, Amma left Sholeh alone because she was a married woman and therefore a grown-up. But I was unmarried, a mere child of thirty-six, so Amma followed me around the house, trying to put sesame oil on my skin, comb my wild, curly hair, or affix bindis to my forehead to make me look "more Indian." I loved the attention, but I ended up looking like an oily pink-skinned dimwit who was trying just a little too hard.

Amma didn't need me to need her the way my own mother did—that dynamic so many grown daughters encounter with their mothers. She was just curious and wanted to be helpful. I know that if we didn't have a language barrier, Amma would have been a good listener, offering me sage advice about love and life, but we couldn't communicate without Bijuraj's help translating. Even so, Amma managed to teach us how to make a delicious chai tea.

The lack of boundaries I had with my own mother made me the kind of person who was easily motherable. Amma was there when I woke up in the morning; at night, when I got ready for bed, she stood next to me in the bathroom, smiling at me in the mirror. The first time she saw me take out my contact lens, she screamed in terror. Then she laughed in delight when I showed her the lens. She asked me to repeat this, putting the lens back in and taking it out, again and again as she looked on, squealing in horror and glee, clapping her hands as if I had performed a fantastic trick.

While I was the proverbial apple of Amma's eye, the literary men of Kochi were smitten by Sholeh. Bijuraj had arranged for Sholeh to give a talk at a bookstore in town. It happened to coincide with the culmination of the local elephant festival, where a procession of fifty elephants would take to the streets. I am ashamed to admit it, but I was a little annoyed. This was not a very generous attitude, but I wanted instead to see the parade I had read about.

The bookstore set chairs up outside, and the event was standing-room only with more than a hundred Indians, mostly men, gathered there to see Sholeh, who delivered an eloquent lecture on the political situation in Iran, literature, and the relationships between East and West. The audience listened with intent, intellectually hungry, engaged in the world of literature. They were entranced by Sholeh. And I was entranced, the sweat rolling down my back and the heat making my head light, by watching them watch her.

Afterward, Sholeh was ushered into the Communist bookstore, where the likes of Che Guevara, Fidel Castro, and Saddam Hussein looked out from book covers on the shelves. A crowd of reporters fought to take Sholeh's picture, film her, ask her questions. One reporter thrust a microphone into her face. I took pictures of everyone taking pictures of her.

The next day, we watched Sholeh's interview on television with Bijuraj and his family. Amma and I clapped for her. During the filming, I had sat with Sholeh, so along the bottom of the television screen ran the script: *Iranian Poet Sholeh Wolpé and American Writer Suzanne Roberts*. My first poetry book had not yet come out, so the title "American Writer" was a bit generous, but still I felt proud. "This station is broadcast all the way to London," Bijuraj said. "I bet there are millions of people watching." We all agreed what a wonderful thing this was.

And not a one of us anticipated that homeland security might be concerned by a sweaty want-to-be-writer with a bindi affixed to her forehead.

I would find this out a week later in the Frankfurt airport, when the gate agent stopped me from boarding the Los Angeles–bound plane and questioned me because I had made it onto the "no-fly" list. My no-fly status would follow me around the world for the next two years, and I would be interrogated each time I tried to return to the United States. My brother-in-law Britt saw this as a coup d'état. "A terrorist in the family!" he said with glee, but this was coming from someone who had tattooed his Medicare card onto his forearm as a protest against the bureaucracy of the U.S. healthcare system. When asked to show his card, Britt rolls up his sleeve and says, "I keep it handy. It's right here."

Eventually, homeland security removed me from the list, along with the errant toddlers and the suspicious little old ladies.

After Sholeh's talk, the bookstore invited us to a party to celebrate the posthumously published writings of Saddam Hussein, who had become a martyr in these parts of India because of his recent execution. We declined the invitation and said our good-byes, even though the men of Kochi could have talked to Sholeh all night. We hurried off to catch the end of the elephant festival.

When we got there, it was hot, crowded, and loud, but worst of all, the giant chains hobbling the elephants made me cry. The sad animals wore gold-plated caparisons and glittering head gear. Mahouts sat behind their ears, holding silk parasols and whipping the anxious animals into submission. If I had done my research, I would have known to stay away; this was not a place for people who love elephants, or for anyone, really. "This isn't what I was hoping for," I told Sholeh. The giant, bedazzled elephants struggled against their shackles, stressed out by the jubilant crowd. I would later learn that dozens of elephants in the state of Kerala die every year due to a lack of food, water, and medical treatment and that authorities have not been quick to act because they equate elephants with tourism.

We told Bijuraj we had seen enough and wanted to leave. We had to run back across the busy intersection—whenever you cross a road in India, you are taking your life into your hands—and were nearly hit by a tour bus.

When it was time to go, Bijuraj begged us not to leave Kochi. Bijuraj himself had become a bit of a celebrity. His house was a magnet for journalists who wanted to interview Sholeh and have a peek at me, the "American Writer," a title that made me cringe every time Bijuraj used it. But mostly, Bijuraj wanted us to stay because his family loved us. And we loved them.

Here is the epitome of Indian hospitality: upon learning of our upcoming arrival, the family had installed a Western toilet upstairs just for us. They were disappointed because Sholeh and I used the Eastern toilet downstairs, which was closer to our room. When I heard about the other toilet, though, I made the trip up the stairs whenever possible. In response to Amma's proud smile, I would say, "Fantastic toilet." Even though we couldn't understand each other's words, she knew what I was saying. She would smile and I would smile, and that was enough. It struck me as odd that I could become so attached to Amma, who knew about ten English words, including "no," "doughter," and "eat." And this, of course, was a much bigger vocabulary than my repertoire of one Malayalam word: "Amma." But sometimes words aren't necessary. Sometimes they get in the way of what is essential.

When our driver picked us up, Bijuraj and Amma waved good-bye to us from their shady front patio. Amma blew us kisses that Sholeh pretended to catch. As we drove off, Sholeh said, "They were so lovely, weren't they?"

I nodded, glad that Sholeh trusted the world the way she did—and what a wonderful thing that can be.

Coming of Age in the Guna Yala Islands

San Blas Islands, Panama, December 2009

A woman stood on the dock, holding quivering fish by their tails—the scales like stacked coins, the green eyes like marbles. The gills fanned at the useless air. A cage hovered over the water, the pig inside it unable to turn around. Lanterns burned yellow in the filtered evening light.

Our hotel's owner had brought us to this island from one of the tourist islands by boat, told us we should see how the locals lived, said there would be a haircutting ceremony, a chance to drink rum with the Guna people. He waved to us as we got off the boat, and we followed a local guide. He said he would return in a couple of hours.

Tom and I paid our arrival taxes and walked through the narrow, treeless streets. Clapboard and rusting tin houses with palm-frond thatched roofs leaned against each other, the small island packed so tightly that there was no view from the streets to the sea, no way to know you were on an island—so unlike the islands for tourists, where palms swayed in front of bungalows steps from the water.

Children smiled and waved; they spoke the local language and called the only Spanish words they knew: "Hola, hola. ¿Nombre? ¿País?" They ran past, their laughter ringing through the maze of streets. An albino girl fled from a group of older boys. She wore the colorful *molas* the girls and women wore, and beads crawled up her pinkish skin. She was sunburned, mottled with insect bites—the pink flares like fireworks. The boys teased her, snatched at her budding chest. Her stringy blonde hair hung from under an orange headscarf, and her blue eyes seemed transparent. She screamed as she disappeared down the tangle of streets, her shouts echoing, part nervous laughter, part squealing fear.

I wanted to follow them, to tell the boys to stop terrorizing her. But I didn't have words they would understand. I couldn't do anything. I later learned that the Guna people have a high incidence rate of albinism. In Guna mythology, albinos are considered a special race of people with the specific duty of defending the moon against a dragon who tries to eat it during a lunar eclipse. It didn't seem like this mythology protected the girl from adolescent taunting and mocking—the language of being different that all of the world understands.

Earlier that day, I had asked a Guna chief about their laws, asked what they would do, for example, if a man raped a woman. He told me that never happened. I asked again, but what if it did? A villager who knew Guna and Spanish translated for us. He told me the chief said they would give the rapist advice. I repeated the answer to make sure I understood correctly, said it back to him slowly in Spanish: "¿Dar consejos?"

"Yes," the translator had said, "that's right. But sometimes, they also have to clean the streets. As punishment."

Tom and I ducked under the canvas to enter the tent where the haircutting celebration was underway. We were the only tourists there, but I had learned that sometimes it is an honor to have outsiders at such celebrations. The darkness knitted across the outside world. The backlit sky disappeared. Only the tips of cigarettes burned orange and the flicker of candles, the wax melting into empty beer cans. Smoke hovered, disappearing and reappearing like a memory. A man played a hand flute in the dark corner. Another man shook a gourd of beads. The elders unfolded themselves from the low wooden benches, poured Seco Herrerano into split coconut shells. The men lined up on the dirt floor, clutching their rum. They sang, "Woo-woo-woo-woo," shuffling along the ground, the earth polished smooth by bare feet. They stooped their shoulders, came together, raised their coconuts, drank. The song, "Idomalando," a chant for health. The dance, an ancient ritual: part bird, part man, part god.

The painted and pierced women drank and smoked and gossiped on their side of the tent. Earlier in the day, they were stitching colorful *molas*—fish, parrots, *el borracho* playing a flute. They sold them at the tourist islands. Now they sat arm in arm at the fiesta, waiting for the haircutting ceremony to begin. They swayed on their benches, giggling to one another like schoolgirls, leaning into each other, laughing over the din of drinking. The patterned *molas*—skirts and headscarves with geometric beading—glimmered blue, yellow, purple, sequins of light interrupting the darkness.

A man tossed his cigarette onto the dirt floor, put it out with his bare foot. He poured rum into a coconut bowl and walked around to bring others this offering. Our guide said it was important that everyone enjoy the ceremony, this rite of passage from girl to woman. He said, "Be sure to hold the rum with both hands." I sipped it until it burned into my throat and stomach, a fire spreading into my limbs.

I told Tom I needed to get some air. I stumbled out of the dark tent and into the gauzy light, passing two old women. Gold rings hung from their septa, and orange makeup blazed along triangular cheekbones, down the length of their noses. One of the women sucked hard on a cigarette, swayed down the dusty street, said, "Borracha." Drunk. It was impossible to know if she meant the friend she was leaning on, herself, or me. The smoke hung in the air like a question.

I returned to the tent, waiting for the girl to enter, imagining the sheared hair falling like rain, signaling her passage into womanhood.

She never appeared, and I didn't have the language to ask.

I would later learn this haircutting ceremony was only part of the coming-of-age ritual, which lasts four full days. During this time the girl's family, if they can afford it, must feed and supply drinks to the village and to tourists like us. On the third day, the girl's hair is cut, the ritual hidden by a committee of women. If she has already gotten her period, she never enters her own celebration. She sits facing east, scarves covering her head and face until her long hair is cut, leaving only a narrow strip bordering the forehead. The ceremony allows for a long break, so groups of women can peer in to see the girl and drink their share of *chicha*, a fermented beverage. Afterward, the haircutter finally removes the rest of the hair, leaving the girl completely bald. As adults, Guna women wear short hair, covered by a bright headscarf.

I tried to picture the secret ritual, the twelve-year-old girl stone-faced as she watched her childhood spiral to the dusty ground. Crossing the boundary between long-haired girl and short-haired woman among her friends and family, hidden but saved—at least for now—from becoming a tourist attraction.

Getting There and Away

~~~~~~

Good girls go to heaven, bad girls
go everywhere.

MAE WEST

Dangerous for a Woman Alone

When I arrived in Lima, I heard the same question from just about every taxi driver: "Are you married?" A single woman in her midthirties, traveling around South America alone, was too perplexing and led to many other questions, so I learned to lie and say I was married.

But then the taxi drivers asked where my husband was and why he would allow me to travel alone. I would say he was in the hotel room. That he didn't feel well.

"I hope he feels better soon," the taxi drivers would say.

"Me too. Thanks." I said this so many times, I started to believe I really did have a sick husband waiting in the hotel room.

One taxi driver asked, "And he lets you go to the museum alone?"

"He's very modern." I was proud of myself that I remembered how to say that in Spanish.

Another taxi swerved in front of us. The driver slammed on the breaks and shouted, "¡Tonto!" Then he turned to me and said, "It's because I'm an official taxi. They're just jealous. They give me no respect."

I nodded and said, "I hate that."

Then he yelled, "Bastard!" out the window and asked me the next logical question: "Do the young people in your country have sex before they're married?"

"Only sometimes." I was glad I was a married woman with a husband back at the hotel. I added, "And judging by all the young people making out on the park benches, they do here, too." I remembered more Spanish than I thought, which would get me into trouble. I was much better off traveling alone with limited language skills—I tended to say too much and ask too many questions.

That's when the taxi driver clicked his tongue and wagged his finger, and I went back to pretending I didn't understand.

I had heard Lima was dangerous, mostly from my mother, who knew nothing about Peru, or anywhere else in Latin America. However, I found Lima to be a beautiful and historic city, full of colonial buildings, parks, and beaches where the sky filled with hang gliders. When I told my mother that, she said, "Don't you dare try it."

I wasn't worried about being on my own on the streets or riding in taxis. I was terrified, though, of being alone and getting sick. I tried to assure myself. I had just traveled through India and wasn't sick once. I had even gained weight! I would surely be fine in Peru. But still, it was a worry I couldn't shake.

Aside from wandering around the old city and the swanky Miraflores with its cafés, bars, and bookshops, I also visited the national museums, which were filled with gold, violence, an impressive collection of penises, and the excavated grave of El Señor de Sipán (or the Lord of Sipán), who was buried with two warriors, a guard, his head soldier, three young women dressed in ceremonial clothes, two sacrificial llamas, and a pet dog, all of whom would accompany the king to his next life.

I couldn't stop thinking about those three young women. And the dog.

I flew from Lima to Cusco, and when I arrived at the airport, a small boy asked me to buy his postcards. "I'm the artist. Look." He showed me the name signed in the corner of his pretty postcards. "I'm Hernan." He gestured to himself. I asked him how many he sold on a good day, and he thought about it for a minute and said, "Seven, maybe eight."

I bought ten cards and caught a taxi. A woman wearing a golf shirt embossed with the name of a tour company jumped into my taxi with me. She convinced me not to stay at the hotel I told her I had booked. "That's dangerous for a woman alone." She directed the driver to another hotel, one that was "very clean and safe." I had become accustomed to this hotel switch-out scam. There was no reason not to stay wherever it was this woman took me; I didn't have reservations, so I might as well help her earn her commission. The hotel she brought me to had bright yellow walls and a courtyard filled with fake flowers and a sad caged parrot named Rodrigo. "Breakfast included," she said, smiling. I booked a room with an en-suite bathroom for $25 a night.

I left my pack at the hotel, found an internet café, and wrote to Tom, letting him know I'd arrived. Sholeh had emailed me, saying that the lovely young Indian writer who had hosted the dinner party we'd attended in New Delhi that January had died suddenly. *They said it was food poisoning*, Sholeh wrote. *Her poor husband. It's just awful. She was 27. She was so, so young.*

I reread the email. It didn't seem possible. I could only picture her alive, there in the candlelit living room. Her wine-stained smile, a wisp of hair falling over the flash of her dark eyes. A hula hoop orbiting her body, in time with Indian music playing from the stereo. Her death was (and still remains) a mystery. I thought about the way we all continue living, as if our own deaths are far, far away, but we never know if that's true or not. I remembered a haiku from the eighteenth-century Japanese poet Issa: "On a branch/floating downriver/a cricket singing."

And I thought about how we must keep singing, even if it's true that in doing so, we are serenading our own deaths—the song in our laughter and the fall of water always impossibly near.

I answered Sholeh's email, letting her know I had received the sad and shocking news. Then I wrote a long email to my mother, describing the museum with the king buried with his people. I bought a bottle of water. When I opened it, there wasn't that usual catch—as if the seal was broken—but I told myself to stop worrying. It didn't taste like bottled water; there was an earthiness, but I didn't want to be paranoid, so I continued the message to my mother, and I drank the water.

I walked out onto the plaza and found a quiet café where I could sit and write in my journal. I looked out over the Plaza de Armas, originally the center of the Incan empire. In the 1500s the Spanish conquerors added two churches, La Compañia and the Cathedral. People gathered in the flower-filled gardens, sat on the park benches, and leaned against the wall of the fountain. Shops selling alpaca sweaters and postcards lined the square. Vendors followed tourists, begging them to buy their wares. The streetlamps flickered on. I couldn't stop thinking about our lovely Indian hostess.

I had been in Peru just over a week, and already I felt lonely, but I knew a little bit of loneliness was good for me. Besides, I had brought my journal and book of poems to keep me company, and Sandra was coming to meet me in a few days. We were planning to hike the Inca Trail to Machu Picchu and then sail to the Galápagos. From there, I would spend some time alone in Quito and then return to Peru for two months of language school in Cusco. There would be a lot of air travel over the next three months, but the flights were cheap. I tried not to think about how much I hated flying. Logically, I knew flying was safe, but my young grandmother had died in a commercial airline crash before I was born, so I also knew in an intimate way what could happen. My fear was both irrational and rational.

In the café, I ordered coca leaf tea with a piece of dry lemon cake and ate it in the dim light. Being alone also meant no one knew where I was—the certain freedom that comes only with loneliness. I read Sylvia Plath, who said, "Perhaps when we find ourselves wanting everything, it is because we are dangerously close to wanting nothing." I wrote in my journal: *The margin between wanting everything and wanting nothing grows fainter and fainter.*

Just before midnight, the boy who had been selling postcards in the airport wandered past the café window. I waved to him, and he came in through the glass doors. The bartender motioned for him to leave, and I said, "It's okay. I know him."

I didn't *know* him, of course; I had just met him in the airport like all the other tourists had. But I knew him better than anyone else in Peru. He walked to my small table. "Hola, Hernan," I said. The boy looked confused at first, and then we both laughed. I asked him where his parents were. He said his mother was out selling finger puppets. His father was dead. "How old are you?" I asked.

He told me he was eleven, or directly translated from the Spanish, he had eleven years, and it seemed he really did have those years. A woman in a brightly colored dress with a poncho and traditional hat approached the café; she stopped and looked in at us. She carried a plastic bag filled with finger puppets.

I pointed at the woman on the other side of the windows and asked, "Is that your mother?"

He nodded.

I waved to her, and she approached me. "It's so late," I told her.

"Lady," she said in English, "would you like to buy a finger puppet?"

I shook my head.

"Candy or coca leaves?" she asked, showing me her box. The waiter looked at me with tired eyes, and I guessed at his thoughts: *Another gringa who doesn't have a clue.*

"I already bought postcards," I said, "but the next time I see you, I'll buy something else from you. I'm out of money now." It was true. I had spent what I brought on tea and lemon cake.

"Please?" The mother held my gaze.

"Next time," I said, which turned out to be true. In a few weeks, I would buy finger puppets from her in the plaza.

But that night, they left the café together, and I walked the two blocks back to my hostel. The cathedral glowed yellow. The cold air bit at the back of my neck, and I wrapped my scarf around me. I felt a pang of longing, but I didn't wish for something else. Everything I needed was right there in the moment, being present in my body without wanting anything else from the world. And being happy wasn't something I needed to chase; rather, the key was to redefine happiness, the kind that could coexist with loneliness and with longing.

As I got ready for bed, my stomach started to rumble. And then cramp. Probably the dry lemon cake, I thought. I lay down on the narrow bed but couldn't get comfortable. I tried to sleep but within an hour, I doubled over in pain—not a stomachache but stomach pain. One minute I was freezing and shivering; the next, I was drenched with sweat. I crawled to the bathroom and managed to get onto the toilet before the violent explosion from both ends. I tried to aim for the bathtub while still on the toilet, but I couldn't reach it, so vomit splattered on the cracking linoleum. I threw up into the trash can, and in between brutal heaves, I cried. I thought about how glad I was to have paid extra for my own bathroom.

I remembered the broken seal on the water bottle. Not worrying and being careless are two different things. I laughed a little at this thought, this irony; then I threw up again and cried some more. I had eaten chicken earlier before I left Lima, too. Maybe I had salmonella? Was that something I could die from? I thought about the beautiful twenty-seven-year-old dinner party hostess and her hula hoop. Sitting on that toilet, shivering, I was sure I was dying, and nothing could be done about it.

I couldn't make it back to the bed, so between vomiting and diarrhea, I slept on the bathroom floor. I had made such a mess; I hoped I wouldn't die there. It was embarrassing to think about someone finding me like that. How vain, I thought, laughed, and then puked again.

In the morning, I still couldn't move without the surge of nausea, the weakness. I wanted to go down to the front desk to let them know I was sick, but I couldn't make it out of my room. I traveled with Cipro and Imodium, but I couldn't keep anything down. I ran out of drinking water, so I treated tap water with the iodine tablets I'd brought. Finally, the maid came, and I managed to open the door, tell her I was very sick. That I needed toilet paper and towels. She came back with the towels and toilet paper and told me to take chicken soup. I nodded and thanked her. Chicken, I thought as I hobbled back to the bathroom, that's funny.

I still felt sick through the next day, and I couldn't make it out of my room to use the phones or email at the internet café, so I called Tom from my flip phone, even though I knew it would be expensive. This was 2007, and FaceTime hadn't yet been invented. I felt like someone should know I was sick, and my mother would worry too much. Tom, being practical to the extreme, wouldn't over-worry since it would do no good. But he would show concern. I felt sorry for myself and wanted sympathy.

I told Tom I was sick, but the phone call kept disconnecting. I fell asleep again on the bathroom floor.

I woke sometime later to my phone ringing; Tom's normally calm voice sounded frantic. "Are you all right?"

"I don't feel so well. How are you?" I tried to sound as normal as possible. I knew I shouldn't have called. What could he have done for me? Though talking to him made me feel like he was taking care of me. It didn't matter that he wasn't actually there—he was there for me in a way that mattered.

"I've been worried. I couldn't get through. My phone isn't set up for international calls. I had to go buy a phone card at the gas station. Are you going to be okay?"

"I'm not dead yet."

"When's Sandra getting there?"

"Tomorrow," I said. "I'll be okay."

"Are you sure?"

"It's my South America weight loss plan."

"Well, I know you must be okay, or you wouldn't be making jokes."

Humor was my family's go-to for dealing with difficult situations. When we were making arrangements for my father's cremation at the funeral parlor, my mother whispered to me, "Maybe if we can find out where they've got him kept, we can break him out of here and do it ourselves. Think of the money we'd save."

And years later, my mother would be on her own deathbed, joking about "popping off" right before she did. We made jokes to bear the unbearable. Humor relies on an element of surprise, a mystery. And there is nothing as mysterious as death.

Keith—the editor I traveled to Mongolia with—told me that to truly live, we cannot be afraid of death. But I don't think that's quite right. Instead, we have to let the fear in without letting it take over. I learned to do the scary thing, not just in spite of my fear but sometimes because of it. I survived being sick—the thing that had scared me most about traveling alone. It was a test I finally passed.

And after my own illness, I realized I shouldn't have left my imaginary husband back at the hotel room alone so many times.

A Wee Scottish Tour

Glen Coe Valley, Scotland, July 2018

"No, really, I'm good at this," I tell Tom, pushing in front of him to stick out my thumb. The cars rush past on the busy A82, a narrow highway winding through the Scottish Highlands. We are on day six of our ninety-five-mile West Highland Way hike and have just walked from Tyndrum to the Glen Coe Valley in the rain. The inn I booked is in Glencoe Village, about ten miles down the road.

As we hiked down the misty path, the bus pulled away, and there wouldn't be another for hours. Hitchhiking is now our only option.

"Yeah, whatever," Tom says. "I'll give you six cars."

"And then what?" I ask, waving my thumb at passing vehicles.

"Then I'll do it." Tom is very practical.

The green mountains hover above us, and the rain becomes a white, steady mist. Peaks appear and disappear behind intermittent clouds. I catch myself thinking that this would be such a lovely place in the summer and then remember it's July.

"One more car," Tom says. "Then I'm taking over."

The next car pulls to the side, a slate-blue Peugeot, and I do a little joyful jump to celebrate, singing, "You see, you see, you see!"

A very fat, gray-haired man with a red nose is driving. He looks like a garden gnome. "Get in," he shouts. "Do you want your packs in the back?"

Tom tells him we can carry them on our laps, and I climb in the back seat. Tom opens the driver's side door, and we laugh, remembering it's the opposite in Scotland. We settle in, and we're off. I'm happy we'll be at our inn soon. I'm wet and cold, and I have to pee. I look around the car. Spilled food splashes the upholstery, and a few sweaters, hats, and an umbrella are scattered about. A plastic bag of something else sits on the seat next to me, but I don't dare sneak a peek.

Our driver tells us the Scottish always pick up hitchhikers, that they are the friendliest people in the world. We smile and agree. "Thank you," we say. I look out the window and think about my hot shower and glass of wine at the inn.

Our driver tells us he lives outside of Glasgow, and I wonder why he's out here in the Highlands, but I don't ask. "This is my favorite part of Scotland," he says. "There's the mountain where *Skyfall* was filmed. I'll take you for a picture."

How nice.

"That one there?" Tom points to a giant roundish mountain with a scoured, craggy top and a skirt of grass below.

"Aye," the driver nods. It seems like he jerks the wheel a bit, but perhaps he's just excited about James Bond. We pull over, and Tom gets out for a photo. I remain in the back with my pack on my lap, and for a second I think if we take off without Tom, I'll be alone in the car with a stranger. I tell myself not to worry—my usual mantra. Even after hiking nineteen miles, I could easily outrun this man. I'm a bit chubby myself, but the driver is like a beanbag in suspenders.

Then I wonder how I'll get back to Tom after I've jumped from the car and run.

Tom gets back in, and the driver asks, "Did you get a good one?" Tom looks at his phone and says he thinks so.

"You think that's good," our driver says, "wait until you see the rest." The rest?

We are on a one-lane road alongside a cliff overlooking a small river, which our driver tells us is the River Etive. I ask him, "Is this an alternative scenic route to Glencoe Village?"

"Nope."

Okie dokie.

I'm shivering in my wet shirt, so I take out my puffy jacket and hat and put them on. Because Tom is midwestern nice, he keeps saying, "Wow, thank you so much. This is beautiful," which is likely prolonging our tour. And Tom's right—it *is* beautiful. The glacier-scraped volcanic cones jut into the patchy blue sky. The sunlight through the clearing clouds makes the grass an electric green. But I'm freezing, and I'm wondering where we're going.

We have pulled over again, and Tom is outside taking a photograph of the stream cutting below a glacial moraine. Without turning around, the driver wags his phone at me and says, "No reception here. No one can get a hold of you if they wanted to."

I smile and nod at him through the rearview mirror. He just means that this place is remote, right? Not that he's holding us captive and we can't call for help. I tell myself again not to worry. And to enjoy this. That this is the joy of traveling—these unexpected surprises.

Then I remember the plastic bag on the seat next to me. And I wonder what's in it. I think about the things that would fit into the white sack. An axe? Some knives? A dead baby?

After Tom returns, I decide if we're all friends, the driver won't try to kill us, so I say, "I'm Suzanne. And this is Tom."

"Oh yes, I'm Hugh. Hugh MacDonald."

"Nice to meet you," we all say. Hugh and Tom shake hands.

Hugh keeps driving, pulling over to avoid oncoming traffic on the narrow road. We wind farther into the valley, alongside the bubbling river. Scottish thistle pops purple against the bright green moor. The blue sky appears and vanishes between passing clouds. This is easily one of the most scenic places I have ever been. I try to enjoy this impromptu tour but have internal fights with myself, as usual.

"I would love to see this in the winter," I say. "It must be beautiful."

"Aye," Hugh says and throws his phone at me. "Have a look at my photos."

I scroll through the pictures. The snowy landscape looks like something out of a fantasyland. "These are amazing."

"Aye." Hugh nods.

There are also pictures of what look like reindeer, very close up. I wonder if they're stock photos. We're in a pullout again, and Tom gets out and takes pictures of a stone bridge and the mountains beyond.

I give Hugh his phone back. I don't say anything about the reindeer, but I do ask, "So how long does this road go on? Does it meet up with the main road?"

"The main road? No. It's a wee way to the car park and then a turnaround. You haven't seen anything yet!"

I try to accept this tour, but I devise a plan to get away from the car as soon as possible in order to use the natural toilet. I'm thinking about this when Hugh asks, "Are you having a good time, dear?"

"Oh yes," I say, because is there really another answer?

Hugh tells us about the volcanoes, the glaciers, and the avalanche paths. Glacial fans spread at the base of the rocky mountains.

"What time are we meeting Susan and Chris?" I ask Tom. This is a risk. Susan and Chris are Scottish friends we met on the trail, but we have no plans to meet up until we arrive in Kinlochleven the next day. I hope Tom gets the clue, that he doesn't say, "What are you talking about?"

But thankfully Tom says, "3:30, I think," and I breathe a sigh of relief that I married the right man after all.

I look at my watch. It's now 3:00. I say, "But they might not be there until 4:00. We probably have a little time." I sit back, feeling satisfied that at least I have a date in an hour.

"There, there!" Hugh jerks the car to the side of the road and reaches for the white plastic sack next to me. He grabs the bag and plops it into Tom's lap, shouting, "Deer. Feed the deer!"

The bag is full of carrots.

I'm from a place with abundant wildlife and know not to feed them, so I ask, "Feed the deer?"

"Yes," Hugh says. "It's not like we're feeding them biscuits. That's not good for deer, but these are carrots!"

I figure Hugh knows more about Scottish deer than I do, so Tom and I approach the fence where three of them graze. Tom throws carrots toward the animals. The deer look startled, but then they begin sniffing the air. Tom throws more. "No, no, no," Hugh says, struggling out of the car and waddling over. "Give me that!" Tom hands over what's left in the bag. "They'll smell it and come to you," Hugh tells us. By then, a white Clydesdale across the field has seen what's happening and gallops toward us. The horse noses over the fence.

We feed the horse carrots, and Hugh is not at all happy about this. "Don't give them all to Duncan!" Clearly, we have turned our attention to the wrong ungulate.

"The horse is Duncan?" I ask.

"Aye." Hugh tries to take a carrot from the bag, but he can't because of his extreme muscle tremors, which I am only now noticing. Parkinson's? I wonder. Too much drink? Tom tries to help him get the bag open, but by now Hugh knows we don't know what we're doing when it comes to feeding the Scottish wildlife. The deer come closer, though Duncan is hogging all the carrots. Hugh ends up spilling the rest out on the other side of the fence. I look around, hoping for a place I can go behind a bush and pee, but Hugh says, "Oh well. Take some pictures." I have missed my opportunity to use the natural toilet.

Hugh seems disappointed in us. I wonder if he regrets picking us up.

We get back into the Peugeot, and we finally head back toward the highway. "Are you having a good time, dear?" he asks me again, and it's clear I'm not grateful enough for this impromptu Highlands tour, so I say, once again, "Oh yes."

When cars come from the opposite direction, the one closest to a turnout must back up. We have to do this many times, sometimes backing over the gravel right to the edge of the cliff. I think about Hugh's tremors, how shaky he is maneuvering the car.

I sometimes can't stop the stories in my head, and this is the tale that comes to me: Hugh loves to feed the deer but because of his medical condition and how very dangerous driving has become, his wife told him he could go feed the deer this last time. He would have to go alone because having anyone else in the car would be too dangerous. She is at home in her Glasgow suburb, wondering if he's going over the cliff this time. And I am wondering the same.

Then I notice the fawn. "A baby," I say, pointing out the window before realizing this will surely prolong our tour.

Seeing that we are out of carrots, I wonder what Hugh will do. He swerves over into a passing place and tells Tom, "Roll your window down." He hands Tom a roll of Polo mints and says, "Give them to the deer."

"The mints?" Tom asks.

"Yes," Hugh says. "Deer love mints."

Tom holds out a mint, and the doe approaches the car. Her spotted fawn stands back, watching.

"Hiya, Bambi." Hugh waves to the fawn.

"Mints are bad for deer," I say. "Don't give that deer Polo mints."

But Tom does as Hugh asks, and Hugh's right—deer love mints, so much that she's willing to take the treat from Tom's hand. Hugh can't get a picture because of his shaky hands, so he throws me his phone, saying, "Take a picture. And get the fawn."

We drive off again, and I see two more deer emerge from the fern, but I don't say a word. Hugh tells us he sends his photographs to his local paper, and sometimes they print them. I tell him I got some good ones for him.

"Deer are my favorite animal," he says.

I want to tell him he shouldn't feed them mints, that mints are worse even than biscuits, but I don't say anything else.

We drive back to the highway, and Hugh says, "I have two more spots to take you before I vanish."

"I have to pee," I say.

"What?" Hugh asks.

"She has to use the toilet," Tom says.

And it's 4:00, I think. We are late meeting Susan and Chris! But it's pretend Susan and Chris. Real Susan and Chris are in their glamping pod at the base of the ski resort, dealing with the midges.

"Just a waterfall and a view of the valley," Hugh says.

We drive through the valley, which is chock-full of camper vans, RVs, and hikers. I hope Hugh doesn't have a twitch and run into an oncoming car. He pulls over again and instructs us to climb a metal fence, walk one hundred meters, and take a picture of the waterfall. We do as we're told. I tell Tom I really do have to use the bathroom.

When we get back in, Tom tells Hugh again, "We better hurry. She has to use the toilet."

"Just one more stop." Hugh holds up a chubby finger.

After a while, we pull a U-turn into a small gravel parking place, and now we're looking back up the glen. The mist drapes over the mountaintops, reflecting in the River Coe. I get out to take one last photograph. Finally, we pull back onto the A82 toward our inn.

Hugh drops us off, we thank him, and I run inside to use the toilet. The drinks at the pub aren't all that great, and neither is the food. Susan and Chris aren't there to tell us stories about their Scottish lives, so we sit alone. We leave the pub and go to bed early. I scroll through my pictures, and the last one of the valley is the single most beautiful photograph of our three-week trip to Scotland. I think about Hugh, the very real possibility of his loneliness, and how he just wanted to share this with us—the magical landscape and feeding the deer, his very favorite thing in the world.

Scary Flyer

In Flight, December 2011

Even though he usually puts up with you, your husband says you are terrible to fly with. You call yourself a "scary flyer" when you really mean "scared." But others on the plane with you might agree when you say you are scary.

Because you have been called "The Next Great Travel Writer" by a national magazine, your friends label you a paradox and a contradiction in terms when you tell them you must have the window seat, so you can watch the wing. Something in you believes your very gaze will hold the plane in the air. Behind your back, your friends call you a freak. Strangers on the plane buy you Bloody Marys because whenever the aircraft makes its usual takeoff or flying or landing noises, you grab whoever is within reach and ask, "What was that? Did you hear that? Is that normal?" Or worse: "Do you think we're going down?"

But on your latest flight, you do not do that. You do something else that will prompt your husband to buy you the extra legroom, so you can sit in Economy Plus on your next flight. Alone.

You tell him the altercation with the teenager wasn't your fault. You tell him that when perfectly nice rats are contained in close quarters, they become afraid and aggressive, to which your husband counters: "You are not a rat."

You guess her to be about fourteen, which you find out later is too young for the emergency exit aisle seat she occupies. She wears pink braces and too much black eyeliner, making her look like a skinny metal-mouthed raccoon.

You are on an evening flight, reading poetry and minding your own business. The poetry makes you feel superior, as if you will be granted entrance into a special reading room in purgatory if your plane should crash. The image of the resulting fireball, with you inside it, crowds out the verses before you, but you try to focus. The teenager reclines her seat into your knees, disturbing your concentration.

You push back. That's when the struggle begins.

She leans forward and then throws all the weight of her skinny body onto your knees. Later, purple bruises will bloom on them. But right now, you push back. You have been lifting weights at the gym, and you can handle 135 pounds on the leg press. This is far heavier than the girl. She changes tactics. She bounces back and forth onto your knees, quickly, backforthbackforthbackforth. You hold strong, poetry book clutched in your hands, sweating a little from the exertion but feeling satisfied.

She jumps up from the seat, which flies forward with the counterweight of your legs.

"What the fuck?" she shouts.

You continue to read and ignore her. Or *pretend* to ignore her, feeling smug because you read poems and even write poems, as if this redeems you somehow even though you are being as big an asshole as the teenager. Bigger, in fact, since you *are* bigger and should know better.

"You better move your feet," she says. Your cabin reading light glints off her braces.

"My feet are not on your chair." This is true or your knees would not ache so.

"You better stop fucking kicking my chair."

"I don't know what you're talking about," you answer without looking up. Under your breath but loud enough for her to hear, you say, "Charming."

Your husband pretends to sleep through this. If he were asleep, you would know because his mouth would be hanging open with little gargling noises coming out. But his mouth is closed, so you know he's faking. If he wasn't faking and was really asleep, you might tell the girl she is a boring, entitled little fuck who is wearing too much eyeliner. So there! But even if you could say this without getting in trouble with your husband, the flight attendants would probably have to become involved, and you have no desire to be featured in the evening news: *Poet and Teenager Fight over Reclining Seat.* So you say nothing more and pretend to read poems.

The airplane pushback continues until she stands up again and says, "Fucking stop it."

"Maybe you should put your seat up a little. You're in the exit aisle. You have plenty of room." You say this without looking up.

"I'm not sleeping sitting up." You translate this in your head: *My comfort is more important than yours.* The good news in this for you is that you have been able to concentrate on something other than the plane's bubbling passage over "unstable air," which is what your captain has called it.

Even though you recently fought the urge to steal small jars of jams and jellies from your hotel to prove you are not, in fact, becoming your mother, you do just what your mother would do in this situation: you put a curse on the girl. You are careful with this, considering where you both are.

Lucky for you and your relationship with your husband, the plane's engines reverse, signaling your approach and landing. You know this noise well because you have inquired about it so many times. The flight attendant asks everyone to put their seat backs in the upright position. Yours already is, but you can hear the small cry of defeat in the girl's voice. Your knees ache, but you know you have won.

Even if your husband is mad at you, you consider the pushback fight an improvement over what you normally do on a plane, which is to panic while pretending to read, your heart rattling around in the cage of your ribs, your palms and armpits drenched with a sweat that smells like fear. Sometimes, if you deem it an appropriate time of day for drinking at either your departure or your arrival destination's time zone—which turns out to be often—you drink too many miniature bottles of wine.

As you wait for the thump of the wheels on the tarmac, you picture rats crowded into coach. They are seat-belted into rat-sized airplane seats reading their rat poems. And they are angry. But they are also hoping someone will buy them a Bloody Mary, wondering if there will be peanuts this time.

El Borracho

León, Nicaragua, December 2008

We boarded the collective bus; Tom sat in the front middle seat, and I squeezed in the back, between a woman carrying a large basket of fruit and a sleeping man holding a small orange backpack on his lap. The man smelled like tequila. I hated the stale smell of hard alcohol, so I tried to scoot closer to the woman and her fruit. She looked at me, annoyed. I wanted to tell her why I was encroaching, but she just kept staring out her window.

The man woke up, shook his head, and looked at me.

I thought I should be friendly, so I asked, "Where are you going?"

"León," he said.

"We're going there, too." I was pleased to practice my Spanish, even if it was with a drunk person. I tried to explain to him that Tom and I had been to Nicaragua together before, but this was our first time traveling to León. I pointed to the back of Tom's bald head. I continued, telling the man that I'd always wanted to visit the grave of the Nicaraguan poet Rubén Darío.

He looked confused by my poor Spanish and said, "I'm going to see my father."

"How nice. Does he live in León?"

"My father in heaven," he said.

"Heaven?" In Spanish, it's the same word for "sky" and "heaven," so I wasn't exactly sure what he meant.

"Yes," he said. "I am going to see my father in heaven."

"Great," was all I could think to say. Tom was asleep in front of me, but even if he had been awake, he wouldn't have understood our conversation. The man next to me fell asleep again, too. I looked past him out the window.

As I usually do, I made up stories in my head. This man, I told myself, was going to a church or cemetery in León, where he would visit his father's grave. I had wanted to go to León because Rubén Darío grew up there, returned when he was dying, and was buried there. I hoped to visit his grave, so this drunk man and I had this in common. But this man had been drinking because visiting a parent's grave makes for a hard trip—maybe even more difficult because for the past decade, they had been estranged. And hadn't Darío himself been an alcoholic? Just as I was satisfied with my make-believe story, the man woke up with a snort, looked at me, and said, "And I'm taking you with me."

"Me?" I pointed to myself.

"Yes."

"Where?" I asked.

"To see my father in heaven."

"No, you're going alone." I emphasized the word *solo*, the Spanish word for "alone." I also wondered if I should be using the formal or the friendly "you." Though I usually default to the formal except with children, I decided this situation called for friendly, so I used *tú* instead of *usted*. Plus, he was younger than me. And drunk, which had to count for something, linguistically speaking. I looked over at Tom, who was still asleep.

"I have a gun here," he said, patting his backpack, "and I'm going to go see my father in heaven, and you're coming with me."

I repeated what I thought he said, hoping there was some misunderstanding. He nodded and smiled, indicating I had understood. At first I felt a rush of pleasure, as I always do when I comprehend something correctly in Spanish.

But that faded very quickly.

Then he laughed, covering his mouth as if he had just experienced some private joke. I looked to the lady with the fruit, and she continued to gaze out her window. She must've known what was happening. I stared at her, but her body language said, *You're on your own with this one, sister.*

The drunk, whom I now thought of as El Borracho because I might as well enjoy my Spanish-speaking skills if I was about to be murdered, grinned at me for a while, sometimes giggling behind his hand.

He passed out again, and we pulled into a gas station. I shook Tom's shoulder and said, "We're getting out."

"We aren't in León yet, are we?" he asked, but I was already scrambling past the woman with her fruit. Tom climbed out after me. "What's going on with you? Why are you acting so crazy?"

"I'll tell you later. Let's get a taxi."

"Why did we get out of the bus?"

"Come with me," I said and headed over to the side of the road to hail a cab. Little girls selling soft drinks in plastic bags gathered around us, asking us to please buy their beverages. "Refrescos," they said. "¿Por qué no? ¿Por favor?"

A taxi pulled up, and the little girls tried to climb in with us. Tom waved them away, and they looked at me, pleading. The driver shouted at them, and they tumbled out of the taxi.

I told Tom about the drunk man on the bus. "What are you talking about now?" he asked.

"He said he was going to heaven and that he was taking me with him."

"Are you sure you understood him correctly?" Tom asked.

"I'm sure."

"Maybe you misunderstood?"

"I didn't," I said.

"Was he speaking in Spanish?"

I asked the taxi driver—in Spanish—to drop us off at the central park. The driver tried to get us to come with him to a hotel he knew about, but I told him we were staying with friends. Then I turned to Tom, and I said, "Yes, in Spanish."

"Let me guess. You were the one who started talking to him first?"

We paid the taxi driver, and I ignored Tom's question, which wasn't a real question because he already knew me well enough to know the answer.

We started walking through town, and I asked, "Isn't it beautiful here?" Vendors crowded the streets around the eighteenth-century Catedral Basílica de la Asunción. We wandered past fruit baskets, children's toys, fireworks, caged yellow and green parakeets. "Let's find a place to eat and look at the guidebook for a place to stay," I said, and Tom agreed.

We went into a restaurant and put our packs on the floor next to us. I ordered a piece of pizza, and Tom ordered ceviche.

"I can't eat this," I said when my pizza came. "It's like cardboard."

"That's what you get for ordering pizza in Nicaragua. You want some of this?" Tom asked.

"No way." I shook my head.

"Why not?"

"We're too far away from the ocean to eat fish."

"Not that far," Tom said.

"Far enough."

The hotel we chose, La Casona Colonial, had a tiled fountain sputtering in the leafy garden. The room's dark wood furniture looked like it dated back to Rubén Darío's time. A ceiling fan spun over the *cama matrimonial*. It seemed so romantic until Tom said, "I don't feel so good."

"You don't want to go walk around?" I asked.

"No, you go without me."

I dropped my pack and walked out into the streets. I wondered where El Borracho was, but mostly I worried about Tom. I bought soda water and crackers for him. By the time I returned, Tom was lying on the concrete floor of the bathroom, his head in the toilet. I could see him there on the floor because the door to the bathroom was a swinging wooden flap like you'd find at the entrance to a saloon, so it didn't offer much in the way of privacy. I asked him if I could help him, but he said he wanted to be alone.

I went to bed and listened as cockroach legs scuttled on the tile floor. A wooden cross hung on the yellow wall. The ceiling fan whirled above. The fountain outside bubbled, a mosaic of water and night. Broken shades clattered against the windows. The television picked up an American station. Spanish subtitles scrolled along the screen. A plane circled Boston, the landing gear stuck. I would find out later that a woman I went to graduate school with was on the plane. Luckily, it landed safely. I reached for the remote, turned off the television. The sounds of retching swelled from the bathroom, and I tried not to worry about Tom but did anyway.

For two days, I meandered through the streets alone, past the colonial buildings and churches. I kept coming back to check on Tom, bringing him crackers, bottled water, toilet paper, clean towels. "Thanks for being so nice," he said.

"De nada," I told him, it's nothing, and I meant it. I worried about him and whether or not I should try to get him medical help until he finally said, "I think I'm starting to feel better."

On the last day, Tom still wasn't up to sightseeing, so I visited Rubén Darío's grave on my own. Darío had been interred in the city's cathedral and placed under a sculpture of a marble lion. When Tom asked me why I wanted to visit his grave, I said only that he was a poet I liked, hoping that answer was enough.

Darío traveled the world, took many lovers, suffered the loss of children, and then returned to his hometown and died of alcoholism at forty-nine. I had become interested in him when I taught a class in Salamanca on the Spanish poet Federico García Lorca, who had been deeply influenced by Darío. One of the things Lorca admired about Darío was his faith in art, the way he thought poetry could save him. Both poets met early, unfortunate deaths—Franco ordered the thirty-eight-year-old Lorca shot in 1936. Art hadn't protected them, had in fact helped lead Lorca to his demise, but that wasn't what it meant to be saved. Poetry can't save us from our mortality; rather, art creates something out of nothing, giving meaning to our lives. But this, too, is fleeting. My own father had been a writer and an alcoholic. He said he felt like the world was sandpaper on his skin. That he was living in a black hole.

My father died when I was twenty-four, so I was too young to understand. Too young to forgive him for his drinking. Yet I could withhold those same judgements for the Nicaraguan poet and accept the shadowy figure of Darío for who he had been. I didn't realize it at the time, but my ability to see the whole person, the man who was both broken and brilliant, the drunk and the poet, helped pave my path to forgiving my own father.

I left the cathedral and walked to the Iglesia el Calvario. I sat in a wooden pew and stared up at the harvest murals and a lifelike Christ flanked by the two thieves who had been crucified along with him. The church bells rang, and the birds flew to and from the rafters of the ceiling. I wondered if El Borracho had made it to see his father in *el cielo*—or maybe it was just a metaphor?

Since Rubén Darío was known as the father of the nineteenth-century Spanish American Modernismo movement, hadn't I also come to León to visit my own poet father in heaven? How would that sound, translated in my broken Spanish?

It didn't matter. As I had learned from my parents, the true story was the one you believed.

Dangers and Annoyances

~~~~~~

Perhaps travel cannot prevent bigotry,
but by demonstrating that all peoples cry,
laugh, eat, worry, and die, it can introduce
the idea that if we try and understand each
other, we may even become friends.

MAYA ANGELOU

Avoiding danger is no safer in the long
run than outright exposure. The fearful
are caught as often as the bold.

HELEN KELLER

The Riffraff in the Magical Kingdom

Celebration, United States, June 2008

Cohabitation was a trial, as there were probably no two people more afraid of commitment than us. The plan was that I would move in with Tom for the summer and write my dissertation while he was at work. What better place to write a dissertation than Florida in the summer? And we could see if we could make the relationship work without the comfortable buffer of a country between us. I also hoped that even though Tom found me "difficult," I would prove to be a good partner.

On my first day of living in Celebration with him, I poisoned myself.

Celebration is a Disney-planned community. Houses squeeze in close to each other, adorned with shutters that are not really shutters. Chimneys dart from roofs of houses without fireplaces. Porch chairs sit empty under ceiling fans. Plaster pillars hold up nothing. White picket fences line sidewalks where miniature poodles and Pekinese wearing sunglasses and yellow rain slickers trot by man-made ponds on their way to the Dog Bark Bakery. Tight-lipped women push strollers past fountains, and golf carts zoom by the toll plaza at the entrance to the freeway. Epiphytes and cormorants cling to old cypress trees at the edge of the asphalt. Downtown you can find ladies hats, baby clothes, antique-looking jewelry and dolls, old-fashioned ice cream, ale, an art deco movie house, and English tea—nostalgia for a time that never existed. You cannot find gasoline, a pharmacy, or groceries.

At a café, I overheard an old woman ask a waiter for water for her terrier. When he brought it, she said, "Oh no, I only give Rocky spring water. Never water from the tap."

I drank tap water all summer.

In Celebration, Monday is the day the lawns are trimmed, Tuesday is the day the leaves are blown, Wednesday is recycling. Nothing happens on Thursday. Friday, the shrubs are shaped. Every evening at eight o'clock, a pesticide called Biomist fills the streets and ball fields. Nine o'clock begins the fifteen-minute fireworks display. During the holidays, the life-size nativity scene plays "A King Is Born." Mary and Joseph rock baby Jesus with mechanical stride. Children make angels in foamy snow blown from machines on lampposts that surround the man-made lake downtown.

When I have a big project in front of me, I do everything I can think of before actually sitting down and writing. This includes doing things I wouldn't normally consider, like cleaning. Even though I usually have no problem ignoring dust and fur balls floating along the floorboards, I tell myself that I can't possibly write in a dirty house. I also thought cleaning Tom's apartment would earn me some girlfriend points. I tackled the bathroom first.

But I couldn't finish the toilet because I started to feel so sick, I thought I was dying. I considered calling one of my sisters, but I knew they would worry, and what could they do from California? I debated whether or not I should bother Tom at work. I decided this wasn't normal, that it was better to call Tom than for him to come home to my dead body on his bathroom floor.

Tom asked, "Did you feel sick when you got up this morning?"

"No," I said, my forehead on the edge of the toilet.

"What's wrong, exactly?"

"My eyes are burning and my throat hurts. And I feel like I'm going to throw up. It's probably just vertigo, but I feel bad—really bad."

"What were you doing right before you got sick?" Tom asked.

"I was cleaning." The bathroom tile felt cold on my back, and the ceiling spun.

"What were you cleaning?"

"The bathroom." I closed my eyes, but it made the spinning worse.

"What did you use?"

"The stuff you had. The powder and the spray. I mixed it in the toilet."

"You did what? Read me the labels," Tom said in a more urgent way than his usual practical manner.

I sat up and grabbed the cleaning products from the sink. "Ajax with bleach and Windex with ammonia." I lay back down on the floor, wondering why he was so worried about cleaning products at a time like this. Was he worried I didn't clean the toilet correctly? I was annoyed.

"You didn't use those together," he said.

"What? Why are you asking me all these questions?"

"Where are you now?"

"Lying on the bathroom floor."

"You need to get up and go outside onto the balcony. Can you do that?"

"Yes," I said, not knowing why. I rose from the bathroom floor and staggered outside, despite the nausea, vertigo, and coughing. The thick air felt suffocating. I turned on the outside porch fan and sat on the ground. The hot, humid air circled above me.

Despite his important job and busy schedule, Tom was home within twenty minutes. I was still lying on the balcony in my pajamas.

"Are you feeling better?" he asked.

I nodded.

"You didn't know you can't mix bleach and ammonia?"

I shook my head. I told him I thought he asked about cleaning products to see if I was doing a thorough job.

"How could you not know that? Everyone knows that."

I started to cry. "You *do* want a midwestern wife."

"What are you talking about? Why do you keep asking me that?"

"I don't know. I'm just not good at cleaning." It seemed like maybe my ex-husband, Craig, had been right when he told me that once Tom got to know me, he wouldn't want me.

"You're procrastinating on your dissertation, that's what I think," Tom said.

"You think I made myself sick on purpose?" I closed my eyes and then opened them, trying to decide which way made the vertigo worse.

But it was true: the only thing less appealing than scrubbing a toilet was writing a dissertation. Tom said, "You don't have to clean my apartment. Just write." I nodded.

"Promise me," he said. "You won't try cleaning anything again?"

I agreed, and with that he left and went back to work. Everyone who has ever tried to write a book knows that cleaning is like sharpening pencils. And who knew you couldn't mix bleach with ammonia?

Everyone did, according to Tom.

My second day in Celebration went by without much fanfare. I got a rejection for some poems, the shaky scrawl saying: *These poems seem unfinished.* We also got a notice on the door that read: *There is an unauthorized object on the balcony that is subject to fine.* Said object was my yoga mat. Without being able to clean my way through procrastination, I ventured out, looking for a place to walk without sidewalks but finding only golf courses and parking lots.

That evening, Tom and I ate dinner at the English pub downtown. We sat at the bar, and I said to the pretty blonde bartender, "It seems like people here sure drink a lot." She assured me this was indeed the case. I told Tom about getting lost on my walk. "I know a place we can walk on trails," he said. "We'll go over the weekend."

We did, in fact, hike in this park, which I called the "man hookup" park. From what I could tell, aside from us, the only people who frequented the park—and they mostly stuck to the parking lot—were men looking for companionship, including one who wore hiking boots, a backpack, and nothing else. Tom asked me how I knew that's what they were doing. I said, "I may not know much about cleaning products, but I know someone looking for a date when I see it."

My third day in Celebration, the property manager had to call Tom at work, and I knew I was coming dangerously close to being sent home.

But the fight wasn't my fault, at least not entirely so.

I had been at the pool, taking notes on Ann Radcliffe for my dissertation. A little girl humped the concrete edge of the pool. Her mother chatted on the phone, sneaking drinks of a cocktail she kept hidden under her plastic chair. A man across the water answered his phone. "You *are* fucking kidding me, right?" he said, then, "Tim, how could you do this to me?" then he howled, "Tiiiimmmmm." It was easy enough to gather that Tim enjoyed lunch with another young man, which prompted much frantic text messaging. A plane flew by and wrote *Jesus Loves U* in the sky. I wanted to point this out to the distraught young man but then thought better of it. He was still busy texting. A cardinal sang from a nearby tree, a lizard busied himself with push-ups on the lounge chair next to me, and a blue heron landed in the swimming pool. She realized her mistake and flew off again.

A boy walked by, outside the pool's gates. He carried a coffee can with a homemade sign that read: *Help Fight Muscular Dystrophy*. He went door-to-door, asking the neighbors, "Would you like to help fight muscular dystrophy?" An older man with long greasy hair trailed him by about half a block.

I couldn't concentrate on *The Mysteries of Udolpho*, so I went next door to the gym—both the gym and the pool were in the same gated area, exclusively for the residents of Tom's apartment complex. I peeked in and saw a big, tanned, blonde woman walking on the treadmill. I went to the bathroom to change into my gym clothes, and by the time I returned, the gym was empty, though Oprah still blasted from one television, cartoons from another. I turned off both televisions, put in my earbuds, and started to run on the treadmill.

The blonde woman returned with three children in tow, who wore bathing suits and were dripping wet. The smallest one got on the treadmill next to me. She jogged alongside me in her swimsuit and bare feet. While she stared at me, which was more unnerving than it sounds, I took out one of my earbuds and said, "You know, you shouldn't play on the equipment without shoes. You could get hurt."

I was just trying to be nice. In a passive aggressive way.

The little girl smirked at me. That's when the blonde woman stomped over, and though I was listening to my music, I could tell by the waving of her arms, her facial expressions, and the manic movement of her mouth that she was shouting.

Again I took out one of my earbuds and said, "Excuse me? Are you talking to me?"

"Talking to you? Yes—after you stole my treadmill and turned off my shows, you *dare* speak to my children?"

"Your children shouldn't be on the equipment without shoes," I said.

"How dare you!"

I returned to my music and tried to ignore her, but by this time, all three of her children were standing with her, pointing at me and saying who knows what.

"Listen, it was for their safety that I said something." Then, though I probably shouldn't have, I added, "You know, you should thank me."

"Thank you? You are not to speak to my children. Who are you? A *renter*?"

"No, I'm not a renter." I was still running but out of breath by now.

"Oh, so you're an owner? Then how come I've never seen you before?"

"My boyfriend is." Suddenly Tom's weird choice to buy an apartment in Celebration, Florida, gave me cause to gloat. I wiped my entitled brow.

"That's lower than being a renter! You're a bad influence on my children." This struck me as interesting because I hadn't had enough contact with her bratty brood to influence them one way or the other. In my memory, she also said something about living in sin. Then she asked me this: "Have you been drinking too much?" She made a motion of slamming back a shot.

"Are you crazy?" I asked, though it seemed obvious enough. Perhaps I had been drinking too much, like the rest of Celebration, but I wasn't sure what that had to do with this. I certainly hadn't had anything to drink that day.

At least not yet.

"How *dare* you!" she said again, and with that, she strutted out of the gym with her three children dripping behind her. I watched as she headed into the office of the building manager. I wasn't about to have her tell her side of the story without getting to tell mine, so I also went into the freezing, air-conditioned office. I could hear the woman yelling, saying how I had stolen her treadmill, turned off Oprah and her children's cartoons, dared to speak to her children. When she saw me, she said, "And she's not an owner. She's not even a renter. She's just a . . . visitor."

"I didn't say that." I tried to catch my breath.

"Oh really. Then what did you say?" She put her hand on her hip. Her children giggled as if she had really shown me.

"I said my fiancé owned one of the units."

"You didn't say fiancé before. I bet he isn't even your fiancé!"

She was right, of course, but I couldn't take it back now.

"Listen ladies," the apartment manager said. "It sounds like there's been a disagreement here."

"No kidding," the woman said. "You should call her so-called fiancé, to make sure she didn't sneak in."

"I have a key." I held it up for proof. "I didn't sneak in."

"What is your boyfriend's name?" she asked.

"Fiancé." I half-believed it myself by now. Then I told the manager Tom's name.

"Do you mind if I call him?" he asked.

"He's at work." I turned to the woman and said, "He has a very important job."

The manager said, "I'm sure he does. I'm sure this has just been a misunderstanding."

At that, the woman turned for the door and said over her shoulder, "This place is being overrun by the riffraff."

"It sure is," I called to the woman and her wet little brutes who trailed after her. They all left the building, the outside humidity rushing in like a hot wave as she opened the glass door.

"She's crazy," I told the manager.

"She seemed very angry," he said.

"And crazy. I didn't start it." Couldn't he see that she had started it? I hoped that the manager wouldn't use the term "fiancé" when he called Tom. If he did, I would just have to explain. Or deny that I had said it. I practiced saying, "Oh, he probably just assumed that."

I left and reclaimed my spot on the treadmill. But before I began to run, I left Tom a voicemail, warning him that he might be getting a call from the property manager. "It wasn't my fault . . ." Then I called my mother, because I knew that even though she

was Oprah's number one fan, she would side with me uncon-
ditionally. Sometimes a lack of boundaries has its advantages. I
could tell her the story any way I chose, and both of us—if it made
me look good and the blonde woman look bad—would prefer this
version of the truth.

The manager did in fact call Tom, but luckily when he came
home that night, Tom just laughed and said, "What's going to
happen tomorrow?"

On my fourth day, a notice at the pool read: *The pool is not in com-
pliance with Florida Health Code, Chapter 69 E-9 and may endanger
the health, safety, and welfare of persons using this facility. The pool
is closed.* I guessed that one of the blonde woman's children shit
in the pool but was never able to confirm my suspicions.

From then on, I took to lying on the carpet in Tom's apartment,
writing my dissertation. I experimented with turning off the air
conditioner and letting the sweat pool between my breasts. When
Tom came home, he asked, "What the hell is going on? Is the air
conditioner broken?" I told him I was practicing climate acceptance. He went around closing the windows and said, "Do you
know how fast mold will start growing on the carpet?"

For the rest of the summer, I wrote, taking breaks from the air
conditioning to swim in the pool (after they reopened it) and jog
past the golf course in the sweltering heat. At night, Tom and I
drank white wine on the small balcony, covering our glasses with
our palms when the Biomist truck came by to spray. I called the
city to ask what was in Biomist, and the lady on the phone said,
"It's Biomist."

I said, "Yes, but what's *in* Biomist?"

She told me she didn't understand my question and hung up.
Later, I would do some research and find out the main ingredient
in the nightly spray was permethrin, which has been declared
"completely safe" in that it only causes skin rash in humans and

kills insects and aquatic life indiscriminately, including honey bees.

By the end of the summer, I was tan, fit, and my pile of papers had become a dissertation. I learned to write poems to procrastinate on my project, so I ended up with a poetry collection, too. I saw the blonde woman just once more, from across the crowded pub, because it's a small world after all. She looked like she had drunk a few too many, and she didn't recognize me, or at least pretended not to, because everyone in Celebration is too happy to be bothered by the riffraff.

Middle-Aged Vagabonding

San Blas Islands, Panama, December 2009

"It's so cute," the pretty young traveler told us as we got off the boat, "that *you're* staying here." She was one of the twenty-somethings staying on Sunidup Island, off the coast of Panama. With 378 islands in the San Blas Archipelago, the Gunas say there's an island for every day of the year. Most of these islands remain uninhabited; the occupied ones are autonomous reservations for the Guna people, and a few of them host travelers. There are the young party islands and the more expensive, luxury places, which attract older visitors. Tom and I opted for the cheaper accommodations because that's how we'd always traveled.

It was there on Sunidup Island that we learned we had outgrown shoestring adventures. We were twice as old as everyone else on the island, so I didn't have to ask what this pretty blonde meant by "cute."

We squeezed a two-week holiday into our busy work schedules and were traveling around Panama without an itinerary like we might have done back when we had less money and more time. On a bus, we'd read about the San Blas Islands, or Kuna Islands as they were known then, and decided to go on a whim. In Panama City, we met with a travel agent named Junior, whom we found in our guidebook. When we chose the cheaper option, he said, "I'm not sure that's the right island for you."

We shrugged it off. What did Junior know about us?

"No, really," he said.

We assured him we'd be fine, that we were used to roughing it. We had developed a smugness that comes with shoestring travel, that feeling we were making a smaller environmental impact, or had gained a greater understanding of the local culture because we spent less money.

Not until we saw which tourists got off the boat with us did we know what Junior had meant. Not a one of them was a day over twenty-one, many of them still teenagers.

Maybe we didn't want to admit that we were, in fact, getting old.

When we stepped onto Sunidup Island, it didn't matter that we were much older than everyone else because of the travel-brochure beauty. All the travel writing clichés were true. Aquamarine water lapped onto white powdery sand. Palm trees curved over the sea, heavy with coconuts. Cabins with sandy floors scattered around the island. And that sounded good, too—the sand between our toes.

The small island took about twenty minutes to walk around, which we did with our backpacks because our cabin didn't have a door. We sat outside our cabaña, drinking rum and watching the Guna women paddle by in dugout canoes. No one asked us if we wanted to play volleyball or participate in a shot-put contest with a coconut, and that was fine by us. We could just sit there, still living out our shoestring dreams.

Tom and I had gotten engaged the month before, and we talked about what we wanted from the rest of our lives. "What do you think about kids?" I asked.

"Seems kind of selfish," Tom said.

"Not to have them?" That's what I had constantly heard: if you were a woman who didn't want children, you must be selfish.

"No," he said. "The earth has enough problems. I'm not sure how I feel about adding to them."

This talk of children was in the abstract because I had recently turned thirty-nine, and though certainly women my age were having children, I didn't know if I wanted to be one of them. I knew a life of travel and one of children were in opposition, or at least the latter made the former a lot more difficult. I also knew having kids was much worse for the planet than travel. And while we couldn't make that decision for anyone else, we could make it for ourselves. Tom and I smiled at each other, clinked glasses, and drank our sticky, sweet rum.

The sun set, and that's when the drinking games began, led by Tony, the island's host. He was a gorgeous young Guna man who never wore anything but turquoise board shorts, beaded ankle bracelets, and a shark's tooth necklace. He had one long braid. "I used to have two," he said. "But I cut it off by mistake when I was chopping a coconut in two—made me so mad. I'd been growing it for twenty-two years."

"You mean since you were born?" I asked.

"Yeah," he smiled.

Tony bragged about his sexual prowess. "I've had girlfriends from all over," he told me. "That's how come I can speak four languages: Guna, Spanish, French, and English. I even had a Jewish girlfriend once." He counted them off on his fingers.

"You speak Hebrew?" I asked.

"Nah, only one girl, that," he said, holding up one finger.

"All those women came to your island?" I asked.

"Not all. Once, I went to Barcelona, and everyone, they thought I was from the Amazon. They didn't know I could speak Spanish. I pretended I didn't, so I could hear what they said about me. And the women? They all talked about how beautiful I was."

"I'm sure they did," I said, and he smiled. He *was* beautiful, and I supposed that if I was twenty years younger, I would have gotten in line behind the French and Spanish girls, bringing his Jewish count to two.

Tom and I shared our cabaña with mosquitoes, and the welts swelled across my back and shoulders, on my ankles and feet. Two overlapping twin mattresses on plywood served as our bed, and our sand floor meant our sheets were full of it; toes in the sand sounds awfully romantic until you consider the other crevices of the human body. Romance isn't exactly the result unless you have a sandpaper fetish.

Tony had devised the nightly drinking game, to which Tom and I were not invited. But the community area was right outside our cabaña, so we had no trouble hearing every word. Each participant had to down an entire beer in three seconds, while everyone else shouted, "One, two, three"—or in Tony's accent, "One, two, tree," which everyone else found so charming, they copied it. If someone didn't finish his or her beer, he or she would endure what Tony called "the punishment," which meant drinking rum to yet another count of "one, two, tree." The other choice of punishment was skinny-dipping in the sea, which meant a lot more whooping and hollering. Meanwhile, the generators ran, smelling of gasoline, and the speakers— located about three feet from our cabaña—blasted the same loop.

We tried to sleep on the lopsided twin mattresses, which would have been impossible even if it had been quiet. One thing about being older was that I was now much more protective of my rest. I tried to ignore the sand in my crotch and wrapped my head in the paper-thin pillows. Even with earplugs, the bad covers of "Birth-day" and "Get Up, Stand Up" reverberated in my head.

It was two o'clock in the morning now, and I asked Tom, "Can you sleep?" I scratched at the bites on my ankles until they bled.

"Yeah, right," he said. "Who can sleep?"

It was clear we were the only ones on the island trying to do just that. It was like being on a drunken backpacker version of *Survivor*, and I wanted to be voted off the island. Around three o'clock, I sat up in our lopsided bed and said, "I can't take it."

"I know. It's loud," Tom said.

"And this bed. What's up with this fucking bed?" I stood up and shined the baneful bed with my flashlight. "Maybe it would be bet-ter if we piled these mattresses on top of each other and slept on it like a twin rather than a double sloping down from the middle."

Tom squinted into the light. "Whatever you want." Whenever he said these three words, it was because he knew I was on the verge of losing it.

"You have to get up," I told him, so Tom stood and waited in the sand while I pulled the twin mattresses on top of each other.

"Just don't get sand everywhere," Tom said.

"I can't help it; there's sand every-fucking-where. What am I supposed to do?" A crab dropped from our bed and into the sand, scurrying across my mosquito-bitten feet. "Fuuuucccckkk!" I screamed.

"Are you having a moment?"

From outside came more "one, two, tree" and then a cover of the Eagles' "Hotel California" that sounded like it was being sung by a chorus of seals.

"Yes, I'm having a fucking moment. I can't stay here another night." That was how we referred to it when I lost my shit: I was *having a moment*.

What we didn't know then was that the San Blas Islands were under threat from the rising seas. In our lifetimes, perhaps, the indigenous people will have to be relocated, and the islands will disappear, making my "moment" seem even more selfish and self-indulgent. In time, Tony might have to leave behind his way of life and go to Panama City or someplace else to start an entirely new kind of life. He would no longer be the charming island host; instead, he would be another indigenous person looking for work, along with the fishermen and coconut farmers and artists who created the colorful *molas*.

It would be two years before anyone studied this climate-change catastrophe in the San Blas Islands, and it wouldn't be widely reported in the news for another five. What I did know was that the Gunas' ancestral homeland had become a playground for both young backpackers and rich tourists. Each time we bought *molas* from the women who paddled dugout canoes, I told myself tourism was helpful to them; it was an important part of their economy. This was true, of course: the money from my modern, mechanized lifestyle would help them in the short term, while my plane ride there contributed to their demise. Since then, I have thought about the way I have created a life around travel, for better and for worse, and I wrestle with the ethical question looming: if I care about the environment, should I travel at all?

This is a question I don't want to ask, but I must. I go around and around, looking for a way out of this dilemma, but every path leads to another justification, another what-about-this? I tell myself that though there are environmental costs of travel, there are also social benefits. We realize that while there may be cultural differences, the core of who we are as human beings remains the same. We hate what we fear, but we cannot fear what we know. And maybe it isn't even hate or fear that are the problems but indifference. If you have never been to the San Blas Islands, the land is an abstraction, the people, statistics. When I think about the fate of the islands, I see Tony—his one long braid, the afternoon light glinting off his shark's tooth necklace, and the easy way he smiled and gathered his guests around him, sharing the beauty of his island and the magic of its rum.

I want to say this: we never had those children, their little feet widening our own carbon footprints. But I also know this is true: we can bargain our way out of anything. Having no children means even more travel, maybe not exactly balancing the scales, but still. Tom and I know we have to find a new way into our middle-aged vagabonding years, one that includes fewer plane trips, more overland travel, longer stays, less consumerism.

It's hard to separate what I know now and what I knew then; memory shifts with knowledge. I do know that I wasn't reacting out of any kind of environmental or cultural stewardship. I was mad because there was a crab in my bed and sand in my crotch.

Sassy at Burning Man

Black Rock City, United States, September 2017

The morning after it happened, the men at my Burning Man camp said some version of this: *Show me who he is, and I will break his arms.* Our unofficial camp leader, a woman a few years older than me, said: "We don't have to be assholes to him. We can give him a chance to see what he did was wrong and help him be a better person."

This is what's wrong with women, or at least what has been wrong with me. This is what I have always done—"help" men become better versions of themselves, which amounts to accepting unacceptable behavior.

I wasn't playing along anymore.

I said, "That was his mother's job, and quite frankly, she did a shitty job. He's a sexual predator, and if he comes near me again, I'm calling law enforcement—not a Black Rock Ranger but the police—and having him removed from the playa."

In my own way, I was being one of those women-blaming women. His mother's fault? I realize that was so very wrong as well. You know whose job it was to make sure he was a good person? It was his own fucking job.

At Burning Man, you're supposed to resolve your issues with a Black Rock Ranger, someone who can help negotiate problems on the playa, but I was beyond that. I wanted to call someone with handcuffs and a squad car, someone who could take him away. But would they? I didn't know.

I know what you're thinking about Burning Man. And if you haven't been there, I probably can't convince you that before this

247

incident, it felt like one of the safest places I have ever been. But let's say stereotypes mean more than my lived experience, that I was a woman in a place that wasn't safe. How safe is the disco, the bar, the street at night? How safe is the workplace, the classroom, the church, the synagogue, or the mosque?

Any place can be the wrong place. I guess I have always known that but never wanted to accept the knowledge and everything that goes along with it. That is, until recently. I was forty-six years old at that Burning Man. Old enough to know better.

The afternoon after I confronted him, I rode my beach cruiser across the playa, an ancient lakebed. Wind tumbled into a cloud on the distant horizon—a dust storm. But I wasn't afraid, even though I probably should have been. I headed for deep playa alone, past the art structures and mutant vehicles—a bumblebee, the wooden phoenix, a wise owl, and the one-eyed cyclops blasting house music. I could have been caught in a whiteout, but I didn't care. I was too angry to be afraid. And I was thinking, *That fucker!*

But then I realized I had finally done the thing that for so many years I could not do—I not only stood my ground with a man; I did so without apology.

It had taken me too long to get here, but now there was only this thought: *Here I am at last.*

I was camping with friends from my hometown, and our Burning Man gift (Burning Man runs on a gift economy) was a bar we called Tahoe Twisted G-Spot, which doesn't make sense anywhere except at Burning Man. My friend Tammy and I were scheduled to bartend; she stood behind the bar, and I went out onto the dusty street to bark in our "customers," though because this was our gift, the drinks were free. I shouted into the megaphone: "Get your drinks here! Organic juice and vodka. Bad advice. Cupcakes." A man in a sarong and a straw hat came walking up, though it was more of a swagger. He wanted a drink and advice. I told him to tell me a problem, and I would solve it. I love nothing more than to give advice. If I can't solve my own problems, then the next best thing is to solve someone else's.

He told me about his neighbor at Burning Man, how he had been with her but didn't want to sleep with her again. I told him to be up-front with her, that there were plenty of other men, I guessed, who would gladly stand in and become her new Burning Man boyfriend. The man with the straw hat told me that was terrible advice and continued his swagger to the bar. I went back to shouting pithy slogans into my megaphone.

I should have realized at that very moment he was seeing how far he could go with me because "been with her" and "slept with her" are my interpretations, my approximation of his language—he said he fucked her. Didn't he? I'm not sure, but looking back I think, yes, he must have said it in this way. Even my memory has learned to translate for men.

This is also where I tell myself I should have known better, but I'm done blaming myself.

When my bar shift was over, I poured myself a vodka with organic juice and pulled up a lawn chair next to this man with the sarong and straw hat. We introduced ourselves, using our Burning Man names. I told him I was Sassy. He went by Dizzy. We were about the same age and ended up talking about the music of our youth and then moved on to other aspects of popular culture from the '70s, '80s, and '90s—the Bee Gees, roller-skating parties, the time the Brady Bunch stole the Hawaiian idol and were cursed until they returned it. And all those *Twilight Zone* episodes! It's fun to remember these things with somebody else, especially with organic juice and vodka in your hand, the sun on your shoulders, the desert stretched out before you.

I want to say this: it's okay to sit down next to a handsome stranger and laugh with him. It means nothing other than you are sitting down and laughing. Maybe it's for myself that I am saying this.

His pupils were pinpricks. I guessed he was on something, but I don't know how to read pupils. I had to use the restroom, and he said he did, too, so we walked to the porta-potties together. Within minutes, a dust storm built on the horizon before us, and by the time we finished in the porta-potties, we had to run through a whiteout and back to my camp for cover. We banged on the door of my friend's RV, seeking refuge.

By now, Dizzy was complimenting everything from my freckles to my feet, but none of it seemed overly flirtatious—as least that's what I told myself. He was a massage therapist and kept telling me he could see I was tense. I told him I was happily married and that he was not allowed to touch me. Yes, I said those words: "You are not allowed to touch me." Burning Man can be a sexually charged place but also a place that promotes boundaries. I wanted to be clear, and I was.

In the RV, Dizzy gave Tammy a shoulder massage, and I felt relieved that his attention had turned elsewhere. I told myself he was on something—maybe ecstasy—and he just wanted to touch someone. It had nothing to do with me.

After the dust storm, I said I was going out onto the playa. The sun was setting, and the light would be perfect for photographs. He asked, "Can I come with you?" I told him I was taking my bike. He said his bike was at a camp next door. I shrugged and said, "Sure, why not?"

We watched a giant marionette strut across the playa and then stopped at a dome with fish-eye lens holes. I went inside to take a photograph. Just as I did, Dizzy stood outside in front of the small window and flashed me his dick.

"Seriously?" I said even though no one was listening. I was shocked and then angry. *Fuck him*, I thought. *I have to get away from him.*

And I will say this also: his dick was not impressive.

While I was still kneeling at the small window, I deleted the blurry picture off my camera—I wanted to erase him. I came out of the dome, and Dizzy was there, facing the other way, massaging a woman's shoulders. I saw this as my chance to escape. I got onto my bicycle and pedaled away without his notice.

On my way back, I ran into friends at a party, so I stayed and listened to music for a while. By the time I returned to my camp, it was dark. Dizzy was there, sitting at our makeshift bar with some of the others. He came up to me and said, "You left because you were jealous, right? You saw me talking to those other girls, and you got mad." He smiled as if this pleased him.

"I was mad," I said, "but not because of that."

"Then what?" This time, he smiled in that way men do when they are trying to be charming. When they are trying to get beneath our skin.

I didn't want my campmates to hear this exchange; I was afraid someone would say that getting flashed at Burning Man was no big deal. Hadn't I enjoyed coffee and eggs with the shirt-cocking neighbor? I knew this was different but wasn't sure how to explain it. Dizzy and I stood in the shadow of an RV, and I said, "You flashed me."

"I didn't mean anything by it," he said. But he laughed, as if I were being silly, making such a fuss. Especially at Burning Man!

And then I did that thing I wish I did not do—I told him we could be friends, that his attention was flattering. The same shit I had been saying for years to men who acted like assholes: *It's okay. You're okay. Don't worry, I'll shoulder this again.*

And had I really told myself that we could be friends because we both liked the same episode of *The Twilight Zone*? Was that enough to make up for the dick flash?

As a young woman, I believed my charm was my power and that if I was assertive, I would give up the only power I held. This is where I want to apologize to other women because I never properly stood up for myself. I let men think that the lines they crossed—into sexual harassment, assault, predation—were annoying but, on the whole, all right.

But here's the thing: it was never all right.

"Just don't do anything like that again," I think I said to Dizzy, there in the dusty light of the nearby RV. Somehow, I never had the right words—only the shame I felt. Or maybe I was too embarrassed to make a fuss. I mean, shouldn't I be grateful that someone was paying attention to me? Wouldn't that give me power like my mother had suggested? And if it went badly, as it so often did, wasn't that somehow my fault?

Dizzy agreed that he wouldn't do it again. We might even have hugged. I hope we didn't, but I can't say for sure. By then, I had had a couple drinks. And I was in a hurry, leaving again to cross the playa on my bicycle for my friend Blondie's memorial at Celestial Bodies Bar. I do know this for sure: Dizzy asked me if he could go with me, and I said he couldn't. He hadn't even known Blondie. I went to my pickup truck, got some water, a sweater, more lights for my bike, and I pedaled off.

After Blondie's memorial, I rode back across the playa to my own camp. Glowing neon colors from art structures, decorated bicycles, and art cars flickered like a carnival of lights in the darkness. It was near midnight, and for many, the party was just getting started, but I was ready to go to sleep. I returned to camp, and Dizzy still sat at our bar, but I was able to sneak past to where I was parked without him spotting me. I brushed my teeth and then crawled into the back of my truck and fell asleep.

When I told my husband about my plans to sleep in the back of the truck, he said, "But it doesn't lock. Someone can reach in." I said that this was Burning Man—no one would ever do such a thing. I would be completely safe. This was my eighth year at Burning Man, and I had never felt threatened. I may have even called my husband silly.

But from a deep sleep I emerged, thinking I heard someone trying to get into the cab of the truck. I shrugged it off and turned over—maybe one of my campmates came home drunk and mistook my truck for theirs?

Then a few minutes later, someone turned the latches on the camper shell, opened the window, and started to pull down the tailgate. I shot up: "Who's there? Who is it?"

"It's me."

"Me? Me?" I said. "There's no one here named Me."

Only my husband, my mother, and sometimes my best friend called themselves by the name *Me*, and none of them were out on the playa.

"It's me," he repeated and then gave me a name I had never heard before. Then he said, "It's me, Dizzy," realizing I didn't know his real name.

That's when I started yelling, "Get out of here!"

I repeated my screams even louder, and he finally shut the gate and the back window. I lay there, stiff as a hairbrush, afraid to go back to sleep. And this is what I thought: *He can come back and rape me if he wants*. I thought about what might make a possible weapon: my Swiss Army knife, the lantern, a bottle of wine? I stayed like that, clutching the sheet around my neck, a wine bottle at the ready, terrified until dawn.

The next morning, I asked my campmates if anyone had heard me shouting, and no one had. Everyone wore earplugs, and with BANG, the drum set camp next door, no one heard me scream. I just hoped I wouldn't see Dizzy again.

The next afternoon, I was putting my things into my bike basket, getting ready to ride away, and Dizzy appeared back at my truck. He said, "I just wanted to apologize for scaring you. I didn't mean to. Everyone was asleep, and I just wanted to see if you wanted to go out on the playa."

"Listen," I said. "You did scare me, and you better never come near me again, or do that to anyone else on the playa. Or anywhere else."

"I apologized," he repeated, as if he should get a Boy Scout badge.

"I'm glad," I said. "But you came, uninvited, into my camp, into my personal space. Where I was sleeping. I set boundary after boundary with you. Please go away, and don't come back here again. If I see you near my camp, I'm calling the police."

"I said I was sorry."

"I know." My voice was now shaking even though I'd rehearsed this in case he came by. "Now go away. If you don't go away now, I'll scream. We have a Black Rock Ranger in camp, and I'll have him call law enforcement. Not a ranger but the police."

At that he walked away. Then he stopped, turned around, and walked back toward me. I stared at him, incredulous. I tried to attach my water bottle onto my bike basket with a carabineer, but I was trembling.

"Does that mean you're mad at me?" he asked.

I laughed. "Mad? Mad? Yes, I'm mad. And I'm going to stay mad. Like forever. Go away." I pointed out toward the dusty road. "Now. Get out of here. I mean it. Go."

And it was true: I wasn't cajoled or flattered. I was pissed off. And this was new. And I felt something else new: a surge of real power.

He turned and left, and I hopped onto my bicycle and pedaled away without looking back. I had planned to bike across the playa to visit my friend Jim at Patsy's, his local gayborhood bar, but instead I headed for deep playa—no longer frightened, only angry.

I realized I had finally stood up for myself. Dizzy had expected me to make him feel better when he came back and asked me if I was angry. A younger me would have said some version of this: *It's okay. Don't worry about it.* Or I might have complimented him for his courageous act of apology: *I'm sorry. Thank you. I'm flattered.*

Flattered? Yuck. As if all it takes to prove our worth as women is the attention of a man—any man, even one who made inappropriate advances, who was most probably high on drugs, and who tried to make light of predatory behavior.

And who didn't even have a nice dick. It's okay for me to say that again, right?

After saying, "That's okay," my younger self would have scrutinized every detail, trying to decide if the situation wasn't her fault, if she hadn't been the one to blame. Like she did with her junior high science classmate who grabbed her developing breasts during dissections. And the time she had been told she was a "tease" in a Hawaiian hotel room and barely escaped, clothes ripped. And the time her college genetics professor tried to kiss her in the elevator, and the female dean said there was nothing to be done, so she had to accept a failing grade because she'd said no. And the random pussy grabs in crowded elevators and city streets, the thousand catcalls, and all the rest. Was she too friendly? The neckline of her dress too low? The paint on her toenails too flirty?

My younger self believed she had to be worthy of a man's wanting—just enough without asking for too much. And when he crossed the line, it had to be her fault.

These memories flipped through my mind as I bicycled across the playa. I passed a cruise ship art car and then an island oasis that blasted tropical music; revelers danced under papier-mâché palm trees in the hot sun. A distant drumbeat echoed across the ancient lakebed. I tasted the alkaline playa dust and smoke from the smoldering fires of the previous evening's burns. And I cringed at all the moments in my life where I acted flattered in the face of sexual harassment.

The etymology of the word "flatter" comes from the old French *flater*, which means "to deceive; caress; fondle; throw and fling (to the ground)." A later definition is "to give a pleasing but false impression." As it turns out, it always *was* flattery. But now I finally understood it for what it was: deceit and being flung to the ground.

As I pedaled, the burden of my transgressions lifted—as if I could see my life through another porthole, the shame I carried no longer mine.

I rode into a wind of my own making.

Hiking Home

South Lake Tahoe, United States, July 2011

"We'd better find cover," Tom said when the hail started. The trail clung to the edge of the ridge, exposed. The distance between thunder claps and flashes narrowed. The gray sky fell as rain, then hail, soaking and freezing us. We were on the last day of a two-hundred-mile backpacking trip, hiking from Yosemite to Tahoe. We were in the final twenty-mile stretch; that day, we planned to hike to our front door in South Lake Tahoe. This was how we'd agreed to celebrate our first wedding anniversary.

"Here," Tom said, pointing to an outcropping of rocks. We crawled under the granite and sat on our packs. The boulders had fallen down the side of the mountain and leaned against one another, creating a space beneath just big enough for the three of us—me, Tom, and Ely, our newly adopted chow-shepherd mix. The hail bounced into our small cave, but for the most part, we stayed dry. We couldn't do anything other than what we were doing—sitting on our packs in what we thought was the safest spot around—so what would panicking do? Even so, I asked Tom, "Is this safe?"

"There's nothing else we can do," he said, which also meant, *No, it isn't safe.*

"But we're right under that giant red fir," I pointed. "And what if the lightning strikes the granite above us? Won't we get ground splash?"

"We're okay," Tom said, but what he meant was that we were in the best place in a terrible set of options. The front had moved in too quickly to make it back down, and hovering under this out-cropping of rocks was better than standing out on the exposed trail, if just barely. The rain started to seep into the cracks between the granite and fall in curtains around us. That's when it occurred to me that the water could dislodge the boulders above, and we'd be crushed. I tried to concentrate on the smell of wet minerals and earth, of pine sap and sage, but I could smell only my own fear—a mixture of sweat and salt and insect repellent. I knew enough by now to pull my legs up onto my pack so I wasn't touching the ground. Ely and Tom both fell asleep.

I took out my journal and began to write. I thought about the ways Tom had taken care of me while also allowing me to take care of myself. I felt safe with him, but I had also learned how to feel safe without him. Both were important.

We had a history of electricity—lightning on our first trip kayaking together, then on our wedding day, and on that last night of our honeymoon, when I slept on the carpet of the Bogotá airport because the air traffic control tower had been struck and the planes were grounded. A woman mopped the carpet around me, and I was too tired to care; I only wondered, "Why don't they vacuum instead?" All the seats were taken; it was raining, and the homeless had descended on the benches earlier in the day. The boarding lobbies were locked because it was the middle of the night, so we stayed in the public areas. I wanted to go to a hotel, but because we had only five hours until we could catch another flight, Tom said we should wait at the airport. He told me he would stay awake while I slept. I wrapped myself in my silk sleeping bag liner and lay down on the dirty carpet, my head on his lap. The violent beauty of lightning mapped the key moments of our life together.

Water began to pool beneath my backpack. The ferns and wildflowers were bedraggled from the hailstorm. I wrote the possibilities of our impending doom into my journal, everything from hypothermia to being smashed by a dislodged rock. But as Tom said, there was nothing we could do. I worried about so many things, but my worries never saved me from anything, except maybe my own happiness. The hail turned to rain, blurring out the forest with its gray veil. The air held the smell of burning things, of fire and of ash.

Nothing reminds you of your own mortality like a lightning storm—a shock wave of light, a sky breaking open. The hail started bouncing off the granite again, and lightning flashed so close I could see the afterimage in the dark sky. Tom woke up and said, "Another front moving through. We're probably going to get some close hits."

I counted between each spark of lightning and clap of thunder. Each one was less than a second apart. "Fuck!"

"Shh, with love!" Tom said. To avoid fighting, we had come up with this way for him to ask me to be quiet. I have an "outdoor voice," which has served me well as a backpacking trip leader and ski instructor, though in other situations, my voice can be a little too loud. Even so, I hate to be shushed; saying, "Shh, with love!" is ridiculous enough that I usually laugh instead of get mad.

"I can't help it," I whispered to Tom.

"Does it calm you to write?" he asked. I agreed that it did, even though the rain smeared the ink. "Then keep writing."

A mosquito landed on my knee, unbothered by the lightning storm as she looked for a way to drill into my skin with her proboscis. I watched her for a minute and then brushed her away. The nearby creek bubbled with its white noise. Lightning split open the sky. The dog remained unbothered, too, curled into a ball, asleep.

The electrical storm trundled off into the distance. "Let's go," Tom said. We got our packs on and continued to climb the ridge to Armstrong Pass. A soaked chipmunk lay twitching on the trail, had perhaps fallen from a lightning-struck fir. I looked around at all the blackened trees—a history of storm and fire.

"I think we should pick up the pace," I said. I'm usually slower than Tom, except when there's lightning. We made it over the pass and back down along Saxon Creek. Night fell, and we followed the rainy yellow paths of our headlamps. I kept my eyes trained on the trail but jumped away when the light shone onto a bullfrog, an animal I had never before seen in Tahoe (though it's true I rarely took night hikes and never before on a night as rainy as this). The animal proved that sometimes it takes a long time, and the right circumstances, to see something that's always been there.

The rain finally stopped, and a few stars popped into the clearing sky. The temperature dropped, and the night air felt elastic. Wet pine needles crunched beneath our boots. I was freezing and could see only a few feet in front of me, but I knew that after enough dark steps, I would reach the front door of our house. As far as my headlamp. One step at a time. This would get us home, would lead us through our new marriage. Ely ambled along, wagging his tail. I told Tom, "I love hiking with you and Ely."

"I love having you in my life," he said and took my hand. Rather than giving in to the old insecurities, trying to decide if this was Tom's way of getting out of telling me he loved hiking with me, too, I told my mind to *Shh, with love!*

For the moment, I accepted everything for what it was, walking home together, toward the yellow glow of our porch light.

Acknowledgments

Many thanks to Robert Taylor and the rest of the University of Nebraska Press team. I am grateful for your support and professionalism. Thank you for believing in my work once again. And my gratitude to copy editor Sara Springsteen for both a keen eye and responding to my neurotic emails with grace.

And many thanks to my family, friends, colleagues, mentors, and editors who read drafts of the essays in this book, offering valuable insight and suggestions, as well as to some of my best writing cheerleaders and confidants: Marcela de Lira Astorga, Jason Bell, Keith Bellows, Kristin Bennett, Nancy Bodily, Laurie Braaten, Michael Branch, Gayle Brandeis, Elaine Butler, Mary Cook, Niesha Davis, Tammy DeGiovanni, Deborah Dexter, Christine Dobrowolski, Camille T. Dungy, Kate Evans, Hattie Fletcher, Carolyn Forché, Patty Gilbertson, Kristine Gillette, Margaret Greene, Maggie Hakansson, Lee and Lisa Herrick, Wendy Holmquist, Sue Kloss, Ilyse Kusnetz, Britt Leach, Catherine Roberts Leach, Debby Liberman, Rebecca Board Liljenstolpe, Lauren Lindley, BK Loren, Krista Lukas, Tammy Lundquist, Jim Malloy, Andy Maness, Joe McGee, Kathryn Miles, David Miller, Optimism One, Gailmarie Pahmeier, Suzanne Parker, Eve Quesnel, Jessica Rinker, Cynthia Roberts, Ann Ronald, Terre Ryan, June Sylvester Saraceno, Phyllis Shafer, Patricia Smith, Lois Snedden, Liv Spikes, Jen Spina, and Brian Turner.

And a special thank you to my writing group, The Wordy Girls, Ann Marie Brown and Kim Wyatt, for all the writerly camaraderie, retreats, lobster macaroni and cheese, hikes, jalapeño margaritas, friendship, and love. I don't know where I would be without you—probably lost somewhere in the desert.

Also, gratitude for the sisterhood of the Betties, the GDC, and the Coven. Your friendship sustains me.

And to the creative writing students I have taught over the years: you have inspired me with your curiosity and your determination more than you will ever know.

Many thanks, too, to Bijuraj and Amma for hosting Sholeh and me in India; to the Prague Summer Program, where I started this book; and to Al and Lynne Landwehr for offering me your sweet little cabin in Astoria for a DIY writing residency, where I worked on many of these essays during a rainy spring break.

Finally, all my love and gratitude to my intrepid travel partners who agreed to let me tell their stories along with my own: Sandra Breylinger, Sholeh Wolpé, Tracy Young, and my mother, Sheila Roberts. And especially to Thomas Greene, my forever Practical Boyfriend. I am so grateful for your continued support of me and my writing and for allowing me to write about us even though you would rather I didn't. Thank you for getting me and for making me want to be a better person. You are my everything, and I love you more than these words can say.

Source Acknowledgments

I would like to thank the editors of the following journals and anthologies, where parts of this book, some in a slightly different form or with alternative titles, have been previously published:

The Bark Magazine: parts of "Hiking Home"

Best Women's Travel Writing, Volume 9: "The Love Test"

Best Women's Travel Writing, Volume 12: "My Mother Is My Wingman"

Creative Nonfiction: "Hotel Cádiz"

Litro: parts of "Three Hours to Burn a Body"

Longreads: "The Call of the Coquí"

Matador: "Bargaining, or the Third Stage of Grief"; "Bellagio People"; "Gone Missing"; "The Grand Elephant Festival"; parts of "In Search of Genghis Khan"; "The Love Test"; "Loving the Lie"; "My Mother Is My Wingman"; "One Degree of Separation"; "One Hundred Boyfriends"; "The Peruvian Blackout"; "Prague and the Unbearable Lousiness of the Tourist"; "Scared Shitless"; "Scary Flyer"; "Stretching the Thigh Fat"; parts of "Three Hours to Burn a Body"; "A Wee Scottish Tour"

National Geographic Intelligent Travel: parts of "In Search of Genghis Khan"

National Geographic Traveler: parts of "Three Hours to Burn a Body"

1966: "The Illuminations"

The Normal School: "Sassy at Burning Man"